# Nationalism and Self-Gover

SUNY series in National Identities

Thomas M. Wilson, editor

# Nationalism and Self-Government

## The Politics of Autonomy in Scotland and Catalonia

Scott L. Greer

State University of New York Press

Published by
State University of New York Press, Albany

For information, address State University of New York Press, Albany, NY
www.sunypress.edu

Production by Kelli Williams
Marketing by Anne M. Valentine

**Library of Congress Cataloging-in-Publication Data**

Greer, Scott L.
   Nationalism and self-government : the politics of autonomy in Scotland and
Catalonia / Scott L. Greer.
        p. cm. — (SUNY series in national identities)
   Includes bibliographical references and index.
   ISBN-13: 978-0-7914-7047-3 (hardcover : alk. paper)
   ISBN-13: 978-0-7914-7048-0 (pbk. : alk. paper)
   1. Self-determination, National—Scotland.   2. Scotland—History—Autonomy
and independence movements.   3. Scotland—Politics and government—
20th century.   4. Catalonia (Spain)—Politics and government—20th century.
5. Catalonia (Spain)—History—Autonomy and independence movements.
6. Nationalism—Spain—Catalonia—History.   I. Title.

JN1228.G74 2007
320.9411—dc22                                                          2006021933

# Contents

*To Scott A. Greer*
*Who I hoped would have liked this.*

# Acknowledgments

This book has taken the better part of ten years, and trying to thank the people who helped me with it would come close to writing an autobiography

The first thanks of any qualitative researcher must go to informants. With every interview I am more grateful to the busy people who take the time to share their knowledge and perspective, and exercise their intelligence, just so that academic research may be better. I am very lucky to have met so many serious people in politics, society, and public service who were willing to be forthcoming and responsive without trying to control or distort my work.

At Northwestern, Charles Ragin was gracious and endlessly helpful in the years he worked with me. Kathleen Thelen's advice and support gave form to the work while Edward Gibson's advice and comments were constantly helpful. Albert Hunter's conversation and enthusiasm, in Chicago and in London, was always inspiring.

I first arrived in Spain with little more than the friendship of Marta Dueñas and Anna Olmedillo Vila—and that, it turns out, was almost all I needed. I left Spain profoundly grateful for their help and support, and moreover the friendship of Oscar Barberà, Pere Fabra, Raquel Gallego, Iolanda Garcia, Manuel Tornedijo and the other participants in the ICPS seminar on political parties. Josep Llobera and Salvador Giner both helped me out greatly at the start of the research. Joan Subirats' comments and support have been indispensable throughout. The library of the UPF was my school of Catalan politics; I certainly appreciate that component of Catalan higher education policy. And my anonymized thanks to the two journalists who helped me with contacts and the intricacies of Catalan politics.

In the UK, Helen Daines, Ralph and Gillian Davidson, Andy Gillespie, Robert Hazell, Chris Nottingham, Mark Sandford, John Tomaney, and Kevin Woods all played their crucial roles in the research. David Borchard, Charlie Jeffery, James Mitchell, and Alan Trench, in particular, taught me an enormous amount in many long and highly entertaining conversations. David McCrone of the University of Edinburgh graciously hosted me in 1998 and did a lot to set me straight about how Scotland actually worked.

I did quite a lot of research for and wrote most of this book while at the Constitution Unit and School of Public Policy, University College London; my thanks to all of my colleagues and the administrators there, who made it a pleasure to do this work. The opportunity to participate in the Unit's two large devolution networks, funded by the Leverhulme Trust and ESRC, was invaluable, particularly for the opportunity it gave me to work with those scholars.

Holly Jarman and Elin Royles kindly took time off from their own work—time I know they didn't have to spare—to read and comment on the whole draft. My thanks!

Qualitative, comparative research, and the training for qualitative researchers, is expensive, and I owe enormous thanks to the funders who were willing to support my work. The Council for European Studies, the Ford Foundation's area studies grant to Northwestern University, Northwestern University, and Northwestern's Center for International and Comparative Studies made possible the original research work. The bulk of research was funded by the Social Science Research Council through its valuable IDRF program. The research also benefited from spillover from other research I did in 2001-2005 with the support of the Economic and Social Research Council's program on Devolution and Constitutional Change, the Leverhulme Trust, and the Nuffield Trust.

Parts of this work have been presented at the American Political Science Association and its British Politics Group; the Law and Society Association; the Society for the Advancement of Socioeconomics; the UCL School of Public Policy; and Northwestern University.

I owe thanks to Llewellyn Somers, Michael Rinella, and two anonymous reviewers for SUNY—to the former for patience and skill, to the latter for good advice. My new colleagues at Michigan provided a welcoming environment for the final revisions, and the UM librarians rapidly made themselves indispensable. Pat Dempsey put the final text together.

Finally, I cannot imagine this work without the generosity, inspiration, and conversation of Tyler Colman, the whole Derluguian family, Robert Fannion, Margitta Mätzke, Christina Nyström, and Alan Trench. Long conversations with Alan, Robert and Margitta also explain why my argument makes any sense. Nor can I imagine this work without the patience, advice, and support of my mother, Ann Greer.

And given that I have thanked people who I know do not agree with me (or each other) on important points, I hasten to add that they are not to blame for errors or silliness in what follows.

# Chapter One

# Autonomy and Its Explanations

It might be wholly wrong to think of unified nation-states as the world's basic political units or even as a feasible goal, but as a myth and an ambition they are alive and well. The idea of a correspondence between nation and state, that nations have states and states have nations, has been remarkably little diminished by the experiences of recent decades. It might only apply to a few places, such as Iceland and Portugal, but it still has great power over thought and legitimizes frightening politics. If we think each state has a nation, and each nation a state, then the world will be much more likely to put aside liberal democratic principles in order to excuse both homogenizing programs of states and separatist programs of stateless nations.

It might be wholly wrong to think of nationalism as a wave of primordial passion that, once unleashed, cannot be stopped, but, like the idea of the nation-state, it also seems to bear on reality. Abundant and often excellent theories focusing on the illogical, contingent, and constructed nature of nations and nationalisms have been the most common output from the decades of "Great Debate" about nationalism (Schöpflin 2000:3). By explaining it, placing it in history, and showing the contingency of national identity over time, twenty years of work have done much to strip away the idea that national identity is "tribal," fixed and ahistorical. But theories stressing the contingency and political uses of nationalism only go so far—deconstructing national identities might conceivably help to inoculate populations over time but seems unlikely to dampen conflict in Kosovo, Chechnya, or the Basque Country. Any social institution, after all, is ultimately contingent and historical but can still be a strong and very tangible reality in people's lives.

It is these theories' focus on the internal conflicts, malleability, and multiple political uses of nationalism that has excited more applied theorists.

If national identity, nationalist ideas, and nationalist mobilization all respond at least in part to structural conditions and the political opportunity structures facing national leaders, then practical politics and good institutional design might contain or channel nationalism in a liberal direction, avoiding the problems that come with state-seeking nationalism and nation-creating states. Such a view both accords with many findings, and also has the great virtue that it allows us to at least imagine doing something when faced with potentially dangerous conflicts between nations.

Scotland and Catalonia, Spain and the United Kingdom, play a special role in these debates, as exemplars first of the resurgence of stateless nationalisms and then of the use of territorial autonomy to resolve conflicts between state, majority and minority. Both the UK and Spain, faced with nationalist challenges, have created autonomous governments for their minority nations in Scotland, Wales, Catalonia, Galicia, and the Basque Country. They have both increased the political autonomy and representation of the smaller nations while preserving the state as a whole. Internally, meanwhile, the politics and public discourses of Scotland and Catalonia are a world away from their neighbors in, for example, Northern Ireland; in both countries, most intellectuals and leaders take great care to be "civic" and tolerant, eschewing ethnic or sectarian politics in public.

It did not obviously have to be that way, which is why we study these largely successful cases of multinational accommodation in one state. When nationalism erupted in the 1960s and 1970s across the West, after a postwar lull, it seemed to presage a serious threat to modern states. Diverse nationalist movements and parties in Scotland, Wales, Northern Ireland, Catalonia, Quebec, Brittany, Corsica, Flanders, Catalonia, and in the Basque Country, to list just the most discussed, made serious claims for national self-determination and statehood, and in each of those places and others the arrival of politically mobilized nationalists made it easy to imagine their independence. Central states worried while academics and journalists flocked to study the many and contradictory manifestations of the "new nationalisms of the developed West" (Tiryakian and Rogowski 1985). Nationalisms, implicitly assumed to be state-seeking nationalisms, appeared to be everywhere.

The interest of the UK and Spain lies in what happened since (Keating 1992:224; Conversi 2000:138; Sturm 2006:147; Gunther, Montero, and Botella 2004:7). Decades later, the outcome is not quite what an observer in 1970 might have imagined. Nationalism in these places and others across Europe seems to have elided with other concerns to produce not nationstates but regional governments. Like other 1960s and 1970s social movements, they have produced reform rather than radical change. The UK, France, Spain, Belgium, and Canada are all intact, often with nationalist parties ruling some of their regional governments. Rather than pursue the classic and still popular nationalist demand for a state to a successful conclusion, leaders of these mobilized nations have settled, more or less stably, into life as regional governments within larger states. Even as the breakup of the former Soviet Union and Yugoslavia reminded the world of the deadly possibilities of nationalism and the demand for statehood, Scotland and Catalonia were governed by regional parliaments that are popular and well entrenched but a far cry from states. The nationalism of these old nations had somehow merged into a broader trend of regionalization. Meanwhile, other places with little or no nationalism, "new" or otherwise, were pursuing regionalization with success. Corsica had nationalists and the cobbled-together French region of Provence–Alpes–Côte d'Azur (known as PACA) did not, but both were nearly identical regional governments; Cantabria was a newcomer to Spanish political history but was by 2003 under almost the same legal regime as the ancient nation of Catalonia.

What has happened in Europe's stateless nations, then, is the rise of regional government—a type of meso-level government that has been gaining influence worldwide for decades (Sharpe 1993; Keating 1998). It is as if history's wires had become crossed, turning classic nationalist fights for statehood into territorial, elected, agencies charged with social policy, public administration, and regional economic development. The result was regional governments for stateless nations and newly invented regions alike. That raises the question: what created regional governments in these countries? What explains the way the drive for territorial self-determination not only started, but also stopped? *Why, in short, did nationalist mobilization arise and develop momentum but also stop short of secession when it did?*

The answer lies in the relationship between political institutions and the struggles within Scotland and Catalonia, where separatist nationalists are by no means the only forces at play (alternative theories are in chapter two). They are thickly institutionalized, dense societies with complex interwoven interests and networks, and it is both an error and a disservice to them to regard them as simple peoples unified behind any political force. Regional autonomy is a consequence of the politics that play out from strong webs of regional organizations. Their interests, as regional organizations, lie in environmental stability and their own autonomy; this opposes them to both centralization and secession. Autonomy suits them perfectly by guaranteeing both. Where such regional organizations exist, they can be very influential in politics by virtue of the resources they control; in both Scotland and Catalonia, the party systems and institutional arrangements reflect the ability of regional institutional organizations to shape politics. They do this through their elective affinities with parties; coalition-building politicians, searching for strong supports, look for groups that will adopt their interests, and regional organizations are a major such group. If their support is needed for a party to thrive, a successful party will take on their preferences regarding autonomy. Thus, when a nation that could be another case of nationalist secession instead stabilizes with an autonomous regional government, it should be explained by the presence and influence of regional institutionalized organizations whose pull attracts and strengthens parties and thereby undermines that of secessionist movements and centralists alike.

The rest of this chapter makes this argument, linking the high politics of nationhood, self-government, and statehood to the organizations and politics of civil society and public policy. Public policy actually matters in high politics; if nation identifies with territory and public policy is territorial and is worth the name, then policy issues can also create nationalist, regionalist, statist, or other coalitions, as much as state and minority nationalist parties that often occupy the limelight. It also makes the point that most people in a society are not concerned about their national identity most of the time, but that the politics of public policy, and the frustrations of regionally concentrated groups, also matter. Scotland and Catalonia—and Quebec, Flanders, and others—are not just nations. They are also societies. And at least in these comparatively rich societies of Western Europe, dense as they are with autonomous organizations, policy and diverse organizational interests that cannot be easily reduced to class or nation also matter. In such societies, it is an analytic error to leave out them and their systematic preferences when explaining either stability or change. In societies without such dense networks of autonomous organizations, it might be an error to adopt institutional solutions that rely upon them to guarantee stability. And, if it is correct, then there are dramatic implications for our understanding of the institutional arrangements, such as regional autonomy, that work in different kinds of multinational states and societies, and for our understanding of the worldwide trend toward decentralization of government and administraton.

## REGIONS AND GOVERNANCE

So the outcomes in Scotland and Catalonia, while they are to some extent probably driven by nationalism, are actually regionalization. Regionalization, a subspecies of authority migration, is the process of creating new meso-level governments, between the levels of the central state and the local level (Sharpe 1993; Harvie 1994; Balme 1996; Marks, Hooghe, and Blank 1996; Nay 1997; Keating 1998; Le Galès and Lequesne 1998; Negriér and Jouve 1998; Loyer and Villanova 1999; Bukowski and Rajagopalan 2000; Bukowski, Piattoni, and Smyrl 2002; Gerber and Kollman 2004). It has been growing (Simeon 2005:18). While, in 1970, Western Europe's only regionally decentralized states were federal Germany and Austria, by 2002, Spain, Italy, France, Belgium, and the UK had established regions. These regional governments occupy a territorial level not traditionally present in these states' diverse histories, and their rise redistributes power, accountability, and responsibility while reshaping politics and society. The confusion in the discussion of their rise is that they have blossomed and flourish with or without nations behind them; Andalucia is as much of a protagonist in Spanish politics as Catalonia, and German Länder are powerful actors in a decreasingly homogeneous country (Jeffery 2003).[1]

The question is what has been driving the rise of these governments and to what end? There are functional explanations, which focus on the idea that the nation-state is too small for the big things and too big for the small things (Guiberneau 1995). The argument takes two variations: one proposing that regions are better units for the provision of important public goods (Balme 1996; Gobetti 1996) (and which often conflates economic or social regions with the inherited regional borders) and the other that the decline in geopolitical and economic usefulness of the state affords regions, particularly those with stateless nations, more protagonism as actors. More recent work focuses on the politics, identifying central states (V. Wright 1997; Mitchneck, Solnick, and Stoner-Weiss 2001; Boone 2003), parties (van Houten 1999; Meguid 2002; O'Neill 2003) or regional politicians' networks and activities (Bukowski, Piattoni, and Smyrl 2002) as agents of change that explain particular regional outcomes.

There are also more technical justifications for decentralization (Manor 1999). They come primarily from public finance, which focus on the likely misallocation of public resources when they are allocated centrally (the null hypothesis is that central allocation will produce over- or underprovision due to spatial variation and lack of information; Oates 1999; Wincott 2006). Finally, there is an abundant tradition of democratic theory that proposes participation is better in smaller units, with Machiavelli, Proudhon, and Montesquieu among those who have argued for small polities (Dahl 1967). So regionalization might, at least under some conditions, create better public administration, better democracy, and also reduce ethnonational strife. The conditions under which regions come into existence and get their powers, and their effects, though, remain relatively unclear—as one well-placed observer argued, we "know a great deal about what happens in regional politics. We are less well placed to offer generalizable explanations of how and why developments in regional politics take place" (Jeffery 2002:vii).

Perhaps the most important thing asked of autonomous governments in multinational states, ahead of their economic development, public administration, or social policy concerns, is that they reduce the likelihood of secession or conflict. One practical and theoretical debate to which the Scottish and Catalan experiences and turn to regionalization matter is the one about the conditions under which territorial autonomy arrangements stave off or limit conflict. Repeated upsurges of national and group conflict around the world have justified decades of scholarly and practical work on institutional solutions to ethnic conflict. There are a variety of solutions to the problems that emerge when nation and state do not correspond, ranging from the extremes of making the population correspond to the state through genocide or mass expulsions to making the state correspond to the populaton by secession (McGarry and O'Leary 1993).

One of the most common proposals, desirable because it prevents state breakup while permitting cultural autonomy, is federalism or territorial decentralization to ethnic groups (G. Smith 1995). It is intuitive enough to argue that a measure of national self-government should satisfy most people (Lijphart 1977; Lapidoth 1996:121–125; Keating 2001; O'Leary 2003) and there is empirical evidence in both case studies (Bajpai 1997; Conversi 2000; Mitra 2000; Watts 2000) and cross-national studies (Cohen 1997; Bermeo 2002; Saideman et al. 2002:97; Amoretti and Bermeo 2004). Political autonomy for minority nations would mean that "groups, states, or nations would govern themselves while participating in supranational political institutions . . . in order to solve common problems. . . . It is not that federalism eliminates all ethnic conflict. Rather, it provides mechanisms by which this type of conflict can be checked by groups committed to maintaining an interconnected system without necessarily trampling on the interests of minorities" (Jusdanis 2001). The idea is logical (Hechter 2000) and historical precedents, above all the enormous history of indirect rule in sophisticated empires throughout history, suggest that it has promise. Empirically, states such as Canada have been able to manage the tensions between diverse populations for many years via federalism; "granting a substantial measure of autonomy and self-government to distinct groups within the polity may in fact contribute to enhanced unity . . . all the evidence points to the fact that, if there had not already been provincial autonomy, the [Quebec separatist] movement would have been much stronger, not weaker" (Watts 2000:48).

The reason is simple enough; modern states' abilities to penetrate individual life are so great that they are almost certain to routinely touch sensitive areas of culture and group life with their educational, regulatory, legal, economic, and other policies (Bendix 1969; Gellner 1983; B. Anderson 1991; Jusdanis 2001). If these policies clash with the group's practices, then they will become a point of contention and the state will clash with that group. Since the state is likely to be reflecting some other nation when it does so, and possibly some other nationalism, the result is all of the ingredients required for conflict in divided societies—unless the state devolves responsibility for these intrusive functions onto the minority groups. Once they are allocated in ways that cleave to national divisions, there is no necessary reason the different nations cannot share a currency or foreign policy.

In such circumstances, federalism can be thought to mitigate the security dilemma, in which mutual mistrust leads to increasingly defensive and aggressive behavior by each group, which thereby increases mistrust and can eventually explode into violence (Posen 1993; Rothchild and Lake 1998:211–212). Furthermore, such a view of the relationship between state and group suggests what would need to be devolved to a self-governing group—namely, the areas of public policy and administration such as education that are most likely to touch on group preferences and values. Federalism might not be enough to prevent conflict and keep a state intact and decent, but Simeon and Conway find that "federalism does not guarantee 'success' but it is hard to see any form of successful accommodation of multiple nations within a single state that does not include federalism" (Simeon and Conway 2001:364–365). So Alfred Stepan's judgment is that "if countries such as Indonesia, Russia, Nigeria, China and Burma are ever to become stable democracies, they will have to craft workable federal systems" (Stepan 1999:20).

The logic and whole history of indirect rule by the world's empires, the relationship between group identities and practices and the omnipresent modern state apparatus, and the ability of federal systems to flexibly balance different territorial, including national, interests against each other all appear to justify territorial autonomy as a solution. The developing literature on nationalism and territorial politics in comparative politics is, though, broadly skeptical about territorial autonomy as a solution. What do these scholars[2] find wrong with territorial autonomy, that is, autonomy for regional or federal governments whose borders correspond to the territorial extent of a nation?

The chief problem, these studies argue, is that of a "pathology of federalism" that accentuates differences (Watts 1998; also Simeon 2006:31). Creating ethnic units risks making the national groups the bases of politics while reducing healthy cross-cutting interactions between groups and creates insecure minorities in the ethnic units (Roeder 1991:197–199; Lieven and McGarry 1992:72; Schöpflin 1992:183; Agnew 1995:299; Popovski 1995:188; Brubaker 1996:24–25; Leff 1999). Given that cross-cutting cleavages and personal networks are one of the most important obstacles to ethnic violence (Varshney 2001), or in Robin Williams's formula "connection, complementarity, and consensus" are the prerequisites of peace, ethnic or otherwise (2003:235), it is not obvious that we should adopt institutional forms that disconnect national groups from each other. Furthermore, even if these could be defined as appropriate responses to the reality of national identity and mobilization, there is the charge that they create political incentives to polarize politics around the claims of ethnic groups as represented in the new national units. Forcing ethnic entrepreneurs to compete for power in the central state would, by contrast, create incentives to build larger and presumptively less divisive coalitions (Linz and Stepan 1992; Horowitz 2002). The new autonomous units can make their own claims to ethnic purity, or even establish the distinctive public policies such as language education that justify them, and thereby create new security dilemmas for their minorities. Meanwhile, autonomy equips them with many properties of states, save sovereignty; once they have their state-like flags, leaders, institutions of socialization such as schools, and political systems, it is easier to both imagine and attain greater sovereignty, autonomy, or ethnic purity (Cornell 2002:251–252). Snyder (2000:327) summarizes the case against autonomy:

> This method has had a terrible track record, yet it remains popular with liberal problem-solvers, in part because it seems to allow national self-determination without the nasty fuss and bother of full-fledged partition . . . ethnofederalism tends to heighten and politicize ethnic consciousness, creating a self-conscious intelligentsia and the organisational structures of an ethnic state-in-waiting. When mass political participation expands, these ethnofederal structures channel it along an ethnic path. For these reasons, ethnofederalism is at best a last resort that risks fueling rather than appeasing the politicization of ethnicity.

Local units can also be more easily seized by corrupt or eccentric local elites; a key reason for centralized states in the nineteenth century was precisely that they were less vulnerable to capture by retrograde local elites, and it is not wholly accidental that local and regional governments have a reputation in so many countries as sinks of corruption and incompetence. Decentralization can "facilitate regional deviant behavior" to the point of permitting local authoritarian states in some places (von Beyme 2000:38).

So is decentralization a good way to govern a state, multinational or otherwise? Is it useful as a remedy for conflict despite its price? Is it a creator of conflict? The answer, as so often with this kind of debate, is that it depends. The next question is—on what does it depend?

What the current indeterminate answers in the literature suggest is that we should look at the interactions between institutions and societies. If similar institutional forms seem to have different effects, then it might be time to examine the social structures, interest, and socialization that also shapes the actors who confront institutional incentives. Despite their fundamentally institutional nature, the questions about the relationship between federalism and nationality cannot be answered purely in terms of institutional incentives and design (Forsyth 1989:6; Watts 2000:49–50; Simeon and Conway 2001:340; Williams 2003:234). We must include the social forces at work—the people with various kinds of power, the people who seek to mobilize resources to some end, their coalitions and their fallings-out. It is they who respond to incentives and, as often as not, explain the institutions on paper and in reality. The most successful analyses of national and regional politics have always been those that break it down and reveal the complexity and contingency of politics in a nation, whether as an explicit point (Díez Medrano 1995) or not. The society that interacts with the institutions matters because its politics cannot be reduced to individuals and elites facing a set of incentives or a unified nation seeking an appropriate institutional home. It might not seem interesting to point this out, but it is striking how often nations are anthropomorphized or institutions are studied purely for the incentives they present to otherwise undifferentiated and sometimes rational individuals.

## A THEORY OF TERRITORIAL POLITICAL CHANGE

How might we enrich a theory of territorial politics by engaging with the complexity of politics? One way to understand their role is via the logic of resource mobilization and dependencies (Tarrow, Katzenstein, and Graziano 1978; Rhodes 1981). The actions of organizations are powerfully contingent on their resource dependencies. Their preferences and constraints are not to be mechanistically derived from a single variable (such as class or nationality) but are part of complex webs of resource dependencies and mobilization in which organizations maintain themselves. The reasons organizations do what they do—throw their weight in one direction or another—should come from their resource dependencies.

In this, political parties are organizations like any other; their links into society and forms of mobilization give them specific characteristics, resources, and limitations (Panebianco 1988). They can strategically pursue voters, but their activities and existence are shaped by a fact, found in many party studies, that a "key feature of the party system . . . was less their electoral role and more the way they forged and shaped socioeconomic coalitions, policy-making structures, and public policies" (Pempel 1990:14).

They are dependent on other organizations, just like any other, and when they mobilize activists instead, that constrains them, too. Thus, it is a mistake to focus entirely on the electoral strategies of parties, despite its undeniable heuristic and simplifying value. It is a mistake because the axes of conflict, the permissible positions, and the preferences of parties are all constrained by the people who shape politics and parties. Resource dependencies in regional politics are what shape party *preferences* and are thus crucial, and combine with electoral positioning to account for the *intensity* and *timing* of the party actions.

In turn, that means it is too simple to code outcomes such as the Scottish parliament and the competencies of the Catalan regional government as simple electoral plays by parties—parties are more than their electoral strategies. Parties' internal coherence, possible strategies, and possible positions all varied with their own insertion into regional societies. Britain's Labour Party demonstrated this with the 1979 devolution fiasco in Scotland, discussed in chapters two and six, when it tried a regionalist electoral strategy in the face of regional elite opposition to regionalization. It found an electoral strategy unmoored from its local resource dependencies led to humiliation in a referendum that split Labour and failed. The response of statewide parties to nationalist electoral challenges explains Labour's activities in the 1970s—which did not lead to Scottish (or Welsh) autonomy.

## Dependence on Institutions and Its Consquences

Parties can get their resources from two different sources. The first kind of source is stable, institutionalized connections with other institutions. That means reliable connections with institutions that do not have to worry much about self-preservation, whether banks or universities. If the organizations on which parties depend have clear preferences for regional government, those parties will of necessity develop a preference for regional government. Such regional webs of organizations are rare but potent (V. Wright 1997). An organization is regional when the bulk of its resource dependencies are regional—when it depends on relationships with other institutions grounded in the region and/or mobilizes around issues found only in the region (such as nationalism). The extent to which an organization's key resource dependencies are on either a region itself (its population, language, economic specialization) or on other regional organizations is the extent to which an organization is regional. The indicators of an organization's territorial resource dependencies might vary with context, but they should reflect the organization's needs and the conditions under which it receives those resources. Thus, under what conditions does a given organization receive the resources necessary to it—above all, its funds, its staff, its clients or activists, and its political or regulatory role? This entails three questions. First, research must establish empirically what the organization requires: trades unions in both cases here, for example, rely on members, fees, and a particular role in industrial relations law. Second, it should then establish whether those are territorially contingent: in the example of a membership organization, do the members join because the organization is regional or statewide or for some other reason (such as its effect on their wages), are the fees set in some way that is regional or regionally conditioned (such as by region-level bargaining or regulation), and who makes industrial relations law? Third, most organizations seem to have some mixture of resource dependencies; the question is which kind bulk largest in terms of the amount and importance of the resources.

There can be organizations that are so culturally of a place (for regions, the Church of Scotland, for the central state the Spanish military) that a resource dependency test appears beside the point. Nevertheless, there are more elites than those easy cases, and they can surprise—the Comissions Obreres (CCOO) de Catalunya, a union, is both proudly Catalan and is today fundamentally Madrid-oriented by its resource dependencies (on statewide labor negotiations and laws). CCOO could not pursue its main organizational goals, on which its resources are contingent, by privileging the Catalan level. It follows that a resource dependency test is the most useful way to understand the territorial ascription of an organization (and if an organization's loyalties and resource dependencies are out of line, something logically will give when the resource providers demand different loyalty). By using this test of resource dependency, it is possible to establish which organizations are regional and thus which organizations' elites should defend regional autonomy and stability.

If an organization's resource dependencies are not regional, it is opportunistic (dependent on no particular area of territory) or linked to the central state. The Scottish Conservatives and the Partido Popular in Catalonia both depend on funding from their central sibling parties and support from organizations linked to the state. There are other levels of territorial ascription, not generally relevant here, and opportunistic organizations. Local government controls resources that are linked to its territory, and which might or might not reinforce regional governments' demands. Many organizations are opportunistic, with diversified resource dependencies across territory, and would want to stay that way.

Regional organizations will seek autonomy and stability for themselves and, as a condition of this, for the region (compare Logan and Molotch 1987). Regional (predominantly nationalist) social movements will seek to further their goals of greater autonomy for the region, with independence as a likely eventual goal. Most organizations probably find it in their interest to be opportunistic rather than be tied to a particular level of government. Regions, in particular, might not be very appealing; local social goods (such as sanitation and some policing) and state ones (such as macroeconomic policy) are inescapable whereas a region might or might not reflect a natural economic or social zone of interest (Lange 1998; Dupuy and Le Galès 2006). Thus, business groups in Scotland and Catalonia work hard to avoid completely concentrating on one level. Central state organizations, whose fates rise and fall with the central state's extent as the regional ones' depend on the region's autonomy, will defend the central state. There are other groups—local organizations, and now European and even global organizations—but they are extraneous to the argument (although they should matter in explaining other levels of territorial governance, such as the EU and local governments' powers).

An institutionalized organization by definition does not depend on voluntary decisions to assist it (Jepperson 1991:145,148). It does this because expectations of others include its existence (subject to it behaving as expected). It is embedded in a web of relationships with other organizations through which flow resources and support. The mere fact—of organizational leadership—should give it preferences about the political and social environment in which it functions. I assume organizations are corporate actors (whose decisionmakers are elites) with corporate interests in their autonomy, survival, and strength; the latter gives elites an interest in the stability of their environment (i.e., their ability to predict what will affect them, the better to survive and grow) (March and Olsen 1989; Scharpf 1997:64). I posit that environmental stability (in resource flows and institutional framework) and organizational autonomy (to allocate them and self-organize) are what they seek across the board and in addition to whatever else they seek personally or as organizational leaders. This should mean that they seek to preserve the autonomy and the stability of their organizations in politics. In turn, their preferences for autonomy and stability should be connected to the level of government they prefer to have governing them. They will seek a government and a broad political environment responsive to their concerns, and one that does not destabilize their environments.

*Dependence on Collective Action and Its Consequences*

The second way to assemble resources is via collective action-inducing activists to give their time and resources in return for the rewards of belonging to a movement or party with certain principles. To some extent all parties do this, but the extent to which it dominates their resource mobilization varies sharply. Parties that depend on mobilization to the near exclusion of resource dependencies on other stable organizations are movement-parties; rather than depend on institutionalized organizations, they rely on repeated voluntary decisions to assist them. They are more constrained and driven by the goals of their members than by the goals of allied organizations. These include the Scottish National Party and, until 2003, Esquerra Republicana de Catalunya (ERC). They have different constraints related to their resource dependency on collective action; needing to maintain collective action means needing to maintain some combination of the incentives required to win activists and the cultural dynamics that win their continued participation even in the face of a seeming lack of incentives. This in turn means that they will look erratic (as they pursue strategies born of mobilizing and are constrained by the conditions under which they mobilized their existing activists), will reflect activist milieux that can vary quite dramatically but might or might not appeal to regional elites, and will be constantly pushed toward maximalist objectives. Crucially, this means that these parties are almost always weaker (although they can do well, as with the SNP). They lack the resources—the legitimacy, the press, the money, the infrastructure—of parties that are reliant on big outside organizations. That means they lack the stability that comes from dependence on outsiders, whether those outsiders are banks, trades unions, churches or the press. They also therefore are well suited to the protest voters and charismatic leaders who have historically been the core of regionalist parties' support (de Winter 1998).The result is a vicious cycle: weakness and dependence on collective action gives them destabilizing ideologies, which means they do not attract organizational allies, which means they are weak and dependent on collective action.

The key point about weights is that the political contest is stacked against organizations dependent on collective action. Even if the SNP is the main opposition party in Scotland, its ability to bring about a social coalition against it (of all the organizations supporting environmental stability) exceeds its ability to muster its own activists and public support in support of independence. Its dependence on activists means that it looks unstable, and with its commitment to independence (and their commitment), regional organizations find a safer regionalizing partner in Labour while those who seek a protest vote can, in the new Scottish parliament, opt for a Green or a Scottish Socialist Party with more radical élan than a large party like the SNP can have.

*SNP now are the party in charge in Scotland, and have secured a vote on independence in 2014.*

*Summary*

According to this theory, the politics of regionalization is essentially a contest between regional and central organizations. The nationalist movement-parties range between epiphenomenal to the process of regionalization and threatening to the regional and central organizations that structure regional governments. The key actors are the regional institutionalized organizations where they exist. This means both the elites—those who run the organizations—and the people in them. A policy acts on an organization, and that affects its members who can have resources as well as its elites. The vice-chancellors organization that represents British university leaders is far less influential than the combined opinions of their thousands of faculty; if a policy offends universities, both are likely to respond. The hostility of doctors, repeated when chatting over consultations or expressed through leaflets in waiting rooms, matters just as the statements and campaigns of their peak organizations matter. If the organizations are convincingly regional, the members will defend their autonomy and stability as well. They are the only actors bound to a level of government but with preferences that are not directly set by the level of government to which they are bound—they are not necessarily obliged to defend the central state or maintain regional mobilization. They can see threats from both the central state and the nationalists, and thus will adopt stances in territorial politics in response to whatever is the greatest threat—central state centralization or nationalist instability. They matter because of their influence on politics and parties in their regions and in some cases in the state capital, and because they can pivot. Their crucial role ties in with the broader strand of historical sociology led by Stein Rokkan, whose analyses focused on the characteristics of different European states and societies in order to work out what led to integration of peripheries or its failure (Eisenstadt and Rokkan 1973; Rokkan and Urwin 1982, 1983; Flora, Kuhnle, and Urwin 1999). The strength of a distinct regional society, whether due to its dense networks (as in these two cases), or because it was too difficult to assimilate it (as in Wales or Galicia), is just as crucial in their studies across time and space as it is here.

The pressure of regional organizations for autonomy and stability is why the regional government of Scotland and Catalonia took the form that it did—a formalization of the autonomy of their dense networks of territorial institutionalized organizations. In explaining the outcome, the key point is the way dependence on regional organizations both made particular parties, Labour in Scotland and Convergència i Unió in Catalonia, strong in their regions and committed to regionalization. The rise of nationalism in Scotland, and to a lesser extent Catalonia, took scholars and policymakers by surprise, and now their politics of autonomy are what are interesting. These are mysteries only if we focus exclusively on nationalist parties and ideas, since the actual politics of territorial political change in both are difficult to understand without examination of the role of their strong regional societies.

# Chapter Two

# Two Stateless Nations

## Scotland and Catalonia

Scotland and Catalonia are, by any international standards, successful cases of autonomy and toleration in a continent that has historically done poorly in both categories. Europe has spent much of the last 150 years in a sanguineous and immensely destructive process of nation-state formation. The map of European nationalities is infinitely less complicated and intermingled than it was in 1848. Total war, forced population transfer, genocide, and systematic discrimination have done a great deal to match nation with state. The exceptions—the comparatively successful cases of multinational coexistence—consequently are particularly interesting. Almost nobody would outright recommend that Europe complete its process of rearranging nation to fit state, or that other continents pursue that strategy, so studying successful multinational politics and the limits to any given formula has some value.

Scotland and Catalonia are often presented as easily comparable (Moreno 1986; Keating 1996; Guiberneau 1999; Paquin 2001; MacInnes 2004; for introductions to each, see Kellas 1989; M. Lynch 1991; McCrone 1992; Balcells 1996; Devine 1999; McRoberts 2001). They are middle-sized stateless nations (if they were independent, they would be of the scale of Ireland or Denmark) in Western Europe with old identities, relatively recent regional autonomy, nationalist parties that grew up from the late 1960s onward, and many exponents of a "civic nationalism" that asks for autonomy and inclusiveness but neither secession nor xenophobia. Both, furthermore, are clear cases of "bottom-up" regionalization, driven initially by social and political forces in the regions rather than imposed by the state to shift responsibilities or fulfill a political aim of its own (Bullman 1997:9–10; Keating

1997:22–25). In their own domestic politics, they treat themselves as similar, with leaders on reciprocal visits, academic conferences and public events discussing each other, and journalists from the one looking to the other for comparable experiences coping with problems such as racism. It is a "classic comparison" by now, observed one interviewee.

Nevertheless, what might at first appear to be very similar cases are actually something else. They are a pair of very similar outcomes in what would by most explanations have been hopelessly different countries. When looking to factors that could shape a society and its government, the similar outcomes in Scotland and Catalonia become a puzzle.

## LONGUE DURÉE EXPLANATIONS

Going back in history to look at the imperial *longue durée* is not much help in explaining their similar fates. Barcelona was the center of the old kingdom of Aragon, a Western Mediterranean trading power for centuries and an empire that spanned parts of what are now Spain, France, and Italy; the coats of arms of many cities and regions around the Western Mediterranean still bear the heraldry of four red bars on a yellow background that is now the Catalan flag. In 1492, Ferdinand of Aragon—his kingdom suffering from the effects of a ruinous civil war and the crown's overtaxation—wed Isabella (of Castille), uniting the two kingdoms. Around the same time, the development of new Portugese and Spanish global empires undermined the Mediterranean trade routes that had made Aragon's cities powerful and wealthy (Elliott 1963:2–6). Aragon would remain united with Castille despite its rulers' efforts to produce heirs that would split them again (Maltby 2002:7) and would slowly and painfully become integrated parts of the Spanish throne (Núñez and Tortella 2003). When Catalonia's anachronistic ruling classes led a failed 1640–1652 revolt against Spanish efforts to tax them, their efforts narrowly ended in defeat. Later came the 1707–1716 Decrees of the *Nova Planta*. This was a relatively common aspect of statebuilding in Europe. Absolutist monarchies under geopolitical pressure were trying in many countries to rationalize taxation by removing medieval Estates and parliaments that impeded taxation and fragmented public administration (Ertman 1997; van Creveld 1999:99–100). In Catalonia, the decrees came to be remembered as a national disaster with the good reason that they marked the end of distinctive Catalan government and language and a blow to its institutions—the legal system was reduced to a distinct form of private law and the decree pointedly moved the University of Barcelona to Cervera in the interior. In 1833 it would be replaced as an administrative unit by four provinces.

A new and more durable Catalonia had, however, been growing within this framework and would consolidate even in the decadence and death of the Catalano-Aragonese formal institutions. Its novelty and durability, indeed, explain why Catalans have a point when they celebrate the day of their defeat, 11 September, as their national day. The new Catalonia developed as a coherent urban system centered around Barcelona, more or less equivalent to the "principality" that is Catalonia today (García Espuche 1998:412–416). Economic historians would later comment that the resilience of this urban system that is Catalonia is something of a peculiarity in European history. Despite a consistently unfavorable political, economic, and geographic environment, it could always maintain a strong, highly differentiated, and relatively advanced industrial economy (Thomson 1992:310–319). Catalonia would survive, much reduced from the Crown of Aragon to today's principality, and it would survive in good part because of the dynamism of the Barcelona urban area. The other *Països Catalans*—Catalan-speaking lands of the old Aragonese empire in Valencia, the Balearic Islands, Languedoc, and parts of Provence and Sardinia—were too far from the Barcelona urban economy, and were over time largely included in the trajectories of Spain, France, and Italy rather than the principality.

In other words, Catalonia was integral to a very old world system, one that was decaying even before 1492, but was peripheral to the new Atlantic economy. Spain's subsequent decline from its seventeenth-century power would render Catalonia doubly peripheral—not just incorporated into an unimportant and poorly governed part of the Atlantic economy, but also on the wrong side of Iberia, facing the stagnant Mediterranean world. It would also face the political problems that came with Spain's decline, including bleakly comic political instability and *trasformismo* (*turno* in Spanish—the regular undemocratic handovers between two parties) (Carr 1982). It would henceforth survive, in that relatively hostile environment, as an entrepreneurial economy with many family structures that abetted capital accumulation and small business rather than as a great trading power.

It would also fit poorly with the Spanish state; Catalonia was throughout the nineteenth and twentieth centuries more economically progressive and industrial than most of Spain and would regularly produce leaders who, frustrated by the Spanish state, would both try to modernize it and seek Catalan autonomy to escape its problems (Harty 2001). Catalan political activity during the nineteenth century and its political nationalism after 1898 would be driven by reformist impulses, often with a renovating generational tint, to lead Spain out of its quagmire as much as by its own leaders' drive for autonomy (Marfany 1996; Anguera 2000). The breakthrough for Catalan nationalism was 1898, when the loss of Spain's remaining colonies to the United States provoked a wave of self-examination and regenerationist political thought, including a regionalism that swept Catalonia aimed at both modernizing Spain and winning autonomy for Catalonia (Balfour 1996).

Catalonia developed a rich tradition of political thought and action focused on nation, state, and territorial autonomy (Balcells 1988, 1996; Termes 2000) and would unfailingly elect large majorities of its deputies for autonomist, Catalan parties of right or left from 1898. It would also have relatively little chance to pursue either autonomy or modernization, since the rest of Spain would stumble through a series of failed political experiments. Finally, autonomy for Catalonia, a bridge too far for the Spanish far right, helped trigger Franco's military coup and the bloodbath of the Civil War. Franco's "national-catholic," quasifascist regime would determinedly repress Catalan identity and culture from 1939 to 1975.

Scotland's history is very different. Unable to beat the great powers of the seventeenth and eighteenth centuries, it joined (one of) them. Scotland was a small and relatively consolidated state in the seventeenth century, but it was poorly positioned in the kill-or-be-killed geopolitical environment of early modern Europe. Its exports were low in added value and it lacked an empire of any sort that would enrich it. Spanish and English resistance helped to suffocate its one major, and for Scotland hugely expensive, colonial enterprise, the foundation of Darien in Central America. It did, however, have a strategic position and a land frontier with the increasingly powerful English monarchy.[1] This meant that an autonomous Scotland was a permanent potential threat to Protestant England, and Scotland's alliances and connections with England's Catholic rivals France and Spain worried the English. Unification of the crowns in 1603 in the person of James I did not solve the problem, since a purely dynastic connection could be quite unstable. After deteriorating relations in the late seventeenth century and the failure of Darien, which nearly bankrupted much of the Scottish political elite, the pressure on Scotland was enough to persuade its parliament to unite with the English parliament. There were contemporary accusations, and now evidence, that they were bribed—hence the poet Robert Burns's famous accusation that the Scots parliamentarians who voted for the treaty were "such a parcel of rogues in a nation!," for they had been "bought and sold for English gold." Even if they were bribed, and it seems that they were (McLean and McMillan 2005), union was one of the outcomes of the process of geopolitical transformation that was eliminating independent units across Europe at the time, regardless of their desirability, incorruptibility, or national sentiment.

In English usage, the legislation uniting the parliaments is often called the Act of Union; in Scotland it is better known as the Treaty of Union. The difference in nomenclature (and the slow shift over recent decades from Act to Treaty in UK-wide usage) reflected a basic subterranean confusion in the UK. For many Scots, it was a partnership between England and Scotland; for many of the English it was more akin to a union of the peoples.[2] Whether

Scotland would have been better off independent, whether it could have survived independent, and in what ways union was costly are speculative and politically contentious questions that cannot be answered here. What is clear, though, is that Scotland found a relatively successful niche in the expanding British empire; one author, counting Scots in the empire, has even talked of "Scotland's empire" (Devine 2003). Upwardly mobile Scots and upwardly mobile Scots elites discovered the pleasures of an imperial metropole: "magnetised to a conurbation [London] that was at once the site of government and the court, and Britain's biggest port, ship-building centre, money market, and source of print, the different elites of these islands developed, from very early on, a shared avidity for imperial investments, ideas, and adventures" (Colley 2002:11).

The city of Glasgow grew great on transatlantic trade and later on shipbuilding. Scottish youths went to London or the empire and found new horizons there; Dr. Johnson in London insulted his future biographer, the Scot Boswell, by telling him when they met that "the best prospect a Scotsman ever sees is the high road to London." That says something about the Scottish influence on metropolitan life then, but other Scots found wider horizons, including the effective colonization of much of southern Africa or the creation of great colonial trading networks. Back in Scotland, the Scottish Enlightenment changed world intellectual history, with people such as Adam Ferguson, Adam Smith, and David Hume at work in Edinburgh and Glasgow.

Scotland, like other parts of the UK, would become a highly specialized part of the imperial metropole, with its own strong industrial base and also specializing in trade and related sectors such as finance and shipbuilding. Its particular parts of the economy would, however, decline faster than other parts of the UK; Scotland's ability to capture the added value of its products and the benefits of empire was not as great as that of the magnetic conurbation of London, and, like other regions engaged in the work of Britain's great nineteenth century (Manchester, Liverpool, Newcastle, South Wales), it would decline in the twentieth alongside the empire while London moved on to become a worldwide financial and service sector center. The empire—the partnership venture—was declining rapidly and the partnership itself began to look shaky. Oil, a potential substitute for imperial trading ventures in Hong Kong or South Africa, made it seem like Scotland could move, metaphorically, into another line of business—and dissolve the partnership. The impact of decolonization in Britain, so important but difficult to see in everyday life on the island today, is still a topic being studied, but it is not hard to argue that the ties that bound England and Scotland together were also ties that bound them both to empire (Kumar 2003:172). Perhaps Scotland could have followed Ireland and other parts of the empire out from England's shadow into independence.

What Scotland and Catalonia have in common is that many of their key organizations remained regional and were able to carry forward their nation in time. Walker Connor (1994:42) reminds us that nation-building (i.e., the creation of a unified people within a single state) is perhaps better thought of as "nation-destroying," for it demands the elimination of small cultures. Spain failed, and Britain did not really try, to destroy the small nations. Those stateless nations could preserve in their urban networks the institutional and social bases of their articulate distinctiveness.[3] That does not tell us why they both ended with autonomy in their respective states at the end of the twentieth century.

## SOCIAL EXPLANATIONS

These processes were part of the histories of distinct but dissimilar societies. Is there an obvious structural variable, used in analyses of nationalism, territorial mobilization, and territorial politics that would explain a convergent outcome? Consider the most purely cultural explanations of regional political outcomes. There is language, key to Catalan nationalism and identified as a major explanatory variable by Conversi (Conversi 1997). Scotland has no major own language (Gaelic, in the Highlands, is very marginal, and Lallans, or lowland Scots, has not been widely seen as a separate language). Then, there is the distinct religion, a classic prop of nationalist sentiment (Hastings 1997; Gorski 2000). Scotland has a distinct religion; Catalonia does not. Spain is Catholic, whereas the UK is Protestant. This means that the centralization and political force of religion was different—the Spanish Catholic Church has centuries of connection with the Spanish state and political right, whereas the UK has different Protestant churches in Scotland and England as well as a much longer history of strongly organized dissenting churches.

Political economy explanations of territorial political change highlight different factors. A classic one is overdevelopment and underdevelopment. Scotland has periodically been poorer than the rest of the UK and has often had lower wage rates (although not from the 1960s onward, when it has had more internal variation than it has varied overall relative to England and Wales) (Lee 1995:212). Catalonia is unquestionably overdeveloped relative to Spain, although the last decades have seen the gap reduced (Vergés 1998:269). In other words, a theory premised on underdevelopment such as that of Hechter (1999) does not work in either country while one based on overdevelopment, such as that in the last chapter of Gourevitch (1980), that might receive support from Catalonia, does not stand in middling Scotland (see also Page 1977). Sectors are strong explanations in other aspects of political science (Gourevitch 1986; Shafer 1994). While Catalonia and Scotland were early industrializers and both concentrated on textiles, they diverged after the mid-nineteenth century. Catalonia developed light industry while Scotland built a focus on mining, metallurgy, and engineering. Light industry and small textile plants have very different tariff, labor, capital formation and regulatory preferences from heavy industry, mining, and metallurgy, and the societies they create are very different (Díez Medrano 1995). The dominance of the latter in Scotland, added to Scotland's far higher reliance on international trade until the postwar era, give very different casts to their economies and societies. This combined with the level of development; in the 1970s, when the case studies in the next chapter start, Britain was in decline or transition after achieving the world's earliest industrial revolution and Scotland's heavy industry sectors were declining—an explanation canvassed for Scottish nationalism (Breuilly 1993:330–331, 337). But Spain was rapidly industrializing, having only begun to be a predominantly urban population in the first decades of the century, and Catalan industry was thriving.

## POLITICAL EXPLANATIONS

The likelihood that any argument based substantially on changes within the state will hold is reduced by the dramatically different careers of the Spanish and UK states since World War One. The UK has been a parliamentary democracy with mass suffrage for almost a century, and was a democracy of sorts long before that. It has not seen any dramatic regime changes in a very long time. Spain, by contrast, entered the twentieth century as a weak monarchy and passed through an eccentric dictatorship to an unstable republic ended by a bloody civil war that led to the yet bloodier victory of a "national-Catholic" dictator who presided over rapid development and systematic repression of minority nations (Carr and Fusi 1979). Upon his death in 1975, Spain began a lengthy democratic transition that led to its becoming a consolidated polyarchy that entered the EU in 1986. If instability gives nationalists chances, then Scotland poses a problem. If a repressive state hurts them, then Catalonia poses a problem, while if repression helps nationalism, as in the Basque Country (Conversi 1997), then Scotland's nationalists pose a problem.

In addition to this major set of structural differences, other variables decrease the amount of environmental similarity. Spain's state, at the start of the process of regionalization, was a Napoleonic state copied from the French model. Britain's had a far stronger tradition of local autonomy, even allowing for the steady encroachments of the central state on local government during the twentieth century (Bulpitt 1983). Meanwhile, clientelism and local elite dominance figured (and figure) much larger in Spanish history than in British

(Robles Egea 1996), as did abuse of the legal system by the powerful (Maravall 2003). Violence had also been more important in Spanish politics. Finally, Europe is unlikely to have had consistent effects. Spain regionalized before joining the EU, and Britain after—Britain joined in 1973 when authoritarian Spain was, if not quite a pariah, at least unwelcome in European institutions. This sequencing problem goes further—Catalonia's regional government was born in 1977–1980 while Scotland's was born in 1998–1999. Indeed, Scotland's 1979 referendum on regionalization, the same year as Catalonia's, failed. If there is a learning process or demonstration effect linking the two cases, it seems to be a decidedly lagged one.

## OUTCOMES: REGIONAL GOVERNMENT IN SCOTLAND AND CATALONIA

Nevertheless, these two cases have converged on very similar outcomes (Table 2.1). The basic coinage of regional governments' power is power over the center, money, and competencies, or the right to develop and implement policy in an area. This is a more nuanced and robust indicator than a simple tally of the presence or absence of a government, because governments can shade off into nonexistence without crossing a single clear line. Elected officials, legislative powers, budgetary control, competencies and links with other institutions need not vary together and in many cases do not. A simple test of the presence or absence of regional governments would both have unproductive definitional problems on the wider shores (such as whether England's weak, corporatist, and nonelected regional chambers are regional governments) and leaves enormous variation among "existing" regional governments. By contrast, disaggregating governments and paying attention to what they can control gives a better handle on the variations between ethereal English regions and powerful Scotland, between advanced Catalonia and advancing La Rioja.

Table 2.1 presents for illustrative purposes and in highly simplified form the competencies of the Scottish Parliament and Catalan government (*Generalitat*) in policy fields, their own rights to organize themselves, and their power over the center as discussed by Stepan (2001:340–341). That means, for detailed outcomes, the range of competencies of the regional governments detailed in the Statute of Autonomy of Catalonia and the Scotland Act 1998 (for a nontechnical summary of the Scotland Act, see Taylor 1999; for a technical one, Burrows 2000; for the Catalan Statute of Autonomy, Sobrequés and Riera 1982, Vernet i Llobet 1998, Albertí et al. 2000 or, nontechnical and in English, Aja 2001). The design of the Spanish constitution introduces many such restrictions by giving the central state license to legislate basic norms, which in intergovernmental power grabs can

Table 2.1  The Powers of Scotland and Catalonia, 2000

| Competencies | Scotland | Catalonia |
|---|---|---|
| Language | Yes | Yes (qualified) |
| Police/fire | Yes | Yes |
| Justice (legal system) | Yes | No (role in administration) |
| Agriculture/fisheries | Yes | Yes |
| Pensions/social security | No | No |
| Health services | Yes | Yes (qualified) |
| Education | Yes | Yes (qualified) |
| Universities | Yes | Yes (qualified) |
| Research and investigation | Possible | Possible |
| Culture (inc. museums, patrimony) | Yes | Yes |
| EU relations | No | No |
| Transport | Local only | Local only |
| Infrastructure | Local only | Local only |
| Macroeconomic policy | No | No |
| Immigration/citizenship | No | No |
| Regional development | Yes | Yes |
| Planning (spatial) | Yes | Yes (qualified) |
| Industrial policy | Possible | Possible |
| Radio/television | No | No (but done quasi-legally) |
| Environment | Some | Some |
| Finance | No | Some (*caixes d'estalvi/cajas de ahorro*) |
| Industrial/personal regulation (work conditions, privacy) | No | No |

| Structure | Scotland | Catalonia |
|---|---|---|
| Control over local government | Yes | No |
| Control over legislature's own internal structure | No | Some |
| Taxation | Very minimal (funded by block grant and can change income tax rate by 3%) | Very minimal (mostly funded by block grants plus a few marginal taxes) |
| Own civil service | No, qualified (unified UK civil service, but most employees— doctors, police—are not civil servants and are thus effectively employed by the Scottish Executive) | Yes, qualified (the contracts of many are still held over from statewide negotiations) |

*continued on next page*

Table 2.1    The Powers of Scotland and Catalonia, 2000 *(continued)*

| Role in State | Scotland | Catalonia |
|---|---|---|
| Region used as electoral circumscription | For European parliament only | For 20% of ineffective *Senado* |
| A veto in any formal intergovernmental forum | No | No |
| Regional government represented in upper house | No | No |

Note: "Qualified" means restricted by the central state; "possible" means at the discretion of the region.

Sources: Statute of Autonomy of Catalonia and Scotland Act 1998; see also Aja 1999:108; Hazell 2000:3–4; Argullol 2004.

be very detailed. Almost uniquely in the world, the UK has very few such norms (Simeon 2003; Greer 2004:ch. 7, forthcoming).

Both governments have extensive policy autonomy, limited rights to organize and finance themselves, and no real control over the central state. The interesting phenomenon to be explained is that Scotland and Catalonia have such similar outcomes—namely, autonomous regional governments with responsibilities centered in the welfare state.

In financing, both are substantially similar. Each receives the bulk of its budget from the central state according to a set formula, and it comes as a block with few and decreasing sums earmarked. Neither can raise much revenue alone. Scotland has one major tax power, that of varying the income tax rate by 3% (which would raise a very small amount of money relative to the Scottish budget). Most of its budget comes from a formula (the Barnett formula) that gives it new expenditure on a set ratio vis-à-vis new English expenditure (Bell and Christie 2002; Heald and McLeod 2002; House of Lords Select Committee on the Constitution 2002). Catalonia theoretically has extensive tax powers, but a Constitutional Tribunal decision upheld a central state law banning double taxation (i.e., the same source of income being taxed by two levels of government). Since the central state has, over the last five centuries, already tapped most important sources of tax revenue, Catalonia depends for its funds on a formula (set every five years until now, but being changed in the new Statute of Autonomy for Catalonia) that gives it a set percentage of income tax revenues, a percentage that is less than its taxpayers contribute (Vilalta i Ferrer 1998; López-Casanovas 2003; see also the critical Omnium Cultural 1998; Vergés 1998). It will benefit from 2006 reforms that retain the structure but transfer more money. Neither is a bad financing system as regional finance goes, although Scots and Catalan politicians often claim they have greater outflows than inflows and that their autonomy is intolerably crimped. Indeed, some studies propose block grant financing with autonomy over budgeting as the optimal outcome for substate politicians who seek power but no blame (van Houten 1999; Garman, Haggard, and Willis 2001).

So they are formally very similar. They both are primarily administrators of social policy. Both have the bulk of their budgets tied up in health and education. Noticeably, neither has much capacity to redistribute resources across the population in the most important ways governments can, since neither can set pensions or the effective rates of major taxes. Neither has much power over the economy in general. Something else matters: neither is independent. Both have strongly enunciated claims for statehood, established nationalist political parties (the second largest one in Scotland) that explicitly demand it, and regular public discussion of the issue. Yet neither is an independent state, and neither one has attempted to hold a referendum on independence. This is crucial, for explaining convergence on their current model requires not just explaining what started the process of regionalization, but also what appears to have halted it.

## NATIONALISM AND GLOBALIZATION AS CAUSES

Political, economic, and cultural variables associated with statebuilding and nationalism suggest that Scotland and Catalonia should not resemble each other, yet they do. This bodes ill for macro-level theories; in addition to any problems explaining the link between language, sector, or religion and a political outcome, they mostly do not hold for these two star cases of regionalization. What, then, do they have in common or affects them alike? Their most obvious commonality is nationalism, but that concept asks as many questions as it answers when put in comparative perspective. Nationalism, and nationalist ideology as studied by the more intellectually oriented scholars, are inadequate explanations of how Scotland and Catalonia arrived where they are and as suggestions of what they might teach us about the causes and satisfactory resolution of national conflict in the rest of the world. It is in the diversity and complexity of nationalism, nationalist politics, and their societal and political environments, rather than in the mere fact of national identity, that we find the useful and informative explanations. To look somewhere else is to risk misunderstanding the nationalism—who can say which pronouncements truly represent a nation? It is to let state nationalists in liberal states off with no reason, since nationalists attached to an existing liberal state can be just as much nationalists as those who believe in a nation lacking a state. And it risks indulging the tautology that a nation with tolerant, agreeable politics is therefore a nation with a tolerant, agreeable national identity.

## Nationalism

Both Scotland and Catalonia are nations with nationalisms, of course.[4] Both host secessionist parties and many of their politicians freely (and to their own benefit) identify themselves as nationalists. They both have all the infrastructure of political and banal nationalism, from art museums and galleries to flags and weather forecasts that discuss every corner of their territories while ignoring near neighbors (Billig 1995). Nevertheless, pure analyses of nationalist ideology and mobilization in the two countries are an inadequate explanation for the actual regional governments for three reasons.

First, nationalism as often needs explanation as it explains. The most common result of looking to nationalist ideologies to explain outcomes in polities with nationalists is a circular argument that attributes desirable outcomes in areas with a nationalism (essentially, liberal politics and policies in stable societies that tolerate diversity) to desirable properties in the nationalism (its inclusive, civic, nontribal ideas). This view surfaces in self-congratulatory forms everywhere and in many discussions as an opposition between "civic" and "ethnic" or "western" and "eastern" or "inclusive" and "exclusive" nationalisms (Kohn 1945; Ignatieff 1996; see Shulman 2002).

"This attitude is truly lazy," remarks George Schöpflin; "it projects Western illusions and worse . . . and, incidentally gives rise to very poor political analysis." By dividing between two sides of nationalism, as defined by their political outcomes, "one is obscuring the proposition that the so-called civic nations of the West, the positive examples . . . also have ethnic identities; it is just that these are framed by the state and citizenship (civil society)" (Schöpflin 2000:5). It might be an excellent argument in the practical politics of nations and nationalists, but its intellectual usefulness is almost nil because civicness or ethnicness are not definitional attributes of nations or nationalisms. Serious studies of nationalist politics almost uniformly conclude that any group identity has its internal political debates, its demons and its virtues, its potential for bigotry and its potential for inclusion. Both Scottish and Catalan nationalist milieus—whether formally organized by nationalist parties or not—have many intellectuals and activists concerned with maintaining an inclusive, tolerant national identity and stamping down violence or bigotry. That is a political outcome, though; it tells us that Scotland and Catalonia have something to teach us, since some societies do not have such insistent politics of territorial autonomy and tolerance. The mere fact that Scots and Catalans intellectuals and leaders put such effort into maintaining their tolerant, liberal national politics suggests that the explanation for their desirable characteristics and outcomes lies not just in their national identities but also in their politics.

Second, it is unwise to assume that an analysis of a nationalist party or nationalist thought will be a full and generalizable explanation of the rise of regional governments, even those in areas with nationalist mobilization. Studying nationalist parties and movements was an obvious reaction to their appearance and capacity to create change, but it is misleading to conflate their careers a priori with either national identity or territorial political change. The fact that autonomy happened in some areas with mobilized nationalists, and the fact that it can, under some circumstances, quiet nationalist conflict, still do not mean that nationalism causes autonomy in any simple way. At a minimum, there must be an interaction between the nationalist movements and somebody else—not only have Scotland and Catalonia not seen wars of national liberation, but they both won their legal autonomy when a statewide socialist party held the majority of their seats and had put nationalists firmly in second place within their territories. No matter what observation of the rooster may suggest, his crowing probably does not explain the sunrise.

Third, many of the best analyses of nationalism (in general, classics such as Gellner 1983; Hobsbawm 1990; Anderson, B. 1991; A. D. Smith 1991; and, for Scotland and Catalonia, Brand 1978; Díez Medrano 1995; Conversi 1997), are just that: analyses of nationalism. It would be unfair to demand of them an explanation of the legal and organizational form of the Scottish Parliament and Catalan Generalitat. They do, however, suggest that looking at society can explain the form a nationalism takes. They suggest that the mobilization, course, and effects of a national identity are all worth explaining by factors including the structure of the state and society as well as the efforts of intellectuals and others to push its ideas in one direction and another. In other words, all three reasons not to stop at nationalism when explaining regionalization suggest that there should be some social structural variables at work behind both the government and the nationalism.

*Parties?*

Perhaps it is not nationalism *grosso modo* that explains regionalization, and instead it is the clearer and more visible consequence of the presence of a nationalist or regionalist party. The presence of nationalist parties such as the Scottish National Party (SNP) certainly brought national identity and territorial politics to the fore; even if Labour delivered the Scottish Parliament, the "existence of the SNP has forced Labour to pay attention to Scottish matters" (Bennie, Brand, and Mitchell 1997:160). Or, bluntly, "devolution was supposed to kill the Nats dead"—a variously attributed but popular quote in the Scottish Labour Party. There is voluminous evidence (some of it here) that the irruption and force of nationalist parties changed regional politics. It leads to a much clearer hypothesis than simple analyses of nationalism. Namely, it suggests that the presence of nationalist parties as electoral competitors obliges established statewide parties to create regional governments in order to defeat the nationalists. Autonomy is, ironically enough, explained by secessionists' impact on centralists (van Houten 1999; Meguid 2002). This analysis fits with an overall trend toward the study of decentralization decisions (and other aspects of institutional design more generally) through the lens of party preferences and strategies, starting with the fact that almost by definition the decisions in a democratic system will be routed through party politicians (Garman, Haggard, and Willis 2001; O'Neill 2003).

The evidence for this hypothesis is not good enough to take it as a full explanation of politics in the regions with nationalists, in part because of the weakness of any assumption that studying nationalism explains regionalization, for all its descriptive potential as a model of day-to-day politics. The problem is that the societies themselves contain forces that seek to shape political parties. All manner of organizations and political elites can put pressure on a party to change an electorally useful strategy, and resources such as press and money that parties need give them strings with which to tug at a party (chapter three discusses the unfortunate fate of Labour when it tried to pursue an electoral strategy against these pressures in Scotland). Furthermore, nationalist parties tend to be unstable electoral competitors—there is always incentive to hope their threats will go away. The SNP shocked Labour with a 1988 electoral victory in one of Labour's safest constituencies, but Labour could have relaxed after defeating the SNP twice more within months. It would be surprising if parties were able to reshape political power so decisively as a mere electoral play; it certainly does not seem to be reflected in the battles within parties or the pressures others put on them. Meanwhile, the worldwide phenomenon of regionalization has produced strong regional governments in which there are no nationalist parties, and nationalist organizations have failed to advance regional autonomy in other areas (such as Brittany). And, finally, it does not explain how the separate responses of parties to secessionist challengers would lead Scotland, Catalonia, and other regions to develop such similar governments.

*Tidal Movements*

Perhaps the similarity in very different places is explained by common, external, factors bearing upon them that have changed their opportunities or even their societies. There is one literature that fixes the outcome—regionalization—firmly, identifies it as a relatively new phenomenon (from the 1970s, really), and explains it not with traditional analyses of nationalism but with new arguments that bear down on the changing European and international opportunity structures. This is the dominant literature on Western European regionalization (a critical review is Bukowski, Piattoni, and Smyrl 2002). It begins with the claim that convergence on autonomy stems from changes in the international political economy and the role of the state. Implicitly, it grounds its analyses in changes in the international political opportunity structure facing regions. This argument derives from the long debates about globalization that have taken place across academia. Its core is that states matter less—that as factors of production become more mobile, international organizations grow, and culture becomes less rooted, the traditional state form is losing relevance. The decline of geopolitical competition in Europe—the brutal process that led to the end of Catalano-Aragonese rights and Scottish independence—and the decreasing power of European states in the world has made European states less appealing vessels of power, less capable of domination and protection (Collins 1999:106–107). Instead, economic regions are becoming the true political economies for most people and the most relevant social formations for understanding the international political economy. Crossing borders, diverging from their host countries and building thick networks internally, they fulfill many of the functions of an increasingly emaciated state. Few academics have fully endorsed this vision of the declining importance of the state as put by publicists like Ohmae (1995) and the realist resurgence since September 2001 has not helped it, but shades of the argument, complete with poorly specified mechanisms and anthropomorphization of the nation, are common (Hocking 1997; Guiberneau 1999:176–179).

In the more sophisticated discussions, this argument takes the form of the literature on "new regionalism," or "bourgeois regionalism" as Harvie called it (Harvie 1992, 1994). Michael Keating's lucid analysis explains new regionalism as a consequence of the state's power and authority "being eroded from three directions: from above by internationalization; from below by regional and local assertion; and laterally by the advance of the market and civil society. . . . This has produced a new regionalism marked by two linked features: it is not contained within the framework of the nation-state; and it pits regions against each other in a competitive mold" (Keating 1998:72–73). The mechanisms that cause this dynamic are many, but economic regions seem to be the outcome (Balme 1996; Gobetti 1996). The inability or unwillingness of states to redistribute internally, between regions, gives regions no other choice. The arguments should suggest that regional governments will win power as a result of the increase in demand for better government by the firms and societies of regions that are ill-served by states while the supply will come from regional governments that can and would like to supplant the states. Thus, the more exposed to the international economy a region is, the more it should demand a strong regional government and get it; increase in exposure to the global economy should increase the odds of any region becoming assertive. The political process should then reflect resistance to state controls on the region and interests derived from its position in the international economy (and, presumably, frustration with the state) in a way that demonstrably relates to an increasingly open economy.

These dynamics might seem to have an even better chance in Western Europe where the political opportunity structure has, in the 1990s, changed to become friendlier still to regional governments (J. B. Jones and Keating 1995; Hooghe 1996; P. Lynch 1996; Wagstaff 1999; Dardanelli 2005). Many regions and local governments have opened Brussels offices that at a minimum keep tabs on the activities of the EU and act as commercial embassies, and some of the most ambitious, such as that of Catalonia, participate in EU policy discussions because of the depth of research and policy advice they can contribute (Marks et al. 1996; Jeffery 1997b; Granell et al. 2002; Greenwood 2003). EU regional aid programs, while variant across states, have a strong regional dimension that has included the participation of regional governments (Hooghe and Keating 1994; Hooghe 1996). The result was a change in the resources available to regional governments that received aid, as well as a diversification in the sources of such resources. This increase and diversification of aid did have dramatic effects in at least some regions (A. Smith 1995). The EU, meanwhile, brought regions into its core institutions. The Maastricht Treaty creates a Committee of the Regions to give regional and local governments a consultative voice in the EU decisionmaking process (Bourrinet 1997; J. Loughlin 1997).

As a result, it seemed quite likely that the changing international and European opportunity structures combined *would* lead to autonomy. The relative benefits of being a state were decreasing while the costs of becoming one remained high. Catalonia, among other European regions, seized the opportunity and built both a network of international contacts (including the Brussels "embassy") and a powerful ideology of national projection within a multilevel world polity that attracted much attention (Morata 1995:124). Catalonia, along with Rhône-Alpes, Bavaria, and Lombardy formed the most famous of the many pan-European regional groups with the economistically named "Four Motors" club that sought to coordinate policy and interests and exchange ideas across ("new") regions that ostensibly had more in common with each other than with the other regions of Spain, France, Germany, and Italy. When the EU convened a constitutional convention to report in 2003, Catalonia and Scotland were among major European regions to form a lobbying group known in Brussels argot as Reg-Leg, representing "constitutional regions," defined as regions with legislative power. The hypothesis stemming from this argument is that strong regional governments should emerge evenly throughout the EU and the process of their emergence should reflect the regions' demand for policies the state cannot supply and the greater ability of the regions to supply such policies because of resources and legal opportunities stemming from European integration.

This European strategy—slipping around the central state—seemed to work. However, the same Catalan politicians that worked on these projects in the 1990s were cynical about their effects in 2001 interviews ("What we didn't see," said one Catalan nationalist deputy in 2001, "was just how much juridical statehood mattered"). The states continued to be the key actors in a Europe still dominated by the Commission and the Council and academic criticisms of the idea of a third level mounted (J. Anderson 1990; Borras-Alomar, Christiansen, and Rodriguez-Pose 1994; Jeffery 1997a; Smyrl 1997; Greer 2005; Jeffery 2005). Good theories suggested that the first consequence of Europeanization was that regional governments *lost* powers to the EU, a forum where states dominate, and had to fight to get them back (Hooghe and Marks 2001:77–78). Others pointed out that the theories of a "Europe of the regions," insofar as they were about any tangible policy areas, were about structural funds—an area designed specifically to build regional political capacity and integrate regions in policy (Tarrow 2004:50). Most regional governments' ability to influence the important areas of EU politics, such as the internal market or agriculture, was nil.

Political practice certainly emphasized the power of member staes. After devolution, UK and Scottish representatives were not alone in closely coordinating and using the "Reg-Leg" group of constitutional regions as a back door in member state negotiations. That was only rational, given the vastly greater power of member states (Jeffery 2005). Meanwhile, the variation in substate and state responses to European integration cast doubt on its consistent effects; if the political opportunity structure shapes the outcomes, we should see far more consistent outcomes than we do (A. Smith 1995, 1998; Börzel 2002:21,25). The strength of regions in their state's EU policymaking and implementation seems to vary based on the political strength of the regions overall—"where there is high regional autonomy, the EU has strengthened it, and where there is low autonomy, the EU has increased the balance of power in favour of the central government" (Greenwood 2003:234, 265). As for globalization, its consistent effects on regions were elusive (van Houten 2003), the state remained important, and the argument rang hollow anyway for regions such as Scotland and Catalonia that had been integrated into the global economy for centuries.

These globalization- and Europeanization-based analyses, pitching giant aggregates (nations, regions) against complicated, full categories of phenomena (the EU, globalization), end up unable to explain the variation in

regionalization and even nationalisms. They are the macrodeterminist theories that Bukowski, Piattoni, and Smyrl (2002:2) rightly criticize for being "in
danger of forgetting politics."

## Scottish and Catalan Explanations

Macrodeterminism is not the main risk for scholars writing from Scotland
and Catalonia about their experiences. There have been many studies of
Scottish and Catalan government and of the origins of their governments.
They contain theorized and potentially generalizable explanations of regionalism as a phenomena—of not just of change in territorial politics, but of
what stops change in territorial politics. These analyses, with their robust
explanations of the events in each country, eliminate many variables (as case
studies do) and served as a basis for this work's theory of regionalism.

The most common explanation for devolution in Scotland is grounded
in the same concept that authors use to explain Scotland's persistence and
informal autonomy—namely, Scottish civil society. The line of argument
begins with Jack Brand's (1978) analysis of the rise of the SNP and the
influential work of Kellas and Hanham on the distinctive characteristics of
Scottish politics (Hanham 1969; Kellas 1989). Its modern form is pervasive
but most clearly stated in Lindsay Paterson's influential *The Autonomy of
Modern Scotland* and David McCrone's *Understanding Scotland* (McCrone
1992; Paterson 1994). Paterson argues that Scotland, informally, was always
about as autonomous as a small European nation could be, and that Scottish
society both broadly shared English preferences and was capable of adjusting
new developments such as the welfare state to maintain Scottish autonomy.
The UK was particularly congenial for a small country like Scotland; not
only was its empire a great success in general and a great opportunity for
Scots, it also had a long tradition of local autonomy that extended to Scotland itself (Bulpitt 1983).

Extending this theory, the 1980s in Britain saw a major assault on
Scottish autonomy, when Scotland was ruled from London by a Conservative Party that was a minority in Scotland. The successful campaign for a
Scottish parliament was another chapter in the ongoing efforts of Scottish
civil and political society to maintain Scottish autonomy within the British
state. Scotland's autonomy, and Scotland's new parliament, are both chapters in an ongoing story of institutional adaptation to changes in the state
(Paterson 1998). The institutions of Scottish civil society are the mechanisms
that muster the political force to do that. They seek to maintain their autonomy and Scottish distinctiveness, and thus provided massive logistical,
moral, and political support to campaigners for a Scottish parliament. The
activities of the Scottish Constitutional Convention, founded in 1988, are

the summation of this consensus. The convention brought together representatives of Labour and small political parties, the Church of Scotland, and
the unions to demand a Scottish parliament with autonomy. This coalition
was able to add to and canalize Scottish outrage at Conservative policies in
Scotland (Marr 1995; Mitchell 1996; Harvie and Jones 2000). Its ability to
territorialize conflict over policy meant that while Scotland is not significantly
to the left of England, it mobilized against Thatcher's retrenching policies
while a plurality of the English voted for them four times (Jeffery 2006).

Explanations of the outcome in Catalonia rely heavily on three factors:
the character of Catalan nationalism; the party system of Catalonia; and the
context of the Spanish democratic transition. The first ingredient, and probably the most studied in Catalan analyses, is the historical trajectory of Catalan
nationalism. For at least a century, Catalan nationalism has been predominantly moderate and often center-right, with equally strong assertions of Catalan
national identity and commitment to autonomy or participation in an Iberian
federal state (González Casanova 1974, 1988; Giner 1980; Prats i Català 1988;
Díez Medrano 1995; Conversi 1997). This long historical context meant that
there were few takers for a more militant nationalist stance when in the 1970s
the Spanish state itself was the object of contention.

In this context of national moderation, the political negotiations leading
to Spain's pacted democratic transition gave Catalan political forces an opportunity to negotiate autonomy that would satisfy Catalan aspirations within the
new state. Just as the unions negotiated a role for themselves and a legal
framework that would offer the chance of winning their goals, and big businesses and finance did likewise, "Catalonia" negotiated a role for itself (Köhler
2000; McRoberts 2001; Gunther, Montero, and Botella 2004:111; Greer 2006).
The literature in Catalan and a great deal of public debate spends much time
evaluating the influence of different spokespersons, the quality of their strategies for becoming sole spokesperson, and the consequences of their negotiating strategies (for a taste, see Bassets, Culla, and de Riquer 1997; Aracil and
Segura 2000). The consensus point is that Catalonia, through the intentional
political activity of the left and the nationalists, was able to speak with a
sufficiently unified voice and muster enough clout to be given its autonomy
as a condition of the transition (Gibbons 1999:288). Not only were Catalans
at the table, the other negotiators could not ignore Catalan demands. The
forces that did this negotiating, and that then went on to implement the bare
bones of the settlement, were political parties—above all Convergència i Unió
(CiU), the coalition of nationalist parties that ruled Catalonia from 1980 to
2004. Thus, the electoral evolution of Spanish parties and CiU's support for
the last Socialist and first Partido Popular governments are a central topic in
the explanations of the development of the state of the autonomies and its
current problems (Caminal Badia 1998b).

These fall in with a somewhat kind of different analysis, which is of the development of the Spanish "state of the autonomies" in general. These are studies of how Spain developed its particular overall territorial settlement and surmounted decades of center-periphery conflict or malign alliance. Looking at Spain rather than Catalonia, they discuss the same main variables, but with different emphases—the moderate character of "peripheral nationalisms" is less important than the willingness to compromise evident in the pacted Transition and subsequent politics, and the nationalist political parties play seconds to the statewide parties that both lead the nonnationalist autonomous communities and "vertebrate" the political system (Moreno 1988; Aja 1999; Grau i Creus 2000a, b). In these analyses, Spain finally created the correct formula to govern itself, both with its short-term multitrack development of autonomous communities and with the long-term harmonization of the communities at high levels of autonomous competencies. The motor of this decentralization is party competition, the will of less autonomous regions to emulate Catalonia and the Basque Country, and the will of the Catalans, Basques, and Gallegos to be ahead of the other, "Spanish" autonomous communities; the whole is "multiple ethnoterritorial concurrence" (Moreno 1997:102,118,167; Moreno 2001). It turns out to be a form of good government that works not only for "nationalities" such as Catalonia but also improves the governance of regions such as Murcia or Extremadura that have come to enjoy self-government and allows them to contribute to that of Spain (Moreno 2002). Peripheral nationalist parties still try to distinguish themselves, leading them to cause permanent instability in what Spaniards call *agravio comparativo* (a sort of invidious comparison), but the development and stabilization of the autonomous state might be slowly robbing them of support and campaigning issues (Payne 2000:106; Núñez 2005).

None of this adds up easily to an explanation of regionalism, and certainly not an explanation of how to such different societies emerged with similar forms of governance. But they do fit with the argument of the previous chapter—that the existence of a complex of regional organizations shapes politics in an autonomist direction.

## CONVERGENCE IN TWO WESTERN EUROPEAN REGIONS

In this comparative study, the logic is the same as the one that underlies the well-known "most-different-systems" strategy of Przeworski and Teune (Przeworski and Teune 1970; Ragin, Berg-Schlosser, and de Meur 1996; see also Ragin 1987). The approach is premised on the logic that an explanatory variable can be best isolated when cases vary in as many attributes as possible but share similar outcomes. In other words, if the point is to isolate the main actors in explaining territorial political outcomes, then the goal should be to find two cases that share few attributes and thus preemptively eliminate most potential variables. If an explanation seems to work well in one case, the other is presumptively inhospitable to its working there. Thus, only the hardiest and most useful explanatory concepts will survive analysis of their role in both cases. Part I uses this logic.

Beneath this high level of politics is a second level that affords us the opportunity to test the argument. This is the level of policy fields, where the presence of regional organizations and their influence on parties (based on their ability to supply resources to them) should explain the areas where there is pressure for regionalization. Part II is an explanation of the relationship between the presence of regional organizational networks and the presence of a regional competency and the existence of an identifiable political process that explains the correlation between the presence of regional organizational networks and regional competencies (see the summary in Table 2.2). This analysis is important for three reasons. First, it is the outcome in detail; totalling up competencies across policy fields creates Table 2.1, or the governments of Scotland and Catalonia. Second, it is important because it tests the hypotheses that regional organizational networks, not nationalist social movements, explain regionalization overall, and that their presence is the best predictor of the distribution of competencies in a policy field. I oversample on positive outcomes to gain the benefits of being able to trace processes; negative cases tend never to make it onto the political agenda because there are few people able and willing to start discussion of regionalization. Third, it is therefore important because of the gaps between Scotland and Catalonia, such as in responsibility for law. This can in each case be traced to a difference in the organizational networks of the two countries—in justice, Scotland has long had its own, fiercely independent, legal system tied to the region and Catalonia faces a long-unified Spanish

**Table 2.2   Policy Area Analyses**

| Policy Area | Social Structure of Policy Area | Scotish Outcome, 2000 | Catalan Outcome, 2000 |
|---|---|---|---|
| Education (policy) | Regional/local | Regional | Regional |
| Health | Regional | Regional | Regional |
| Higher Education | Regional | Regional | Regional |
| Law | Scotland—regional Spain—statewide | Regional autonomy entrenched in constitutional law | Statewide |
| Industrial/labor policy | Opportunistic/central | State | State |

judicial corps. Thus, each policy-specific section analyzes the politics of the regional competency in Scotland and Catalonia in education, health, higher education, law, and industrial and labor policy. They provide more parallel tests of explanations and they also substantiate this book's claim that the low politics of organizations and public policy help shape the high politics of constitutions and statehood.

## Data

The best way, it is said, to understand any group of elites and their organizations is to talk to them a great deal — interviews not only bring information, but valuable interpretative information not available from other techniques (Matas Dalmases 1995). The bulk of the new empirical research took the form of semistructured interviews with decisionmakers in political parties and social institutions in Catalonia and Scotland; I did 77 anonymous, semistructured interviews in 2000–2001 in Catalonia, and in Scotland I did 18 in 1998, 4 in 1999, and 43 in 2001 (they also fed into Greer 2004). In Catalonia this included 22 politicians of all parties, 12 civil servants (one in security, two in culture, two in language policy, two in education, two in research policy, two in local government, and one in universities policy), eleven interviews across the health sector, two interviews with journalists, nine interviews with government or academic public lawyers, two interviews with business associations, one with a union representative, and sixteen with retired politicians. All were reconstructed from detailed notes. In Scotland, this included 28 health sector interviewees, 20 politicians, three retired politicians, one lawyer, two Church of Scotland officeholders, two representatives each of unions and business groups, and nine officials outside health (three in culture, four in development, one in finances and one in education). Interviewees were anonymized.

The study used two strategies to identify informants. Initially, I began with policy sectors and political parties and interviewees in those sectors recommended by Scottish and Catalan academics and journalists. From these starting points, I pursued a snowball strategy in which I asked each interviewee for more potential informants. I used a number of techniques to reduce the potential bias of the snowball technique. I sought out leaders of theoretically important organizations such as employers' federations, unions, and each political party as well as responsible civil servants. I also conducted geographically dispersed interviews — with party officials in Lleida in Catalonia, and with officials and politicians in Glasgow and surrounding areas in Scotland as well as in the capital cities. After analysis and deviant case analysis of the interviews, I used published materials and secondary sources to check the information from the interviews; these are cited in the text wherever possible.

## CONCLUSION

The convergence of the dissimilar countries Scotland and Catalonia on a specific model of autonomy—approximately that of an independent administrator of social policy—is no accident. The particular balance between regional self-assertion and submersion in a single state, as well as the particular details of what these regions can and cannot do, are both results of the political processes that create them. The interaction of institutionalized regional and state organizational networks with social movement mobilization produces both the move to autonomy and the blocks to further autonomy or independence.

Chapter two asked how Scotland and Catalonia, two different, strong, and well-established nations, became equally well known for their autonomist solutions and multinational coexistence. Part I then explains the origins of the Catalan and Scottish regional governments by their regional organizations and parties. Part II cuts into the problem differently. It argues that the competencies of Scotland and Catalonia reflect the presence and exertions of regional organizations on behalf of autonomy. The logic of the argument—that regional organizations constrain parties, rewarding some demands for autonomy and punishing others—works on the level of individual policies as well as on the "high politics" of creating parliaments and administrations.

It links broad social macrostructures—the form that their centuries of national distinctiveness take today is an ecology of regional organizations that shape their regionalist politics. The result to date has been convergence on autonomy where there are strong and dense regional organizations, no matter what the other social forces in the region seek.[5] The presence of nationalist, secessionist parties, if anything, helps them seek autonomy and rarely poses threats to regional institutionalized organizations' dominance of "regional mobilization." This is because regional organizations, when they are strong, make up the largest group capable of switching sides between centralism and regionalism. They are the pivotal players in the coalitions for or against devolution. Over time, this makes them bulwarks of some sort of autonomy as their interest in autonomy cannot make them wholly centralist allies of the central state, and their interest in stability means they cannot be or support secessionists—especially secessionists in their usual form, that of an unstable party-movement.

The same process, then, that triggers a bottom-up shift to autonomy also stops it. Those who hit the accelerator can also hit the brakes. Once institutional organizations' autonomy is reestablished to their satisfaction, they will have no further incentive to seek autonomy—that is, after all, not what their organizations were established to do. Their lack of interest in environmental

destabilization will, however, remain, and they will continue to oppose secessionist social movements. The consequences of this dynamic for Scotland and
Catalonia, for institutional design and for our understanding of territorial political
change and nationalism, are the subject of the conclusion.

Looking at the interaction of complex and territorial social organizations with visible politics and nationalism casts nationalism and territorial
political change in a new light. High politics are not just a product of high
politics. High politics also comes from the contradictions, conflicts, and
coalitions born of the "low politics" in society. Public policy debates and
frustrations will spill over to shape, retard, or advance constitutional demands as well as national identity or political elite strategies. That means
they must be included in an analysis of the origins of national politics alongside both the activity of the state and the activity of explicitly declared nationalist organizations,

And as long as they are strong enough both vis-à-vis their own societies
and vis-à-vis the central states, the present structure of regional government
should remain. Their influence for devolution is powerful—bottom-up regionalism appears to coincide, in the West, with their presence. Their
influence against secession is powerful—other than a close call in Quebec,
there is no case of a stateless nation in an advanced industrial country actually trying to declare independence. They throw that influence in the direction of their own autonomy and environmental stability. And, to date,
regionalization reflects their preferences. It has been the formalization of
preexisting but threatened elite autonomy.

# Part I

# Politics

The key outcomes in this study are the regional governments of Scotland and Catalonia. The following four chapters focus on the broad political contention that created these governments. They argue that the preferences and activities of regional organizations are crucial to the political development of the two regions, and that their preferences and activities are for formal or informal autonomy. Regional organizations seek their own autonomy and environmental stability, and these preferences are important enough in party politics to make regionalization a winning party strategy and the regionalist party the winning one. Thus, fundamentally, "bottom-up" regional autonomy in multinational states comes about when regional organizations see it as the best way to maintain their own autonomy and stability.

In Scotland, Labour's two attempts to create a devolved government produced very different outcomes. In 1979, Scots voted by a narrow majority to establish a weak government, but the referendum failed to win the necessary turnout. In 1997, there was a resounding victory for a more powerful and less constrained parliament. What had changed was the attitude of Scottish regional organizations. Their autonomy and stability, largely respected to 1979, was challenged by Conservative governments and, as a result, they sought formal support for their autonomy. Their shift to support for devolution brought mainstream Scottish politics and the Labour Party along—antidevolutionists were deprived of regional resources while devolutionists now enjoyed strong support from regional organizations.

In Catalonia, the experience of dictatorship from Madrid, atop more than a century of unsatisfying Spanish politics, created a pool of frustrated Catalan regional organizations and elites who sought their own organizational stability and autonomy via Catalan regional autonomy. Their preference for regional autonomy, and the resources that came with supporting

39

these organizations' autonomist goals, created a party system in which all the key actors supported an autonomist, Catalanist, consensus. They shaped the party system, and the party best able to win their support was able to dominate the Catalan regional government at the first Catalan regional elections. Their support further buttressed it in its efforts throughout the 1980s and 1990s to develop Catalonia's competencies and powers.

The focus necessarily lies on parties; they are the main actors in politics (almost by definition, since it is politicians who legislate) but they operate within the cage of constraints created by their resource dependencies. Seeking opportunities to build ad hoc coalitions and make long-term allies, politicians focus on areas where such allies are available. The parties' behavior is consistent with that proposition. For example, Labour in Scotland was riven when its regional organizational allies disagreed with its devolutionary strategy in the 1970s, but coherent and powerful in the 1990s when its newly devolutionist regional organizational allies starved antidevolutionists of support. The chapters point out how an organizational theory of regional autonomy fits the political histories of Scotland and Catalonia better than theories that stress the changing international opportunity structures, or some sort of assumed characteristics of nationalism (which is one of the main objects of struggle), or simple party politics.

# Chapter Three

# Scotland 1960–1979

## The Road to Nowhere

The arrival of the Scottish National Party (SNP) on the Scottish political stage, most memorably when it seized one of the Labour Party's safest seats in a 1967 by-election, seemed to mark a historic change in Scottish politics. The sudden explosive growth in a party dedicated to full independence for Scotland, and long on the far fringes of politics (Finlay 1994) changed the bounds of the possible. It bred both books about Scottish nationalism's eruption (Brand 1978) and its newly mysterious previous quiescence (Nairn 1981). It forced the UK-wide parties to respond as the SNP ate away at their votes and dominance of the political agenda. They both responded with talk of devolution (the establishment of a Scottish parliament), and a Labour government, after much effort in parliament, passed a bill establishing a Scottish parliament subject to 40% of the Scots electorate approving it in a referendum. Public opinion strongly suggested that they would; it had always been strongly favorable to devolution and the referendum campaign began with strong majorities in favor of passing it. The Scots, however, did not do so. The referendum failed and the Scotland Act 1978 was accordingly repealed.

This era is, then, a negative outcome—no regional government emerged. Instead, two decades of SNP gains and arguments about Scottish devolution ended with the failure of the referendum on the establishment of a Scottish parliament, painful splits in Scottish Labour, the near-destruction of the Scottish National Party, the disintegration of the Labour government that had sponsored the devolution project, and the general election that ushered in the defiantly antidevolutionist government of Margaret Thatcher.

41

The rise and failure of devolution in the 1970s can be attributed to the interaction of the Scottish political parties and the web of Scottish regional organizations such as the trades unions, business, churches, and professions. The key arena was the Labour Party. Scottish regional organizations throughout the period enjoyed stable organizational environments and great autonomy over their own organizations, opposed political destabilization, and were broadly uninterested in the establishment of a parliament. A new parliament offered, to these organizations, the environmental instability of major political change, the prospect of creating an arena tailor-made for the insurgent SNP, and the possibility of diminished autonomy. Direct oversight by a regional parliament might be more onerous than the indirect, and often very attenuated, oversight from Whitehall that characterized Scottish politics at the time (Kellas 1989; Moore and Booth 1989; Midwinter, Keating, and Mitchell 1991; Mitchell 2003; Greer 2004, ch. 3). In other words, it promised to destabilize their environment and possibly decrease their autonomy, and it was of a package with the destabilizing arrival of the movement-party SNP. Labour, however, needed SNP parliamentary votes and very much wanted a mechanism to stop or reverse the nationalist party's growth. So Labour and its regional organizational allies fell out when, in response to the SNP electoral challenge, the Labour leadership tried to push through devolution against the wishes of regional organizations. It succeeded only in creating a weak parliament, was split by the opposition of its allies to its strategy, and failed to win the referendum. Regional organizations, simply by denying the resources Labour needed to campaign in a unified and effective manner, won their preferred outcome—the status quo ante.

## THE ROAD TO NOWHERE

The relationship of the different actors changed sequentially and accounted both for the devolution proposals and their failures. The changes and their political effects up to the failure of the referendum and subsequent 1979 election evolved in four stages, each with a different configuration of actors at work. The first stage was the status quo before the nationalist upsurge; the key actors were strong regional organizations connected to established parties. Up to the 1960s, Scottish organizations were mostly autonomous and existed in a largely stable environment. The second stage begins in the 1960s when a new actor appeared that would disrupt the configuration of politics; the big regional organizations were joined by the SNP as key actors. From the 1960s, the social bases of the long-autonomous Scottish web of organizations eroded, creating the opportunity for the destabilizing, secessionist SNP to grow on the back of mobilized activists and protest voters. Once the SNP had appeared, a third stage began in which regional organizations and established parties had to respond. The parties were all engaged in electoral combat and thus willing to try to ignore objections from their regional resource bases. The result was an uncoordinated pair of responses. Seeking to stop the new party, UK parties experimented with electoral strategies that would use devolution to stifle it. On the other hand, regional organizations had a clear preference for the status quo; this afforded them the autonomy and stability that had been Scotland's lot for centuries, while the alternatives of devolution and secession were destabilization for no obvious gain and were closely linked to the intrinsically unpredictable (for them) and destabilizing SNP. Given their strong linkages to Labour, the result was that Labour began to have vicious internal disputes between unionists and devolutionists.

In the fourth and most dramatic stage, the conflict between Labour's connections to regional organizations and its anti-SNP electoral strategy hobbled both the party and its devolution proposals. The Labour Party's electoral and parliamentary concerns obliged its leadership to try to respond to the SNP with devolution. In the attempt to pass devolution, Labour's parliamentary leadership in London and Scottish regional organizations pulled farther apart, with the party itself strung out uncomfortably in the middle. When Labour formed minority governments between 1974 and 1979, SNP votes could also be crucial and devolution was a policy that might win them despite the party's distrust of measures short of secession. Labour accordingly enacted the Scotland Act of 1978 that would create a parliament subject to a referendum. The political instability of late-1970s Britain, and the rise of the SNP, gave regional organizations still less desire for political change, and they opposed regionalization. Both the struggles in parliament and the referendum campaign showed how split Labour was. Meanwhile, with regional and central organizations campaigning for a No vote, the referendum failed.

*Prelude: Scotland and the Union to 1968*

Before the SNP began to gather strength in the early 1960s, the essential structure of Scottish politics (if not any concrete institutions) had shown some striking consistencies over centuries of apparent change (Hanham 1969; Brand 1978; Kellas 1989; McCrone 1992; Paterson 1994). Indeed, basic structural elements of Scottish politics dated to 1707, when the Treaty of Union combined the Scottish and English parliaments and states into one state—the United Kingdom. The basic impetus for the Treaty was not an English desire to take over Scotland; it was, rather, geopolitical. Scotland was a backdoor to England, an extremely appealing ally to Continental European powers, Scots leaders had a record of allying with them (particularly France), and as a result Scotland was a significant military and diplomatic threat as long as it had any autonomous political leadership. European history is, after all, full of dual monarchies that broke apart. Also, given the overwhelming importance of religion in the Tudor and Stuart periods (during the European Reformation and wars of religion), Scotland posed problems for monarchs trying to establish common religious observance across their various kingdoms. Security and religious threats merged. For example, Scotland's 1637 prayer book, imposed by Charles I, looked unacceptably Catholic to the Scots. It seemed to them, not for the last time, that they were being used as guinea pigs for future English policies. They responded by invading England four times between 1639 and 1651 (Morrill 1996:81–84).

The solution to these conflicts, chosen amid other crises in the Anglo-Scottish relationship, was to combine the parliaments and thereby eliminate separate, and potentially pro-French, Scottish politics. Given this limited aim of securing an exposed flank, English leaders were little interested in assimilating Scotland and willing to trade off a high degree of institutional autonomy for the elimination of its formal statehood (Levack 1987; K. M. Brown 1992; Whatley 1994). The Treaty of Union thus specified that the new United Kingdom parliament would leave the structure of the Scottish aristocracy, church, universities, and law intact—"Union reflected the areas in which the two countries had grown apart" (M. Lynch 1991:317). Scotland could effectively govern itself as long as it posed no threat.

Eventually, the UK parliament would radically reshape all four of those institutions, albeit often on Scots terms. However, the key fact remained that Scotland entered the UK with a distinct institutional trajectory of its own, political elites of its own, and a web of interlocking organizations that dominated Scottish life. Important elements of Scottish society—including education, health, social welfare, higher education, religion, local government, the franchise, and landholding—remained institutionally distinct, run in Scotland by Scots (Paterson 1994). The closely interconnected political elites also could concentrate the political weight of the country in London. As the UK state expanded, Scots parliamentarians reliably maintained this administrative autonomy. The key mechanism they used was the Scottish Office, a Whitehall department charged with running Scotland's affairs and subsuming most of the home departments that served the rest of the UK. It began in the 1880s, when the UK had begun to consolidate welfare institutions into boards appointed by parliament and Scottish parliamentarians worried that this took away Scottish local control. In response, the Scottish Office took over appointments and other functions (Hanham 1965; Mitchell 2003).

Then, as the central state grew and in the twentieth century assumed direct responsibilities for housing, health, education, and oversight of local government, it usually hived off the service in Scotland to the Scottish Office (analyzed in Hutchison 2000; on the processes that brought the central state into local affairs, see the valuable Harris 1983, Bulpitt 1983, and Harrison

1996). The reason was, simply enough, that Scotland's organizations, above all the Church of Scotland, Scottish Trades Unions Congress (STUC), local government, local charities, professions such as law and medicine, and educators, had an interest in remaining separate and autonomous. They could offer significant incentives—activists, funds, infrastructure, legitimacy—to politicians who sided with them in their demands for autonomy and funds. English politicians, meanwhile, only rarely had any interest in how Scotland governed itself. Thus, when confronted with a bloc of Scots demanding institutional distinctiveness and often autonomy, there was no obvious reason for UK governments to object—especially as the policy goals were usually UK-wide and met no more objection in Scotland than elsewhere, and Scots politicians were integrated into larger UK parties (the Whigs, then the Liberals, then the Unionists and Conservatives, then Labour) (Hutchison 1986, 2001; Fry 1987). Where there were no interested, territorially dependent Scottish organizations, as in the introduction of old-age pensions, there was no distinctive Scottish organization. Where there were preexisting Scottish organizations, as in policing, health, law, and agricuture, the result was a Scottish Office competency and very often a divergent Scottish legal regime. In a few cases, predominantly the very oldest institutions such as law and universities, there was a direct relationship between the central state and the institutions in which the central state left the institutions alone yet funded them.

This was not strange in the durable combination of local autonomy and central finance that Britain operated until the 1980s (Bulpitt 1983). The UK, even under Thatcher, tolerated a great deal of diversity in its regional and local government. It was *finance*, not public administration, that was centralized (Döring 2000:200; Mitchell forthcoming). Scotland's regional organizations were quite able to work autonomously within such a regime.

Scottish identity remained clear; in 1950–1951 a "Covenant" petitioning for autonomy had won over 1.7 million signatures (out of a potential electorate of just over three million). Labour ignored it, and paid no electoral penalty for doing so, while the Unionists, by now increasingly assimilated into the UK-wide Conservatives, responded with a reaffirmation of their ongoing strategy of pursuing administrative devolution through the Scottish Office (Mitchell 1996:144–148). The effort made no mark, other than reminding observers that Scottish identity was strong and leaving Labour leaders with the impression that Scottish nationalism was a Conservative cat's-paw.

The main agenda in Scottish politics was, instead, economic development. Many states have connected regional government with regional economic development, but few have done so as persistently as the UK (Tomaney 2006). This probably reflects the deep functional divisions of labor across the UK (not just the internal colonialism that interested Hechter, but also divisions such as the heavier industry and textiles of northern England and the consumer goods and light manufacturing of the Midlands, sectors that went in opposite directions in the 1930s and 1950s) (Hechter 1975). The result was that efforts from the 1920s onward on behalf of Scotland, like other areas outside southeast England, were generally focused on industrial development, whether through efforts to aid its declining industries and urban areas or to introduce new industries. The partial exception was the Highlands and Islands, an area that combined problems of sparse population not found elsewhere in the UK with a deep symbolic claim on many Scots and, most effectively, its own turn-of-the-century Crofter's Party in parliament. The Highlands and Islands therefore could claim special legislative treatment, including what amounted to a national health sevice when policymakers at the start of the twentieth century realized that their insurance-based National Insurance scheme could not work among widely spaced self-employed crofters (McCrae 2003).

This was an agreeable situation for Scottish regional organizations and the densely interconnected elites who ran them. It sustained a web of important regional Scottish organizations with deep roots sunk in society. Scottish law and finance were the nexus of these elites and an important social organization in their own right, a corps of powerful, high-status lawyers whose skills were quite simply useless outside Scotland (and who were immune to competition from outsiders) and who worked well with Edinburgh's bankers, almost the only bankers in the UK who had successfully resisted the City of London. Edinburgh and Glasgow clubs, law firms, company boards, and charities provided social glue and dense communication networks among business and government. The universities anglicized their degrees starting in the 1860s so that their students could pass UK-wide civil service examinations, but retained important differences (undergraduate degrees take a year longer) and primarily Scottish students (Davie 1961; R. D. Anderson 1995). The universities, in addition to their elite formation functions, also retained strong connections to local government; university medical schools, police, and public health were closely tied in a way not found in England, with consequent much closer links between those institutions and between the institutions and the community elites who ran local governments (Carson and Idzikowska 1989; B. White 1994; Greer 2004). The Church of Scotland and various Scottish rival Protestant denominations often spoke for Scotland in lieu of a parliament. They could do this because of the tremendous political weight of religion in Scotland. The congregation elders—generally the notables of regional and local business and professions—were powerful and church norms, such as a ban on alcohol sales on Sundays, had real force (C. G. Brown 1997).

Scotland's institutional distinctiveness and elite interconnection extended to the maintenance of distinct economic circuits long after regional

English economies had been subsumed by London finance, law, and corpo-
rations (compare Stokes 1998). Thus, Scotland had distinct economic regions largely reliant on Scottish banks for financing, and with owners who
intermarried (Checkland 1975; Scott and Hughes 1980; Johnston 2000).
The rise of the industrial economy added new owners in new sectors and a
new element: trades unions. The trades unions settled into being well-
entrenched organizations with joint memberships in the UK-wide Trades
Union Congress and the Scottish Trades Union Congress (STUC) (Harvie
and Wood 1989; Aitken 1997). Labour's nationalization damaged Scotland's
economic autonomy by taking over many big Scottish industries in 1945–
1951, but equally created enormous new services under the Scottish Office
such as a national health care system. Each new Scottish Office competency
automatically created a closed but important Scottish policy arena in which
insiders sought to modify or make policy (Kellas 1989; Midwinter, Keating,
and Mitchell 1991; Holliday 1992) while the Scottish Office was a linchpin
of close networks that were so insider dominated as to resemble corporatism
in their incessant negotiations, if not in actual distributions of power (Moore
and Booth 1989).

## A Challenger Appears: The Rise of the SNP

In the 1950s and early 1960s, however, the situation began to change.
Scotland's institutional autonomy and distinctiveness remained intact, with
little change in its legal status. But the strength of these organizations on the
ground—the ability of Scottish organizations to shape society and aggregate
their demands through the established political parties—eroded. The causes
of the social changes of the 1960s in Scotland (or in most places) are difficult
to understand, but the main processes at work changed the political opportunity structure of Scotland by undermining the power of existing organizations. Economically, Scotland began to bump downward from 1945, with
the number and political influence of many economic organizations decreasing. First, nationalization wiped out the independence of big coal, steel,
and industrial firms, taking with it the old Unionist business elites that ran
them. Second, the industries themselves approached crisis more rapidly than
they did in the rest of Europe; Scottish industry was prone to small facilities,
severe undercapitalization, chronic underinvestment, poor labor relations,
and reluctance to innovate. Even if the state took them over, they often
seemed to require much more radical restructuring than they got. These
were the same causes (and the areas the same areas) as for the 1930s industrial crisis. World War Two's defense procurement had provided a respite
from these problems, but they remained and dragged industry down afterward (while natural resources began to be, simply, exhausted) (Harvie 1993;

Kemp 1993; Lee 1995:35–72). Scottish Unionists in 1959, explaining losses in an election that was good for the English Conservatives, dryly reported that the slogan "Life's better with the Unionists," in some areas, "could not have an impact" (Hutchison 2001:104). The Conservative government responded by commissioning a report by high-profile businessman Sir John Toothill in 1961. It proposed a manufacturing-based strategy that involved a much higher profile and larger role for the state-linked Scottish Development Department; once again, the Unionist response to problems in Scotland was to buttress informal administrative devolution and focus on economic development (Devine 1999:572–573).

Socially, the welfare state diminished the influence of networks such as neighborhoods, charities, and the church. The free medical assistance of the charities with local elites on the boards, which reflected so well on those elites, was no match for the National Health Service after 1945 (Nottingham 2000; Greer 2004). New mass media (which was organized on a UK-wide basis around the BBC) and cheap, effective transport and communications reduced the influence of elders, traditional institutions, and the church (Devine 1999:582–583). The decay of communal institutions such as political party or church social clubs, noted in any society when automobiles, television, and the concept of teenagers arrive, diminished the power of the big regional organizations sponsoring the old social life. "New Towns," large new urban areas built mostly to get people out of congested and declining Glasgow, uprooted large groups from institutionally dense areas to put them in far less organized areas (Robertson 1998), while urban redevelopment undermined old neighborhood authorities such as parish and charities and created giant new peripheral housing projects with transport and infrastructure problems. These social changes accelerated the decay of the Church of Scotland (C. G. Brown 1997:158–174). Once, Scotland had been thought so devout and sabbatarian as to not need legislation prohibiting Sunday opening, but from World War Two onward, shopping hours extended and it became easier to buy alcohol (C. G. Brown 1997:162, 171).

As Brand put it in his classic explanation, economic problems and social change created a propitious environment, while Scottish identity seemed a more promising form of expression than the class ideologies that had dominated politics for thirty years. The SNP then took advantage of this opportunity to frame the problems as ones of nation rather than class (Brand 1978). The SNP, despite having won a seat in a freak by-election in 1945 (when, due to the war coalition, the major parties did not compete against each other and there was a clear anti-incumbent vote that it managed to reap in one constituency), had scarcely been able to contest more than five parliamentary seats or win more than 2% of the vote (Hutchison 2001:85). But from the late 1950s, the dominant coalitions of Scottish society weakened dramatically and the structure of politics began to shift. These changes allowed the SNP to break through by accumulating slack resources, and conditioned the sort of party it would be—a party in opposition to the structure of Scotland, including its organizational networks, and strong in proportion to those networks' weakness.

It had been stifled by the interlocking economic, educational, professional, religious, civic, media, union, and governmental organizations and their parties—Labour and the Unionists (increasingly calling themselves Conservatives). It picked up some resources, principally activists' time and energy, that were left slack by the decay of the older social and political organizations that had absorbed it. The result was a party built on collective action—activists' labor. Its most memorable election victories were in by-elections (held in mid-parliament due to the resignation or death of a sitting MP) because the party could flood the constituency with campaigning activists and avoid the effects of a press focus on the UK parties and their leaders. Its social makeup and electorate were aspirational and cross-class, with nearly even representation from each self-identified group, but with a higher representation of people affected by the decay of older social organizations (e.g., residents of the new towns were more likely to vote for the new party; Hutchison 2001:123). As it became better organized its vote jumped; not only did it convert voters, it also was able to pick up votes from voters who could not previously have supported it. A party that runs candidates in more constituencies wins more voters, and the SNP went from contesting two constituencies in 1951, winning 0.3% of the Scottish vote, to contesting all seventy-one Scottish seats in October 1974, winning 30.4% of the Scottish vote (McCrone 1992:152; see also Table 3.1).

Table 3.1   Party Votes in Scotland, 1950–1997

| Year | Conservative (Unionist) | Labour | Liberals (Liberal Democrats) | SNP |
|---|---|---|---|---|
| 1950 | 44.8 | 46.2 | 6.6 | 0.4 |
| 1951 | 48.6 | 47.9 | 2.7 | 0.3 |
| 1955 | 50.1 | 46.7 | 1.9 | 0.5 |
| 1959 | 47.2 | 46.7 | 4.1 | 0.8 |
| 1964 | 40.6 | 48.7 | 7.6 | 2.4 |
| 1966 | 37.7 | 49.9 | 6.8 | 5 |
| 1970 | 38 | 44.5 | 5.5 | 11.4 |
| 1974 (Feb.) | 32.9 | 36.6 | 8 | 21.9 |
| 1974 (Oct.) | 24.7 | 36.3 | 8.3 | 30.4 |
| 1979 | 31.4 | 41.6 | 9 | 17.3 |
| 1983 | 28.4 | 35.1 | 24.5 (incl. SDP) | 11.8 |
| 1987 | 24 | 42.4 | 19.3 (incl. SDP) | 14 |
| 1992 | 25.6 | 39 | 13.1 | 21.5 |
| 1997 | 17.5 | 45.6 | 13 | 22.1 |

Source: Hutchison 2001:156.

*The Parties Respond: The Decision to Devolve*

The rise of the Scottish National Party, based on collective action and poorly connected to Scotland's regional organizations and posing a challenge to Labour and the Conservatives, meant that the preferences of regional organizations and dominant parties ceased to be so well aligned. The SNP and nationalism had been a ghostly presence in British politics since the 1930s, primarily as a threat used by Secretaries of State for Scotland and other members of the Scottish territorial lobby to extract resources. Its increase in votes and elected representatives in the 1960s made the challenge tangible and deeply threatening. Defeating or at least managing the threat became the preoccupation of many established party leaders, even if that meant they had to pursue strategies that traded off the preferences of their activists and many of the organizations on which they depended.

The problem it posed for the existing web of powerful Scottish organizations was that the SNP's bases and social supports were the reverse of theirs. A sort of photographic negative, the SNP was built on the resources and stances they did not hold. It promised secession and an exit from NATO, opposed entry into the European Economic Community (and supported withdrawal), and while it avoided being seen as a class party or putting much emphasis on economic policy, it was broadly left-wing with large internal fissures (including neoliberals) and youthful members. "We were not at all respectable," commented an elected SNP politician in a 2001 interview. It also contained many internal conflicts around ideology and strategies, and there were no obvious outside resource dependencies constraining it. The result was that it almost immediately won the opposition of many big Scottish organizations that were contented with the informal autonomy they enjoyed, but were worried by the destabilizing rise of the new party and its destabilizing secessionist plans. The major Scottish press, which was unionist or devolutionist and never separatist, treated the party harshly but with fascination (Brand 1978:139–143). Scottish business organizations (above all in the form of the CBI(S), the Confederation of British Industry in Scotland) responded negatively to the prospect of independence or greater Scottish autonomy, coupled as it was with a leftward tug (Mitchell 1990:66–67). Professional organizations for lawyers and medical professionals avoided taking sides, but their individual elites were cold to the prospect of independence, as were the churches. To any of them, the SNP offered little but destabilization; furthermore, it was untrustworthy as it had few links (resource dependencies) with them and was built of groups that they had lost. Interviews suggested that many politically involved organizations, including the CBI(S), Church of Scotland, and STUC, considered devolution in internal debates as an antinationalist strategy but with little seriousness.

That Labour and the Conservatives (and the then-exiguous Liberals) had, between them, excellent links with these Scottish organizations did not mean that the SNP did not pose a serious threat. Riding on good organization and the decrepitude of older parties in areas experiencing social change, it deprived Labour of its control of many local governments for at least short periods of time, won by-elections in the Labour heartlands of Glasgow and the West of Scotland (industrial districts already in steep decline) and in Conservative rural areas, and won media attention with its Scottish message. The response of both of the big parties was to propose devolution schemes that would give them a Scottish identity and respond to any nationalist demands.

The Conservatives were, at the time, a party built on three social pillars. They had the support of conservative rural voters, particularly in the south and east, and of Protestants in the West; they had the support and funds of well-off Scots around Edinburgh and Glasgow, which gave them seats and a strong link with the traditional financial, legal, and industrial elites of the country; and they were an integrated part of a large and centralized UK-wide party that was the party of business and finance. This combination of well-off and conservative voters with native Scottish and UK resources was glued together by classic Unionist ideology, which combined British nationalism and Scottish identity with a strong attachment to Protestantism (seen in the party's strong links with the Northern Irish import of the Orange Order) and imperialism (Seawright 1999; Hutchison 2001:15–16). The Conservatives had a legacy of Scottishness (the monument was the Scottish Office) and of "Unionist nationalism" that saw Scotland as a partner in the Union (the term is from Morton 1999). Party leader Edward Heath tried to appeal to this and stave off nationalist challenge. At a party conference at Perth in 1970, in an 18 May speech and resolution known later as the Declaration of Perth, he committed the Scottish branch of the party, to its surprise, to support for devolution. This came as the SNP ate away at the Conservatives' vote in the rural Northeast, where it was fast becoming the opposition party. This Conservative commitment to home rule for Scotland was plainly adopted for electoral reasons and was hardly entrenched in the party's internal power structure or collective consciousness (Mitchell 1990:52, 56–57). The party's UK-wide and Scottish bases were skeptical of the immediate prospect of devolution, even if it were intellectually feasible to develop a new form of "unionist nationalism" such as had been seen before (in the nineteenth century and in the 1930s when the Conservatives constructed much of the autonomous Scottish Office) (Mitchell 1990:21–26). The "basic principles" Heath enunciated were certainly in keeping with this idea: he specified that defense of the Union and devolution of power were core Conservative and Unionist principles.

Labour also had serious problems with the SNP as it held many more local government areas and constituencies where the SNP was taking advantage of deindustrialization and social change. As the traditional Scottish working class, whose class consciousness and organization had sustained Labour hegemony, began to disintegrate, the SNP was suited to pick up the pieces. Prime Minister Harold Wilson dealt with the challenge by appointing a Royal Commission on the Constitution, known as the Kilbrandon Commission after its second chair. The Labour leadership in Scotland promptly produced an antidevolutionist report and submitted it to the commission just before the 1970 elections turned Labour out (Labour's pro-devolutionist intellectuals such as Gordon Brown were mostly young, relatively weak, and to the left of the party; see the agenda-setting effort of G. Brown 1975). The commission returned a report in 1973, and Labour, in another surprising election, took office in February 1974, just in time to be obliged to respond (Royal Commission on the Constitution (Kilbrandon Commission) 1973). Labour was in a weak parliamentary position and its internal polling suggested it could lose thirteen seats at the next (imminent) election if it did not act on devolution (Keating and Bleiman 1979:165). Scottish Labour's annual conference that year saw intense infighting (ten antidevolution motions, six pro-devolution motions). The question of its stance on devolution remained, effectively, unresolved (Marr 1995:130,136). "Nobody wanted to do it . . . we in the trades unions were very supportive . . . [but] it wasn't the priority" commented a 2002 trades union interviewee of these events.

Then came a blackly amusing event that demonstrated the depth of Labour's splits, the weakness of home-grown devolutionist sentiment in Scottish Labour, and the poor organization of the party (the same poor organization that helped the SNP become such a threat). A scheduled meeting of its Executive was called to discuss a blueprint for devolution sent from London. It coincided with another remarkable event: the Scottish World Cup football team made it to final stages and was playing against Yugoslavia at the same time as the meeting. Eighteen out of the twenty-nine members of the executive absented themselves to watch the game. The remaining eleven had an antidevolutionist majority. The Scottish Labour Party's Executive thus returned a negative reply to London's scheme. Antidevolutionist MP Tam Dalyell, a partisan participant, was withering:

> when the vote was taken, all eyes turned to the one member of the Scottish Executive not to have spoken, the petite and comely Mrs. Sadie Hutton of Glasgow, who had drifted in after doing her morning's shopping. Loyal to her Chairman, and resentful of the pressure that was being put on him from [Labour headquarters] Transport House, she raised her hand. Thus are momentous

decisions actually made! So by six votes to five the Scottish Executive of the Labour Party reaffirmed their policy that an Assembly was "irrelevant to the real needs of the people of Scotland." (Dalyell 1977:101)

Labour's leadership in London forced the Scots to call a special conference with the one goal of passing London's rejected scheme for Scottish devolution in order to avoid suffering electoral damage to the Wilson government. The conference, held in Glasgow's Dalintober Street, duly approved the scheme, in time for the October 1974 elections. At the conference, a representative of the General and Municipal Workers' Union, the first to state how his union would vote (unions had block votes that dwarfed those of party members), explained simply that the union wanted nothing in the way of a Labour government, and would accept devolution if that would make a Labour government's return more likely. The manner of Labour's conversion to devolution shows that despite the demand for devolution among many Scottish Labour intellectuals, the stimulus came from London and Labour's UK-wide strategists (Marr 1995:137–141; McLean 2004).

Keating and Bleiman point out the four reasons for the Dalintober Street decision: conviction; pressure from UK leadership; trades unions' convictions; and electoral fears (Keating and Bleiman 1979:170). The UK leadership was putting pressure on Scottish Labour because of electoral fears. The unions, insulated from the prospective Scottish assembly and interested in an assembly where they would be influential, absolutely wanted to save the Callaghan government; and the electoral fears of party members were also real (recalling that the STUC, despite its organization, is not so much an independent movement as an organization joined by trades unions with memberships in Scotland). This created difficulties for Labour because it created divergence between its new electoral strategy and its resource dependencies. Professional organizations and local government members, who were its core resource suppliers, had cause to be skeptical of devolution on the grounds that it would sever vital links with the UK (through which industrial subsidies flowed) and would diminish their power. At best, they were unions, devolutionist but torn within; at worst they were flatly opposed. The STUC had, in its Kilbrandon Committee written submission, suggested an assembly, but in oral evidence skittered away to suggest that it be merely "deliberative"; it only slowly developed a more positive view (Kellas 1989:148; Royal Commission on the Constitution 1973). On the ground, Labour and SNP activists developed an often passionate dislike of each other that made many Labour activists deeply reluctant "to give an inch to the nats"; to the extent that Labour depended on its more traditional activists, devolution would be made harder. Large parts of the Labour coalition—individual unions, activists, the press, and the public sector—had doubts about devolution, and this turned into a lack of enthusiasm.

In short, the response of both major parties in Scotland to the rise of the SNP was to make halfhearted devolution proposals. Both Labour and the Conservatives had traditions of Scottishness that allowed them to construct ideological cases for devolution, but both faced skeptical memberships and supporters who worried that devolution would end valuable UK links, give the SNP more chances to destabilize Scottish politics, and create a new layer of government that would impinge on their positions. There was, in each party, a substantial current that would have preferred a straight fight between their unionist beliefs and the secessionist SNP. The party leaderships, however, opted to support devolution for electoral reasons. The Liberals held only three seats in the 1970s, all of them in remote island areas, but they had been in favor of devolution for a century.

Or, as journalist Andrew Marr writes, "to understand the 1970s in Scotland it is necessary first to remember that devolution was mostly cooked up in London by busy politicians with only one eye on the pot . . . it was the metropolitan establishment, not the Scots, who seemed the less committed to the status quo. . . . Who most wanted devolution? . . . above all the Yorkshireman Harold Wilson, the Kentish Ted Heath and the Welshman Jim Callaghan" (Marr 1995:121).

*The Contest over Devolution and Its Failure*

The big UK parties' commitments to devolution had remained largely theoretical, existing only on the plane of rhetoric and electoral strategy. This rhetorical commitment avoided a clash between their regional resource dependencies—on comfortable organizations—and their chosen electoral strategies. The crises of the British and world political economies in the 1970s gave them more than enough problems without seeking constitutional change, and in neither party were supporters uniformly enthusiastic. The actual turning point when some sort of devolution act became inevitable was the second election of 1974, when Labour was voted the largest party but still held a parliamentary minority and settled on a limited Scottish assembly as an electoral strategy that would keep the party and its parliamentary support together (Keating and Bleiman 1979:180; for a useful chronology, Drucker and Drucker 1978:204–207). Smaller parties became crucial to passing legislation and avoiding the constantly threatened vote of no confidence. These included the Liberals, the Northern Irish parties, the Welsh nationalists of Plaid Cymru, and the eleven MPs of the SNP. The Labour government spent much of its energy in 1974–1979 trying to keep at least some of that impossible mix of parties on its side. The SNP's parliamentary cohort—

many of whom had never served in elected office before—was plunged into a tense situation that gave them enormous power, but not the power to do what they wanted and declare independence. The problem was that swing votes in the UK parliament were inadequate to pursue secession; the SNP's simple campaigning claim had been that when a majority of Scots voted for them, they would declare independence. They did not have a parliamentary strategy suited to the particular power of a swing party in a hung parliament. "We weren't up to it . . . we made strategic errors," commented an SNP leader in a 2001 interview.

For Labour, this electoral outcome increased the tension between its strategy as an electoral and parliamentary force and its organization and resource dependencies as a party. The Labour leadership's solution to its travails in elections and Westminster was to move ahead with its project for devolution to Scotland and Wales, even as its attention was distracted elsewhere (above all by economic problems, a sterling crisis that sent the government to the IMF for a loan under stringent conditions in 1977, civil war in Northern Ireland, and a wave of labor movement militancy that would regularly knock devolution off of even Scottish front pages; M. Brown 1981:118). The devolution project was explicitly intended to fend off the electoral threat and perhaps solve immediate parliamentary problems, damaging the SNP's base and splitting it, while buying its Westminster votes for other reasons (Kellas 1989:145–147). It seemed like a good strategy, at least electorally and in parliament.

The project incurred immediate scepticism if not opposition from organizations in Scotland that were reluctant to see their environmental stability compromised due to pressure from an insurgent party they distrusted and the temporary problems of a minority government. Scottish businesses almost immediately signaled their dislike of the devolution proposals; the chair of the CBI Scotland and the chair of the Association of Scottish Chambers of Commerce, as well as Sir John Toothill, all were prominent supporters of a new, antidevolutionist, organization called "Scotland Is British" that would later become the core of the antidevolution referendum campaign (Mitchell 1990:81). Regional organizations were otherwise mildly devolutionist or split. The Church of Scotland was positive in public, but had a prominent antidevolutionist group; the result would eventually be a fierce argument over whether to read a statement in support of devolution from pulpits. Remembering those days, a church leader in a May 1998 interview explained that "you remember that we used to be called the 'Tory party at prayer' like the Church of England. There still was a lot of that, a great deal of unionist feeling that meant we could not decide whether our duties . . . meant we should support devolution." The trades unions were also in favor, but worried about the loss of state support and the prospect of parochialism, and many were viscerally opposed to any project associated with "the nats." They were assuaged by the absence of economic powers from the devolution proposals—pork-barrel politics and UK-wide economic management would not be affected by devolution of merely "political" matters (Keating and Bleiman 1979:171). Not even the development agency that subsidized investment was to be immediately handed over, even though Labour hinted at it (Wood 1989:119). The "quality" broadsheet newspapers, the *Scotsman* and *Herald*, and the major tabloids, staffed by many devolutionists, interested in the prospect of a new Scottish political arena to cover and anxious to demonstrate their Scottishness, were almost all in favor, covering the topic in depth and editorializing in favor (M. Smith 1994; see the well-written reminiscences of Ascherson 2002). The local press was roughly split between neutrals, pro-, and antidevolutionists (M. Brown 1981). In other words, apart from the big Scottish-only newspapers and some unions, there was no large social organization *wholly* behind devolution. Regional organizations hedged their bets to the extent that devolution appeared inevitable (as it did, and as is demonstrated in the parties sometimes being more interested in claiming credit than in campaigning), but there is little evidence of any of them voluntarily contributing resources or holding their resource-linked party allies to account for it. Local government, which would clearly lose power and influence, was often opposed—and made up the bulk of any party's elected officials. "They were torn. They were worried about their seats too, just like the MPs, but they liked being in charge," explained a high-level public service manager interviewed in 2002 who had been working with West of Scotland local government in those years.

Both parties felt the lack of support for their devolutionist plans. The Conservative Party was already moving away from their lukewarm commitment to devolution, even before they came under the leadership of Margaret Thatcher. Empowered by the nearly unanimous antidevolutionist sentiments of the businesses on which they depended in Scotland, they declared their opposition to Labour's devolution proposals (with some senior Tories holding out the prospect of a different, better plan of their own) (Macartney 1981:22–23; Mitchell 1990:84–96). Labour, meanwhile, began to fracture. After the pressure of the 1974 elections was off, antidevolutionists began to reemerge and brought along intense internal debates over devolution and the development of a strong Unionist, antidevolutionist tendency (Keating and Bleiman 1979:186). Labour's internal divisions were thus clearly understandable; underneath many members' cultural antipathy to the SNP lay the fundamental problem that Labour's resource dependencies in Scotland were with regional organizations that were contented with their informal autonomy and distrusted the devolution scheme. Labour's key allies, in other words, were lukewarm about or opposed to its electoral strategy, and that empowered antidevolutionist tendencies in the party.

The Labour divisions mean that the battle for devolution was arguably lost in parliament, before the referendum (for this chronicle, see Naughtie 1979, 1980; Bogdanor 1979, chs. 4–7; Bochel, Denver, and Macartney 1981). In its passage, the devolution legislation was rendered unworkable and largely unpassable by Labour MPs who had been emboldened by the lack of enthusiasm of key allies. In a hung parliament under the Westminster system there is an enormous amount of parliamentary gamesmanship as party whips try to muster all their MPs to vote (and deal with rebels who can threaten the whole government) and the smaller parties negotiate for concessions. In this fraught environment, some English and a few Scottish Labour MPs began to work to sabotage the devolution scheme when it was first introduced as a combined bill for Scotland and Wales. Led most publicly by a Scot, Tam Dalyell MP of West Lothian, Labour rebels (almost all of them English) had a major impact in reducing the powers allocated to the proposed Scottish assembly and impelling a decision to have a referendum. Labour MPs from the areas where Labour MPs are usually found—Tyneside, Merseyside, West Midlands, London and Wales (Jordan 1979:26)—fought guerrilla battles against devolution. They had northern English urban metropolitan county governments, such as Tyne and Wear, coordinating and noisily supporting their attack on devolution in an effort to draw attention to their own desires and problems.

The bill was introduced, 1,062 amendments laid down (most from the Government backbenches) and after about 100 hours of work and a week the committee had only completed work on a paltry three and a half clauses of the long bill (Jordan 1979:2,17). Rebels first voted with the opposition to defeat a "guillotine," a motion intended to end this delay by cutting off debate and amendments after a fixed time. This meant that the bill's passage would be drawn out and painful; that it would emerge heavily amended as the Government's whips would have to organize a series of majorities, not including their own rebels, to defeat a long succession of wrecking amendments; that it would be a danger to the Government by multiplying divisions and contested votes; and that the Opposition would probably manage to run out the parliamentary session without anything being passed.

So after the guillotine failed, the government pulled the combined Scotland and Wales bill and reintroduced the bills, with guillotines, as two separate bills legislating devolution for Wales and Scotland. This time, the Liberals had saved the government and devolution by supporting the guillotine—not just because they were devolutionist, but because they appreciated their "place in the sun" and feared electoral destruction if elections were held then (Kerr 1977:114; Sked and Cook 1993:313). Labour was tempted to abandon the project, but reintroduced the bill because it had just undergone heavy defeats in the 1977 local government elections in Scotland and still had no stable parliamentary majority. Thanks to the SNP, there was briefly no large

council under Labour control and Labour leaders felt even more strongly
the need for an electoral response (Marr 1995:156). The amendments process began, although this time with a timetable, and rebels successfully
forced retreats from the original act, including strengthening the powers of
the Secretary of State for Scotland, in a viceregal role, to override the devolved parliament (see chapter seven for their achievements), and allowing
the Orkney and Shetland Islands to opt out of a devolved Scotland. The
most successful wrecking amendment—and one that ultimately proved fa-
tal—was steered by a Scot holding an English seat for Labour, George
Cunningham, which required that the referendum on devolution would
only pass if it won both a majority of votes cast *and* the support of 40% of
the electorate (an unprecedented device in British politics; Bogdanor 1980).
This device, inserted late at night (on Burns night, a major Scottish holiday)
when the Government whips had lost some crucial votes, proved impossible
to remove. It would change the dynamics of the referendum dramatically by
making any undecided abstainer an effective no voter (Cunningham 1989).

   In parliament, what was visible were the deep splits across the UK
Labour Party between devolutionists and Unionists. Many MPs, worried,
kept their heads down and hoped for the clear direction that the original
devolution proposal was supposed to have provided; 80% never put down an
amendment on the first bill at all (Jordan 1979:13). When the Scotland Act
passed, establishing a devolved Scottish parliament subject to a referendum
in Scotland, the divisions in Labour and Scottish society came into play.
What had been a story of the Parliamentary Labour Party, split between a
pro-devolutionist group empowered by the leaders' strategy and some equally
fervent English and Welsh antidevolutionist members empowered by the
party's allies' lack of support, now became a complicated game with
antidevolutionists empowered by the referendum (Keating and Bleiman
1979:186–187). Multiple splits organized themselves around Yes and No
campaigns (Macartney 1981). Labour split in the campaign for the same
reasons it did in the parliament; its key resource dependencies were largely
opposed to the destabilization that devolution and the SNP offered. The
SNP, meanwhile, campaigned but was unable to muster as much enthusiasm as it could because its party leadership had supported an option—
devolution—that had little support among highly mobilized, nationalist
members who wanted independence. Laid atop this problem was that parties
initially were quite confident and wanted to be able to take credit for devolution; Labour periodically used literature advocating a vote for "Labour's
Scottish Assembly" (Dyer 1981:60).

   There were two main Yes campaigns, one made up of Labour supporters (Labour Movement for Yes, LMY) and the other trying to be an umbrella
group but largely composed of SNP supporters (Yes for Scotland, YFS) as

In a vote like this it would be difficult to even mobilize 40% of the electorate.

well as a small Conservative Yes one and the SNP's own independent campaign (Macartney 1981). Their messages were different (the SNP making a slippery slope argument that devolution was a good start, Labour trying to appeal to desires for autonomy as an alternative to secession) and their activists were unlikely to get along well. There was one dominant No campaign, Scotland Says No, composed of Conservatives and business, but there was an important (or at least visible) Labour No campaign, made up of rebels. They could not work together easily either, since the Conservatives and Labour supported the constitutional status quo but shared little else. Labour, to preserve its integrity as a party, avoided obliging activists and constituency parties to exert themselves for the Yes campaign, since that could have provoked a rebellion. The SNP worked more uniformly for a Yes than any other party, although for half a loaf. It allowed its constituency parties to decide whether to campaign with Yes for Scotland or as SNP; in areas where the SNP tended not to campaign as Yes for Scotland (campaigning on its own), there would effectively be three Yes campaigns.

What explained this kaleidoscope of campaigns? The answer is that neither the SNP nor Labour was pursuing a strategy supported by their key resource bases: the SNP's resources were contingent on its supporting independence, and Labour's on its supporting the status quo ante. Both parties swung into action behind their leaders, but their doubts made them weaker than they would otherwise have been (compare the events in chapter four). The SNP was a largely activist party, disconnected from most of Scottish organizational life (or at least its resources) and largely unrewarded by an electoral system that at best gave it fleeting control of areas. Its activists and leaders were thus overwhelmingly motivated by ideology and working for an independent Scotland. The leadership's promises that a devolved parliament would be a stepping-stone clashed with other parts of the Yes campaign, addressing different audiences, and arguing that devolution would end the nationalist threat. But SNP activists did campaign for such a second-best option.

Labour's problem was more interesting; while the SNP was a challenging party, Labour was a key party in the organizational structure of Scotland. Its resource dependencies were on Scottish organizations, above all the trades unions and to a lesser extent the broad public sector—nationalized industries, social welfare professions, local government, education, and law. Each of these organizations was structurally in a stable environment with extensive autonomy, and each could lose one or both under devolution. Trades unions were key in Labour's campaign, and more or less devolutionist over their history (Keating and Bleiman 1979; Kellas 1989:145,154). But they, and those dependent on nationalized industries, faced two particular threats that tempered the advantages of devolution. First, and fundamentally, industrial relations in the UK, along with significant parts of its economy, were in crisis in 1979, and unions were embroiled in combat and negotiations on many fronts. Adding a Scottish parliament threatened yet more instability to organizations that were internally fractured and externally facing an already unstable environment. Second, more concretely, the existence of the Scottish parliament would have opened up a second arena for policy disputes, possibly imperiling hard-won UK-wide patterns in labor relations. It was thus important in their calculations that only devolution could save a Labour government.

The Conservatives and the biggest No coalition were easier to understand. Their resource dependencies were on central state organizations elites and certain groups of Scottish elites that were equally contented with the status quo. The key factor was the support of the broad UK private sector for the Conservatives on the UK level; the prospect of a Scottish parliament making taxation, labor relations, planning, and regulation more complicated and possibly more onerous, combined with their opposition to the destabilizing prospect of secession, meant that these organizations (and their representative bodies—the CBI(s), Scottish Council, and Chambers of Commerce) were instinctively unionist and anti-SNP.

"Of course we were opposed. They wanted to create an extra layer of government and hand it over to the kinds of people running Strathclyde . . . [and] do you realize how socialist the SNP was?" explained a business leader of a financial services association in a 1998 interview. The president of the Glasgow Chamber of Commerce and a committee member of Scotland Is British complained that devolution was the product of a "narrow and emotional nationalism," and that "we believe and fear that the creation of a directly elected Assembly will lead almost inevitably to separation. The proposals are disruptive" (Risk 1977:121–122). He continued that devolution would entail "no advantage to industry and commerce, but the reverse" as it would "undermine" regional development policy and mean "less assistance in steering industry in this direction" while "fear of ultimate separation will discourage, indeed already does discourage, indigenous and inward investment" (123). Finally, it would mean "more taxes, more politicians, more civil servants, worse and disputative government, less influence in government and compelling demands for the break-up of the country" (124). A better plea for autonomy and stability of nonregional organizations would be hard to put; he followed it up by telling his audience, at a University of Edinburgh seminar, that the Chamber of Commerce had surveyed its own members and those of the CBI(S) and that there were "only two expressions of dissent that have been received during all that time by either of these groups, representing 9000-odd members, and one of them was from an otherwise respectable Scottish newspaper" (125).

The result was an extremely well-funded No campaign (Macartney 1981:31) with close links to the Conservative Party. By contrast, in Lothians

(Edinburgh), Yes campaigners had to stop in mid-campaign and hold an auction to raise money (Mullin 1981). Throughout Scotland, Yes campaigners had to buy their literature while No campaigners got it free.

In other words, the key Scottish organizations in the public and private sectors, and central organizations, were broadly agreed that their stable, autonomous (and well-funded) places in the structure of UK politics and public administration were superior to anything that could be gained by creating a new parliament. They might have a general agreement with devolution, but a new parliament would introduce the prospect of a slippery slope to independence, flirting with divergent regulations and taxes, giving a victory to nationalists (including the nationalist-leaning activists found in Labour), and, for the public sector, creating the new parliament by directly changing their own lines of accountability. The big parties were both closely tied to them. While Labour tried to regain its lost voters by watering down devolution but carrying it through, the result was to strain the party's organization. The Conservatives, meanwhile, were more uniformly dependent on central organizations and opposed it. Without such support from the big regional organizations, the groups that filled the gaps in Yes campaigning did not increase the allure of devolution: the tiny Communist Party of Great Britain had a disproportionate impact in campaigns, while in south Aberdeen the Yes leaders were English university lecturers (Dyer 1981; Macartney 1981). Neither group was particularly able to win over Scottish elites or even doubters in the parties.

The same distrust for devolution on the part of regional organizations and central ones alike was seen in their direct campaigning—their views did not just hamstring pro-devolution parties that depended on them, some of them also illustrated their lack of interest in devolution. The Church of Scotland, long Unionist, had many pro-devolutionist clergy, but Conservatives successfully defeated a plan to read a letter from the pulpits before the referendum supporting devolution. The STUC threw organizational resources behind devolution and the Yes campaigns, in large part to keep Labour's UK government successful and in office, but was at a low ebb, with many of its component unions distracted. More to the point, given the STUC's small own resources, were the efforts of other unions, which were "nothing like what they'd do in a general election campaign. Not even close," according to a journalist close to the unions in 2003. Business funded Scotland Says No, giving it a massive financial lead over any other single organization. While no accounts were published for these campaigns, a reasonable estimate suggests that the funds came from individual well-off Scots in industries with central resource dependencies such as finance (which depends on London markets and UK regulation) (Macartney 1981).

The multiple campaigns absorbed almost all the energy of pro- and antidevolutionist groups. Given the relative flexibility of public opinion, these campaigns mattered in their efforts to shape both turnout and the outcome; No campaigners tried to produce a No vote or abstention, and Yes advocates tried to drive up turnout and promote a Yes vote. Their main methods, as in general elections, were advertising, leafletting, and canvassing (home visits by activists). In these efforts, the financing advantage to the No campaigners mattered, while the relatively lower turnout by union and Labour activists interested in other topics compared to general elections dented the efforts of the Yes campaigners.

Scottish public opinion had been positive to devolution and the Scotland Act (hence the initial cockiness of the Yes campaigners and the parties' scuffle for credit). But the No campaign, combined with the 40% rule, eroded support over the course of the campaigning period. The referendum thus lost in most of Scotland. Afterward, the SNP, badly divided and "in a mood of near hysteria," demanded that the UK Labour government go ahead and implement the Scotland Act regardless of the result—a majority of those voting had, indeed, supported devolution (Marr 1995:162). Prime Minister James Callaghan, charged with keeping his party together, refused. Labour rebels were not about to see devolution introduced despite failing the 40% test. The SNP deputies responded by laying down a motion of censure; the Conservatives seized on it; and the government fell, by a vote of 310–311. Callaghan observed that it was the first time he had heard of turkeys—the SNP—voting for an early Christmas. The SNP and Scottish Labour both went into the 1979 general election exhausted, having each felt chronic tension between their resource dependencies and their strategies, between their leaders and their activists, and between their differing parliamentary factions. The Conservatives, on the back of English votes, emerged victorious (and with a jump from 16 to 22 seats in Scotland), the SNP was reduced from 11 to 2 seats, and Labour would be out of power for eighteen years.

*Summary: The Rise and Fall of Devolution*

The key problem for devolutionists was that devolution was a political strategy at variance with the distribution of political resources in Scotland. The devolution debates were direct consequences of the parties' responses to the electoral challenge of the SNP. That challenge arose because of the older organizations' loss of their grip on parts of society; the changes that came with economic decay, the welfare state, secularization, and population movements all freed up resources. The SNP mobilized them. Interpreting the SNP vote as a demand for some Scottish self-government, Labour (and for a while the Conservatives) made promises to support devolution.

The problem, however, was that the big interlocking organizations of Scottish society were content with the formal and informal autonomy they already enjoyed. With no direct Scottish political oversight or accountability, and separate Scottish organizations, their autonomy was great—so long as the state recognized it and consulted them on their fates. Given that the state was, if anything, now more solicitous of them (and more willing to fund trophy developments) in order to inoculate Scotland against further nationalism, they had no reason to support change. A parliament near to them would give the SNP a boost, give them a close-up political master, and destabilize their environment in many unknown ways, from changing planning laws to their workers' educational curriculum. They thus fought not to be included in the remit of the parliament (chapter seven) and, when the referendum came, many fought to stop it or at a minimum denied resources to Yes campaigners.

The most intense pro-devolution regional organizations were the Scottish quality (and some tabloid) newspapers, which were often staffed by confirmed devolutionists; the *Scotsman*, particularly, had a tradition of supporting devolution. In large part this is because they stood to gain so much not only from the establishment of a devolved assembly, but because the press even stands to gain from (or at least find interesting stories in) environmental destabilization (such as debates and articles about the prospect of an independent Scotland). The Scottish newspapers were accordingly generous in coverage and the two most influential broadsheets as well as the tabloid giant *The Daily Record* were in favor (Bochel and Denver 1981; M. Brown 1981; Kemp 1993). Otherwise, regional organizations were skeptical of devolution and showed it in their weak preferences and lack of intensity. Some scaled back their resource flows to the party, depriving it of campaigning resources on which it could usually rely, and lobbied to be excluded (as with professional organizations); others were in favor of a continuing Labour government and willing to pay for it with very limited devolution that would not affect their most important interests (as with most unions); a few fought it outright (such as the financial sector).

## CONCLUSION

Labour had grown to be the party of Scotland's autonomous elites. When it opposed them in the name of electoral strategy, it was shaken and eventually failed to change the governance of Scotland. Labour's problem was that the big, densely interwoven organizations of Scottish society, starting from a firm base in 1707, had successfully, through different political parties, woven a cocoon in which they dominated Scottish policy communities that were relatively insulated from London or from Scottish voters. This satisfied their interest in environmental stability and in autonomy, and they were reluctant to give it up. Their influence, both through denial of support to the Labour strategy and their chilly response to the proposals reduced a healthy opinion poll lead for Yes to a tiny positive margin and a failed referendum, nearly shipwrecked Scotland's biggest party, almost destroyed the SNP, and gave a boost to the declining Conservatives.

The failure to establish a Scottish parliament is a puzzle for explanations of regionalization that stress either the impact of nationalist parties or the international political economy. Parties do not explain the outcome. On the one hand, the political events leading up to the 1979 referendum were clearly driven by the presence of the secessionist SNP and the responses of Labour and the Conservative Party. The big UK parties' leadership both attempted to win over the Scots by promising a devolved parliament, and Labour actually did try. Obviously, this party activity produced no change in how Scotland was governed (and was spectacularly self-defeating for both Labour and the SNP). Furthermore, the view that parties are the autonomous drivers of political outcomes does not seem to receive support from the chaos of internal party politics in the 1970s in Scotland. Devolution divided the major protagonists, with bitter infighting in a SNP split between secessionists and devolutionists and a Labour Party split between devolutionists and unionists. The unusual conditions for success of the referendum—a majority of voters plus a majority of 40% of electors—were born of Labour Party splits. Party strategy arguments explain why devolution was proposed; they do not explain why it failed and nearly took the parties down with it.

Meanwhile, explanations based on opportunities in the international political economy neither suggest neither that devolution would appear on the agenda nor that it would fail. Opportunities-based theories usually argue that regionalization responds to the greater possibilities regions face. The problems are that Scotland was ill equipped to take most of the available chances and that its key resource—oil—was only available to an independent state, not an autonomous region. Scotland was hardly an economy free from the constraints of the state and able to compete with other regions in the 1960s and 1970s. The 1970s were a period of economic decline; the Scottish economy, based in deeply troubled heavy manufacturing sectors, was dominated by state-owned or subsidized enterprises and by any measure was uncompetitive in most fields. It is important to note that the exponential growth of the SNP predated the exploitation of North Sea oil—the rise of the SNP cannot, chronologically, have been a by-product of any economic change that made independence look more desirable (Brand 1978; Hutchison 2001:122–123). The SNP's striking argument was based on the presence of North Sea oil in the oil-hungry 1970s: "It's Scotland's Oil" was their most famous slogan; the image it conjured was of a small and prosperous Scotland freed of the shackles of a declining imperial state. Whether Scotland would have been better off independent is unknown, but it certainly seems that the

UK government tried to conceal the extent to which oil wealth would have *looking* belonged to an independent Scotland. *even further to the future*

But the SNP was right: oil pointed to independence, not devolution. The proposed Scottish Assembly neither played on that potential strength nor responded to its known weaknesses in the rest of the economy. If Scotland's problem was, as it was for a large part of the Scots labor force, industrial decay, then the centralized state was the only lifeline they had—and, indeed, the proposed devolved assembly would have no responsibility for the big state-owned or subsidized industries. If Scotland's one major opportunity was its oil, then a devolved parliament with no say in energy policy was irrelevant and independence beckoned.

The problem with a parties-based analysis is that it overstates the parties' real autonomy from their activists and resource dependencies. It thus understates the variety and power of outside influences on the parties; the SNP was composed of activists who wanted independence, not devolution, and Labour was closely tied to organizations in society that opposed devolution. It focuses too closely on one set of actors—parties—and then artificially limits the strategic constraints they face. The problem with an opportunities-based analysis is that the relationship between the international economy and Scottish government is too complicated for a monism. To explain why devolution proposals arose as an unsatisfactory halfway house, and then failed despite their irrelevance to the economy, required a more detailed analysis of the actors in Scotland, and analysis of the relationship between organizational webs and outcomes, mediated through parties, sufficed. Above all, though, the case of Labour should justify the assumption that parties should be studied as organizations with resource dependencies, as well as electoral game-players.

# Chapter Four

# Scotland 1979–1997

## Centralization and Backlash

> *Thatcher put the Great back in Britain but took the United out of Kingdom.*
>
> > —a UK civil servant in London, 2002

> *If the [Conservative] Party sometimes seems English to some Scots that is because the Union is inevitably dominated by England by reason of its greater population.*
>
> > —Margaret Thatcher

The year 1979 was one of the great watersheds of British politics. The general election put the Conservatives in power for eighteen years and ushered in one of the most dynamic and effective neoliberal regimes the advanced industrial countries have seen. It left the Labour Party in disarray, quashed any idea of Scottish autonomy, and reduced the SNP to two MPs. The new Conservative government of Margaret Thatcher, an intensely polarizing government, set out to undo the postwar consensus on the welfare state and state economic management, orienting politics around a straight left–right fight and in the process undoing the bases of Scotland's quasicorporatism and particular relations with the central state.

Yet, by 1998, there was a positive outcome in the form of a Scottish parliament, a less constrained, more powerful, and more broadly supported body than the defeated Scottish assembly of 1979. The explanation lies in the changing position of regional organizations, which shifted under the new

67

pressures Thatcher brought to bear on them. These pivotal actors shifted to supporting formal devolution because the central state, rather than the SNP, had become the greatest threat to their autonomy and environmental stability. They did so because the agenda of the Thatcher government was largely unresponsive to their interests, often attacked their institutional bases in its policy changes, and overrode the informal autonomy they had enjoyed until it came into office. As a result they shifted *en bloc* to supporting formal devolution, and the Labour Party, dependent on them, shifted along with them. Whereas in 1979 their antagonism to devolution had split Labour, by 1997, they made devolution an obligatory goal for Labour.

The Conservatives under Thatcher exploited the tremendous power of the UK executive, ignoring the many informal conventions and habits that had constrained its operation (including those prescribing Scottish autonomy). In response to this shock, Scottish regional organizations switched to supporting formal institutional autonomy for their region that could adequately defend them against future centralizing governments. This meant that Labour was able to call on their assistance, Labour antidevolutionist rebels were starved of resources, and Labour became yet more powerful in Scotland and more commited to devolution.

This chapter analyzes key periods in the relationship between the central state and Scottish organizations and the consequences for the parties. In the first period, 1979–1987, the government tended not to enter into conflict with Scottish organizations. In the second period from 1987 to 1997, the government, knowingly or not, attacked the bases of Scottish regional organizations, diminishing their autonomy and stability by making major changes with little consultation or deference to them. When the Conservatives began to change policy in areas that in Scotland were regional (such as education, economic development, and health), and led to regional organizational support for devolution campaigns—directly and through support for devolutionists within Labour—they became available to pro-devolutionary coalitions within and with Labour. This regional organizational consensus on devolution became all-enveloping by 1997, such that the Conservatives lost all their Westminster seats, the Labour government enacted devolution as one of its first acts, and the devolution referendum was a landslide in favor. The campaigns with support of regional organizations, such as the Scottish Constitutional Convention, helped highlight the resources of legitimacy, funds, press, and infrastructure available to devolutionist campaigns. Most important, it meant that Labour's internal politics changed. Labour's foundations, local government and the unions above all, swung to devolution, thereby depriving antidevolutionists in Labour of resources and making it almost obligatory for any Labour leader to support devolution to Scotland. Meanwhile, other regional organizations changed the environment, sometimes campaigning (as with the Scottish Constitutional Convention) and otherwise lending legitimacy and sometimes infrastructure to the devolutionist campaigns.

## FROM NO TO YES: THE POLITICS OF PUBLIC POLICY AND THE CONSTITUTION, 1979–1997

Conservative governments of these years pursued policies and policymaking strategies that eroded Scottish organizations' autonomy and stability. The organizations' backlash took the form of support for devolution. In this process, spread over the eighteen years of Conservative rule that began in 1979, there are three key periods. Like the periodization of party politics in the 1970s, the defining characteristic of each period is its particular configuration of central organizations, regional organizations, and the parties that depended on them. The first period runs from 1979 to 1987. In this period, a surprisingly cautious Conservative government coincided with a ruined opposition. Margaret Thatcher's most dramatic policies in these years were in macroeconomic policy, the management (or privatization) of state-owned industrial enterprises, and industrial relations. This meant that most redoubts of Scottish regional organization were left alone. At the same time, the opposition parties were in serious trouble. The SNP was reeling from its referendum and general election defeats and suffered from a factionalism problem. Labour in England (mostly not in Scotland) veered leftward and split. It was dominant in Scotland but almost unelectable across the UK. While this meant there was no effective legislative opposition, the Conservatives avoided picking fights with autonomous Scottish institutions. The second period runs from 1987 to 1997. In this period, the Government began to directly challenge the regional organizations of Scotland while opposition parties began to recover. As a result of the challenge to regional organizations, which they almost never successfully resisted, they began to support formal regional autonomy. The experience of learning just how little influence they had if the government chose to ignore them was brutal for these organizations and their policy communities. The result was both direct mobilization in favor of devolution and a broader shift to support it across Scotland's regional organizations, and a consequent consensus within Labour on devolution (the SNP perked up in these years, but its threat is chronologically unable to explain Labour's shift). The result of this consensus was an electoral earthquake in 1997, when the Conservatives were eliminated in Scotland (and Wales) and Labour came to power with a now-consensual commitment to devolution.

The third period, in 1997, comes between Labour's landslide election and the referendum, which came quickly on the heels of the election (the referendums for Scotland and Wales were the first legislation of the new parliament). This short period demonstrated an amazing degree of consensus;

the nugatory organization of the No campaign and shortage of spokespersons merely confirm the power of regional organizations and their consensus. On the Yes side were the full organization of unions and Labour (often dependent on local government support) and a broader public coalition in the press, churches, and professions in support of devolution that provided infrastructure, legitimacy, and public support to devolutionists. These formal campaigns came atop the long process of regional organizations' opposition to centralized British government since the late 1980s, which had buried the Scottish Conservatives under bad press, formal opposition from many different groups such as voluntary organizations and the professions, and constant suggestions that the Conservatives were an English party. On the No side, there was substantial finance, much of it apparently from the Edinburgh financial sector, but almost no workers, legitimacy, positive press, or even basic infrastructure such as meeting facilities.

In short, the first period did not produce devolution because regional organizations and major parties were largely uninterested. The second period produced a strong Labour commitment to devolution because regional organizations swung to favor it. The third demonstrated the strength of the pro-devolution coalition.

## Thatcherism from Above: 1979–1987

In speaking of Thatcherism, it is easy to talk of an undifferentiated period of turbulence, neoliberalism, and confrontation. The years of her governments were certainly marked by the Conservatives' destruction of the postwar quasicorporatist consensus that governed British politics (Kavanagh 1990). But, in fact, the eighteen years of Conservative rule include at least one analytically useful divide around the 1987 election (my argument for this periodization is from Holliday 1992; the best political analyses of Thatcherism still are Kavanagh 1990 and Beer 1982; for economic policy, Hall 1986, 1992). From 1979 to 1987, the Thatcher government was primarily concerned (in domestic policy) with macroeconomic policy and the shape of the industrial and service economies, meaning that the first two parliaments were dominated by privatization and industrial restructuring; monetarist economic policy (followed more in spirit than in the aggregate); and conflicts with the trades unions that reached their apogee in the strangely medieval battles of mounted police and columns of miners that marked the 1984–1985 miners' strike.

What is striking about this agenda is that it had remarkably little effect on the regional Scottish organizations. There was no challenge to their main institutional redoubts. Macroeconomic policy operated on the level of aggregate economic indicators and had no direct impact on the autonomy and stability of regional organizations in Scotland. Industrial restructuring was painful for Scotland, but did not entail damage to Scottish regional organizations. The damage to those networks had been done in the postwar decades when the industries were nationalized. Industrial restructuring in the 1980s meant the closure of state-owned or state-dependent industries, but not an attack on Scottish regional organizations—"we worried far more about the banks than about any shipyard. It was sad but we knew they were doomed" observed a journalist in 2003. "Glasgow's problem is that it hasn't adapted to any technology since the invention of the diesel engine . . . you can't subsidize that," remarked one West of Scotland public service manager in January 2002. They were fewer central organizations because London had cut off the resources on which they were dependent. Likewise, Thatcher's abolition of regional policy (in which the state steered industry to particular areas via a license system) abolished an attraction of the UK for Scots, but did not directly attack a constituency organized on a Scottish level. Rather, it undermined the Secretary of State's long-term ability to buy off opposition by making a traditional pork-barrel response harder. Finally, the highly personalized battle between Thatcher and the unions, caused by UK-wide tension over both labor relations and industrial restructuring, was not conducted in Scotland per se. Instead, it was fought over large-scale privatizations (such as the UK-wide National Coal Board) and the nature of UK-wide law. The STUC campaigned valiantly (and in a Scottish accent) for the preservation of union rights and state-owned firms in Scotland (Aitken 1997). Above all, this took the form of continuing STUC-led campaigns against specific high-profile closures, which through demonstrations, press events, and local coalitions turned plant names such as Ravenscraig, Bathgate, and Gartcosh into totems of defiant Scottish sentiment among trades unionists and many local communities. But the STUC, and even more so the component unions, were still campaigning for the resources of the center. The issue was UK policy, not Scotland.

Thus, territorial politics was not the main terrain of conflict. Most of Scotland's regional organizations were left alone, including most of the public sector around the welfare state (local government, health, education, law, higher education). Thatcher's first Secretaries of State for Scotland further eased matters; they were old-style Conservative Unionist grandees who were able to work with Scottish policy networks and regional organizations to lobby for funds from London and soften government policy—the traditional role of the Scottish Office and its ministers. Thus, Scottish industrial restructuring was at least somewhat more negotiated, the Scottish Office would lobby for Scottish industry, and unions felt better treated, even if the outcome was much the same (Keating and Jones 1995:102–103). "We always try to keep in touch, tell them what to watch," observed a Scottish Office civil servant in 1998; "we had an easier time than they did down south [England]." "They liked a quiet life . . . they didn't want surprises," agreed a union leader in 2002. The presence of the Scottish Office also meant that the conflict between Thatcher and local government was muted in Scotland; while in England the clash between Whitehall and far-left governments in London, Sheffield, and Liverpool had led to the abolition of metropolitan city governments, in Scotland Labour local governments resisted the Trotskyites and Thatcher's Secretaries of State enacted the policies, but did not pick such public fights (Carmichael 1995:124). A remarkable exchange from 1988 summarizes how well the "Scottish lobby" could work under Thatcherism. Peter Hennessy (1989:465-466) cites an interview with the Chief Executive of the Strathclyde local government (Glasgow and western Scotland) just after Thatcher's third election victory:

> [Hennessy]: "What you've just said reminds me [of the description of Scotland] as the greatest single pressure group in Britain."
>
> [CE] "Why shouldn't it be?"
>
> [Hennessy] "So, despite being Chief Executive of a very heavily Labour dominated regional council, you think that Conservative Malcolm Rifkind is Scotland's megaphone in the Cabinet Room?"
>
> [CE] "Yes, and I think Malcolm Rifkind would see that role for himself as well."

Scots regional organizations were not facing an environment they necessarily liked, but the old mechanisms continued to work (see Kellas 1989; Midwinter, Keating, and Mitchell 1991 for the workings of the Scottish policy system in these years; the irritation Thatcher shows with her Scottish secretaries when she reflects on why "there was no Tartan Toryism" is also evidence; Thatcher 1993:618–624). "We *always* keep lines of communication open," explained a high-ranking Scottish Office civil servant in 1998.

Since Thatcher's policies did not directly and demonstrably affect their autonomy and organizational stability, Scottish regional organizations did not react too negatively. If they did, it was as part of UK-wide policy debates. There was thus little regional organizational support in Scotland for territorial political change. They might or might not have agreed with Thatcher's policies, but were largely unaffected and fought any battles on the UK stage.

The political parties, meanwhile, reflected this position, with Labour fighting a UK-wide battle to reverse Thatcherism (in a singularly inept manner), the Conservatives ascendant in the UK on their economic, social, and foreign policy planks and doing slightly better than usual in Scotland, and the SNP factionalized and deep in the doldrums. Thatcher's form of politics had not created explicit territorial polarization in the sense of alienating regional organizations, for all that she alienated many people in Scotland (and Northern England and Wales). Politics did not polarize around territory (and Scottish autonomy) because no organizations dragged the parties to that position and there was little electoral threat from the SNP.

Labour in these years had a serious problem with a left-wing, Trotskyite, "entryist" group called Militant Tendency that had infiltrated some parts of the English party and caused internal problems as well as winning bad press. Along with a shift to the left among swing party leaders, this led to a radical party manifesto in 1983 that demanded massive nationalization, unilateral withdrawal from the EEC, and nuclear disarmament inter alia. The 1983 election came just after Thatcher's triumph in the Falkland wars, which would probably have won her the election anyway, but the power of the ideological left and the electoral defeat triggered the defectioon of high-profile Labour moderates from the party (to form the Social Democratic Party, or SDP) and more bitter infighting that debilitated much of the party. By 1987, the party's main goal was merely to defeat the SDP-Liberal alliance as the main opposition and reestablish its own internal coherence (for the SDP, Crewe and King 1995; for Labour in the 1980s, Seyd 1987).

In these dramas, Scottish Labour was moderate (Hutchison 2001:147–148). Its dominance by local government and trades unions meant that it was largely immune to radical takeover. To Scottish Labour, the infighting and defeats of UK Labour largely meant that it was excluded from power. It also meant that the party's focus on left–right conflict continued; Scottish Labour's preoccupations came from the left–right conflict within Labour and left–right conflict in Britain. There were strong tugs, then, to left–right politics, both within Labour and in politics polarized around industrial relations and economic policy. Meanwhile there was little pulling Labour toward a preoccupation with territorial politics while the memory of the unpleasant experiences of 1979 reduced its attractiveness as an electoral strategy. Labour thus tended to ignore Scottish autonomy and territorial politics in favor of argument about UK policies within Labour and on the UK level, stopping only to play the "Scottish card" when it could argue that a government policy was bad for Scotland. Its resource dependencies—local government, the unions—were not pushing it while other regional governments were not creating a devolutionist climate.

The Conservatives were ascendant in the UK in these years, and their electoral decay in Scotland (which started in 1959) slowed. They had assembled a strong coalition in the UK, accompanied by a large swathe of English swing voters that allowed them to dominate the decade. This coalition of resources for the party, as it happened, was based on businesses that were, effectively, central organizations or up for grabs. Scotland had an extensive financial sector that looked to the UK state because of its dependence on London for regulation. "You must understand our markets are global. . . . London is our biggest market. We are a specialized center for financial products that mostly pass through the City markets," explained a staff member of a financial services umbrella organization in 1998; in 1999, a civil servant explained that "some of our biggest companies, the Bank of Scotland and the Royal [Royal Bank of Scotland], are very major players in UK finance that think they would suffer. . . . they have threatened to move to England if they feel threatened." Scotland's old regional, industrial, Scottish businesses had been effectively wiped out in the last few decades and the party's elective affinities—the old organizational supports of unionism such as the Orange Order—were in decay (Seawright 1999). The Conservatives were a UK-wide party with a UK-wide coalition of resources that was based largely on its economic activities at the center of the state. Neither its policies nor its structure drove it to stress territorial politics, while its right-wing agenda polarized political debate in general away from Scotland's governance. In a bow to pragmatism, its activities in Scotland were also less disruptive and more consultative, which followed at least the *form* of Scottish politics to date.

Labour and the Conservatives polarized politics on a left–right axis in these years and left Scottish regional organizations' interest in autonomy largely quiescent. They were aided by the collapse of the movement-party that was the SNP. The SNP's threat had driven devolution to the center of UK politics in the 1970s; parties had responded to its threat to their voters and its votes in Westminster. Its threat dramatically diminished in 1979 when it was reduced from eleven to two MPs and from 30.4% to 17.3% of the popular vote (P. Lynch 2002:131, 156). Its organization, already overextended, also collapsed while the party's membership figures (based on the relatively reliable indicator of membership card sales) dropped from 28,091 in 1979 to 19,387 in 1983 and 12,115 in 1987 (P. Lynch 2002:163). This is an indicator of its activists' dispiritedness and the party's political weakness. In a party without business or trades unions support (dependent for many years on a betting scheme named Alba Pools; P. Lynch 2002), it meant serious financial problems with the accompanying weak organization, antiquated campaign methods, and limited public profile. To add to the party's troubles, the reaction of a significant number of activists was to form a faction (the 79 Group) that advocated a swing to the left, while various members experimented with direct illegal action. The details are less important than the fact that the SNP was a party based on activists' voluntary participation, dependent on that resource and unmoored to others. It did not present enough of a threat to make other parties change their strategies overall, and the experience of

1979 had probably raised their threshold for paying attention to Scottish autonomy anyway—reacting to the SNP with devolution had been a disaster for Labour, and fighting it a boon to the Conservatives.

Thatcher's first two governments, then, were not really about Scotland for most political participants. The Conservatives, with an essentially central agenda, and Labour, with an internal and an external left–right conflict, polarized conflict on a left–right axis and on the agenda of Thatcher's policies in macroeconomics, industrial relations, and industrial restructuring as well as English concerns such as local government. The SNP had temporarily collapsed, looking like a social movement-party with an unattainable goal, and was taking time to redevelop an activist base that would fund and work for further challenges. Regional organizations, meanwhile, were able to sit out much of the conflict of these years and exerted no pull to devolution as they were able to view the conflict as a left–right one. This was because they were mostly not directly affected and Thatcher's governments appeared to respect their autonomy and desire to be consulted. In short, these years were the end of an epoch of economic policy in the UK, but in Scottish territorial politics they were more of a reversion to the status quo ante. That was certainly what regional organizations (and the Conservatives) had sought in 1979.

*Thatcherism from Below: 1987–1997*

In 1985, Brand, a devolutionist academic and student of Scottish nationalism, argued that "in every field of Catalan life there is a native elite ready to provide leadership. Scotland has been stripped of its elites" (Brand 1985:292). He was wrong. The elites were there, though, emerged soon enough, and were mostly from the groups that Thatcher would soon threaten. The years after 1987 were dramatically different for them and produced a different kind of politics. This decade saw a combination of action and reaction that effectively undid the basic structure of Scottish politics. The action was that of the central state: after the election of 1987 Thatcher sought to reconstruct policy areas key to Scottish regional organizational networks and her successor John Major (1992–1997), if anything, accelerated the structural changes in British public policy agencies and formulation. *That* provoked a reaction from the Scottish public-sector organizations that loomed so large in the society, elite circles, and politics.

The reaction was that of regional organizations. Before Thatcher, and especially before 1987, they might have disagreed with the policy, but felt consulted, and its implementation was softened for them. After 1987, policy did not respect their autonomy with both the lack of consultation and the attack on their public sector bases. The result was that discrete organizations and the overall network of Scottish regional organizations responded by starting to support formal devolution. Informal inclusion and autonomy had been undone by the activities of the Thatcher and Major governments, so they switched to support for formal devolution. They brought Labour along with them, making it essentially obligatory for any ambitious Labour politician to support a Scottish parliament, and probably influenced public opinion. The outcome was devolution: the Conservative government had effectively created an overwhelming pro-devolution coalition within and outside Labour and, when the Conservatives lost, the Labour Party would arrive committed to creating a Scottish parliament. Scottish regional organizations were pivotal; a few (unions and local government) pushed Labour to unify around devolution while many others (churches, voluntary organizations, professional organizations, press, academics) created an increasingly pro-devolutionist climate through their statements.

## THE POLICIES AND THE RESISTANCE

Between 1987 and 1991, when Thatcher was removed, the institutional map of Britain changed dramatically (see the angry and well-informed Jenkins 1995). Thatcherite public policy in these years was a combination of intense centralization and welfare pluralism designed to increase competition in public services and the power of service users (Rao 1996). The government often ignored established policy communities (including those in Scotland), consulting on its, not their, terms (Richardson 2000:1010). The government's activities created the map of opposition in Scotland and support for devolution. Her educational reforms increased testing and curricular uniformity (somewhat mitigated in Scotland by the different system) and, dramatically, reshaped the university sector by abolishing tenure and incorporating "polytechnics" into the university sector while introducing a funding system based on intrusive performance indicators. In health, the government set out to fundamentally reshape the National Health Service (NHS), switching it from a direct service-providing organization with a workforce in the millions and dominated by professionals, to a market-based structure where supply and demand would reduce costs. This entailed the massive shakeup of introducing new layers of management and hundreds of new organizations as well as urging professionals to accept market-legitimated management dominance and urging former colleagues to compete (Greer 2004:ch. 2). These changes, made without consultation and opposed by almost every party involved in the health service, were tremendously controversial and very slow to be implemented in a resisting Scottish health service.

The personalities were controversial as well; junior minister Malcolm Forsyth (1989–1992) was controversial not only for his refusal to pursue conventional Scottish-office consultative politics, but also because he was imposed as party chair over the heads of Scottish Conservatives. Many Scots concluded that not even the Scottish Conservative and Unionist Party could affect the Conservative government's activities—that, as a Scottish Conservative grandee wrote, "to the scalps of [Argentine general] Galtieri and [miners' leader] Scargill, Margaret Thatcher can now add that of the Scottish Conservative Party" (Harvie and Jones 2000:138–139).

Privatization continued, with electricity and water sold off. The latter was resisted in Scotland and provided campaigners with an issue that had public resonance; Strathclyde organized a referendum in which a majority of voters opposed it. In that case, the government backed down and held onto the water company. Legal reform was also intensely controversial in England and Scotland; in Scotland, however, the government's assault on what it saw as rent-seeking monopolists was taken as an attack on the Scottish profession's autonomy as well as on legal professionalism. The combination of health reforms and entanglement of local and central government involved new players; for example, the social care (social work, elderly care) sector was hit by changes in the funding and structure of local government and health that reduced its reimbursements and caused a breakdown in funding procedures. The Church of Scotland was the biggest contracted provider in social work, operating nursing homes, hospices, daycare, and other services on contract to the NHS and local government. In addition to its objections to its exclusion from policymaking and its objections to Conservative ideology, it was now finding its own budget and institutional coherence battered by the breakdown of funding in social care.

Each of these policies—taking on very large numbers of people (there were around 100,000 people working in the Scottish NHS) and budgets—met with resistance. This was for two reasons. First, the lawyers, educators, health workers, utilities employees, and others affected disagreed with the policy for much the same reasons that their English colleagues disagreed. It was made worse by the weak Conservative support in Scotland; if the English had voted like the Scots, there would not have been a Thatcher government (Greer 2004: table 4.2). However, the second and crucial factor that turned this into a conflict over territorial politics was the *way* the government set about reforming them. It was not responding to problems they perceived; it was not consulting with them; it was therefore dramatically changing their environments and legal natures against their will and without consultation. From 1707 into the Thatcher years, Scottish regional organizations had been key players in policy concerning them. The Conservative government, combining politics of conviction with the crushing formal power of a Westminster executive, ignored this convention and demonstrated how weak Scottish organizations really were. They fought back with conventional lobbying strategies and delayed implementation, trying to modify implementation in Scotland

and minimize its impact, but the effect of Thatcherite policies on these organizations was clear, and the closely interlinked Scottish elites diffused the sense of threat and lack of representation (Holliday 1992).

The water privatization decision, pitching local government against the government, had found public resonance as a Scottish–English conflict. The biggest conflict, though, the poll tax, bubbled over from Thatcher's conflict with English local government (Butler, Adonis, and Travers 1994). Her government had been fighting with local government for years for three reasons: its spending undermined her fiscal plans; its spending appeared on government accounts as liabilities; and its spending was used by left Labour councils to tweak her government's tail (the most impressive example was the Greater London Council in the last months before its abolition took effect, which used the remains of its budget to fund antinuclear, pro-homeless, pro-jobless, and other anti-Thatcherite campaigners). The key to resolving the conflict, for Thatcher, was thus to change local government finance, and the government had been trying various schemes to do this for years. They had failed, and mainly produced legal guerrilla warfare that wrapped central and local government in red tape (M. Loughlin 2000). It began to seem to leading Conservatives that the problem lay in the disconnection between local government accountability and finance. Local government was largely funded by central government or by property taxes that tended to fall on nonvoting businesses, and thus, concluded Conservatives, it had no incentive to be frugal. The government decided to change this by replacing the property tax ("council rates") with a poll tax ("community charge") that applied to all residents of a council. Now, ran the argument, local government would be more accountable and democratic; council spending would be paid by all voters and would not redistribute from nonvoting businesses to voting council-house residents.

This shift in government thinking coincided with a separate problem in Scotland. Scottish properties had not been appraised for years and it was well known that many properties were under-valued. The upcoming scheduled revaluation would hit certain groups hard—especially the elderly whose children who had left home and who lived in private houses around Edinburgh, Glasgow, and Aberdeen where prices had increased. This group, while small numerically, was a large part of the Conservative and Unionist activist base, and the party was about to dramatically increase their taxes. As a result, the government decided to introduce the community charge quickly in Scotland in order to avoid the revaluation. Thus, the community charge arrived a year earlier in Scotland (Harvie and Jones 2000:132–133). The differential treatment—Scotland was now undergoing Thatcherite policy reform *before* England—was enough for local government, the closely linked Labour party, the STUC, officials of the Church of Scotland, and the voluntary sector (nonprofit) to organize a vigorous campaign against the tax, based around a petition and the claim that *Scotland* objected to the policy.

The government ignored them. Eventually the tax would be undone (and would be the undoing of Thatcher), but only after it was introduced in England. A Conservative party rebellion triggered by disastrous public opinion, mass noncompliance, and a riot in London's Trafalgar Square ended Thatcher's career without an election and replaced her with John Major a little over a year later in 1990 (G. W. Jones 1995). Scottish resistance had been lawful, well organized, and unsuccessful while successful English resistance had taken the most obvious form of a riot and local government disobedience. Scots elites noticed their powerlessness, and the Scottish press, especially the increasingly intensely Scottish and pro-devolutionist quality *Herald* and *Scotsman* passed on the lesson to their readers.

After Major's arrival in power, the changes continued. Major privatized the railway system, handing over a deeply unpopular, dysfunctional, and baroque structure that failed to produce visible desirable outcomes but was almost impossible to unpick. His government advanced the managerialist policies of Thatcher (Pollitt 1993), focused on standard-setting and targeting across public administration, and pushed the quasiprivatizing practice of creating "next steps" agencies to run public services in isolation from both public-sector budgeting and, it proved, public-sector accountability. These standards offended professionals such as teachers and doctors while driving home how little they were consulted in policy. Then, the government tightened the criteria for Scotland's block grant so as to reduce the rate of increase, a move that put the Conservatives on the defensive in Scotland (Bennie, Brand, and Mitchell 1997:71). Then, for reasons that are still unclear, in Scotland (and the rest of the UK, on different schedules) the Major government also reorganized local government. This created single-tier governments, which fragmented Scottish government, but inadvertently paved the way for devolution by eliminating rivals such as the giant Strathclyde. In the short term, it outraged local governments, which saw an effort to gerrymander the remaining Conservative votes into control of a few councils. It also "devastated the voluntary sector. There were many groups doing valuable things that depended on Strathclyde and found the new councils were too small to be supporting them. It made a lot of people very angry," remarked a senior Labour politician of the change in a 2003 interveiew.

Throughout this period, an additional governance problem was brewing in Scotland. The UK state relies heavily on quangos, or quasinongovernmental organizations, to operate public policy. These are boards appointed by and accountable to a Secretary of State that fulfill all manner of functions, from running local health services to looking after the canal system or redeveloping cities. Quango appointments were intensely political and afford governments both a vast supply of patronage and a largely hidden way to control public services. In Scotland, as in the rest of the UK, the quango appointments were largely Conservatives, even though the existing powerful organizations of Scotland increasingly tended to sympathize with Labour and the policy reforms of the Conservatives were alienating them further. Scottish medical elites, for example, found that the Scottish NHS was now run by government appointees chosen among the small set of Conservatives. "We were run by Tory ladies . . . the very picture of nice little Edinburgh ladies with old-fashioned ideas" and "they were all Tories . . . and the Tories here are pretty stupid" griped two different health services managers, in 1998 and 2002, illustrating at least perceptions. The government had put ideological and party loyalty above the support of the organizations, and the result was that much of the public sector in Scotland felt itself frozen out of its own governance.

In these years, the activities of the central state directly challenged the autonomy and environmental stability of key Scottish regional organizations—professions, the public sector, unions, local government, and many quangos. It did this by making policy inimical to their public-sector, quasicorporatist preferences without consulting them. They were destabilized by the prospect of major changes being made without their input, and they lost autonomy in the changes as the government sought to control organizations better to push its preferences. They resisted with individual campaigns, such as that of Strathclyde against water privatization, the British Medical Association (BMA) against NHS reform, local governments against restructuring, and the broad Scottish coalition against the poll tax. The Scottish press fulminated (the *Herald*, once the organ of the West of Scotland Unionist business class, devoted a weekly column in the 1990s to Marxist-nationalist Tom Nairn). All these changes in the structure of Scottish governance elicited a reaction stronger than individual campaigns—they swung regional organizations to support formal devolution as a guarantee against more such experiences. The climate in Scotland changed increasingly as the legitimacy and infrastructure of a range of regional organizations became available to support devolutionists. The next section deals with the overspill into party and constitutional politics.

## FROM OPPOSING POLICIES TO SUPPORTING DEVOLUTION

Informal autonomy in a formally centralized state carried the one great drawback that, when the central state decided to abrogate that informal autonomy, there was no way to resist. So Scottish elites, subjected to central assaults, started to seek formal autonomy to buttress their defenses. The support for devolution particularly came with the radical policy changes of

1987–1992, when Scottish regional organizations were finding not just their policy preferences but also their autonomy and stability threatened. To some extent, this coincided with the revival of the SNP, but the timing of SNP surges and their strength relate poorly to the development of the Scottish consensus or its content, while the activities of the central state relate chronologically and in the dramatis personae.

The process involved two rough groups of regional organizations. First were the directly participating, "political" organizations such as the Church of Scotland, local government, newspapers, and the STUC. These organizations were already involved in politics, accustomed to mounting public campaigns and deriving political force from them, and they had little to lose by participating directly in a campaign. Second were other Scottish regional organizations not accustomed to taking public stances on major political issues; they might lobby and participate in insider politics, or even mount specialized campaigns in their policy areas, but they did not habitually campaign and did not work by direct campaigning. These include universities, professional organizations, business groups, and the more specialized lobbying organizations such as the Royal Scottish Society for the Prevention of Cruelty to Children.[1]

The relationship between these groups lies in the small numbers and dense interconnections of Scottish elites. The two groups were subjected to the same Conservative policies, and their ability to communicate magnified the consequences by making all aware of their common plight. The simple mechanism of dinner parties in Edinburgh and Glasgow, let alone Scotland's newspaper and specialized press, conferences, appointed boards and public debates, transmitted a sense of outrage between different sectors. Tacit approval allowed quiet groups like professional organizations to reinforce the determination of noisy ones such as the STUC. "You could feel it in the air in the 1990s. It was bad taste to be a Unionist," remarked a Unionist in 2001. David Seawright comments on how this created a "valence" problem for the Scottish Conservatives—to compete in Scottish politics, a party had to be Scottish, and the Conservatives were seen as English (Seawright 2002).

The development of the key devolutionist coalition came in two parallel and tightly linked ways (overviews are Taylor 1999; Harvie and Jones 2000). First, there was the direct campaign by Scottish organizations for a formal, autonomous, powerful Parliament. Second, there was the internal battle to bring Labour over to devolution.

The first response, the direct campaign for Scottish autonomy, took the form of a pressure-group coalition and constitutional convention that came to be known as the Scottish Constitutional Convention (Mitchell 1996:287–290; K. Wright 1997; Harvie and Jones 2000:153–156). This organization formed as a coalition in 1988 on the basis of an older, marginal, organization called the Campaign for a Scottish Assembly that some low-ranking Labour and SNP figures had formed in 1979 to keep devolutionist ideas alive. The organizers of the CSA realized, as Harvie and Jones put it, that "an article in [their journal] *Radical Scotland* would get nowhere, but what if a group of respected Scots, preferably straddling or above the party battle, should draw up the case?" (Harvie and Jones 2000:148).

They struck at the right time and would give political life then and observers later an indicator of the scope and preferences of dissatisfied Scottish regional organizations. Having started in 1988 and begun by appealing directly to regional organizations, they would be able to channel the increasing irritation of those Scottish regional organizations into their campaign for devolution. They established a committee chaired by a well-connected academic experienced in regional development, and composed of representatives of unions, churches, Liberals, SNP, voluntary organizations, universities, small businesses, and (reflecting the importance of cultural activism in 1980s and 1990s Scotland, and the intellectual bent of the initiators) theater and poetry. A former Scottish Office civil servant who had worked on devolution in the 1970s and was now retired wrote much of the output, a short text called *A Claim of Right for Scotland* (the title had great historic resonance). It argued that Scotland was fundamentally misgoverned by a state that needed radical reform. It called for a constitutional convention to rethink the nature of Scotland's participation in the UK.

The *Claim of Right* was something of a sensation, coming as it did amid Thatcher's policy reforms, and the Scottish Constitutional Convention (SCC) began to coalesce. "It was the catalyst," said one Labour politician in a 2001 interview; "it was supposed to bring politicians together, but it also brought together a wider civil society . . . we united as much of the country as we could," explained a then-Church of Scotland leader in a 1998 interview. The SCC at a minimum had to involve representatives of the major parties, since whatever the power of the STUC or the Church of Scotland, legislation on devolution was the necessary final step and that required parties. The initiative, however, did not lie with parties as electoral actors; it lay with the well-connected organizers. They successfully mustered the most devolutionist members of the Liberal Democrats (successor party of the Liberals and SDP) and Labour as well as groups in society ranging from Gaelic-language groups to the Law Society (a main lawyers' professional organization) but weighed toward local government and unions. Politicians sensed that, on the one hand, there was a powerful coalition to be had for devolution, one with the potential of considerable support from regional organizations and elites, and, on the other, that the constellation of forces in a devolved Scotland might be a better environment for center-left politics and policies. The SNP was reluctant to be drawn into a "devolutionist trap" and preferred to use its new electoral momentum to push for independence. It accordingly stayed out and was showered with criticism for spurning the cross-party group (Mitchell 1996:234–243).

All this happened despite the evident weaknesses of the Constitutional Convention, which was, as Mitchell points out, "unprepared for the most likely outcome of the 1992 election," namely, Conservative victory (Mitchell 1996:287). The SCC might not have galvanized Scots or even made itself known to them, but it did certify elite resistance and territorial politics as legitimate, and autonomy as a goal many Scottish regional organizations now actively wanted. It made it clear and public that regionalization could supply autonomy without being a creature of the destabilizing SNP.

The SCC thus became the point on which regional organizations, the Liberal Democrats, and Labour could agree in pursuit of devolution. Devolution might defend them both against future Thatcherite policy. The SCC appointed a committee of well-known academics to produce a draft of a devolution act, chose an eminent churchman for a chair (the choice, Canon Kenyon Wright, was also well connected in England, which helped stop accusations of anti-Englishness). Its devolutionist proposals initially came out on 30 November 1990. They were studiously practical and basically spoke of self-government over competencies already devolved to the Scottish Office. Its specific, and reassuring, suggestions amounted to replacing the Secretary of State for Scotland with a Parliament. Its radicalism was confined to speaking of a Scottish Parliament, a strong word in Westminster constitutionalism, a commitment to proportional representation, and a gender policy—some adroit maneuver by feminists produced a commitment to institutional mechanisms for increased female representation (A. Brown 1998). It is probably wise to remain agnostic about the effects of the SCC, but it is at least an indicator and was, then as now, an elite rallying point.

Its offering appealed to regional organizations whose chief complaints were already, and would increasingly be, about the intervention of the central state in their affairs. By 1990, they were already in the throes of the poll tax, NHS reform, utilities privatization, and law reform, all imposed from London with only sporadic regard for incumbent policy communities anywhere in the UK (Richardson 2000). The SCC's moderate devolution proposal was a good solution that promised them all autonomy and stability together. The consequence affected public opinion by supplying Scottish framing for resistance to policies and easing campaigns against the various high-profile policies such as the poll tax and the local government reform. The press joined in, with the *Scotsman* especially interested (it sponsored a dramatic debate in Edinburgh that raised the temperature and forced parties to respond) (M. Smith 1994). Above all, though, it made devolution not just a respectable but a favored strategy for regional organizations seeking

autonomy. The final list of participants included 56 local authority representatives, 21 party representatives, 23 trades unionists, and participants from
the Dundee Chamber of Commerce, the Law Society/Faculty of Advocates
(the main legal organizations), two Gaelic groups, the Forum of Private
Businesses, the Federation of Small Businesses, the Scottish churches, and
the Committee of University Principals as well as 59 MPs and 6 members
of the European Parliament (all Labour or Liberal Democrats) (Scottish
Constitutional Convention 1995:34–35). The ensemble was highly respectable and represented important aspects of Scotland's regional organizations,
and that was what mattered.

The second response, the fight for Labour, was intertwined with the
direct elite campaign and the particular career of the party itself. The experience of Thatcherism was silencing, removing, or converting antidevolutionists.
Industries dependent on central state aid were mostly gone; the structures of
UK-wide industrial policy and the groups dependent on it were far weaker. In
1979, Labour antidevolutionists had support in local government and unions
and a friendly climate in much of Scotland; by 1997, the loss of autonomy and
stability had diminished or converted to devolution most of both groups.

Two groups with resources were so dominant within Labour as to be
able to drive much of it. The first was the trades union movement. Increasingly confined to the public services, the trades unions and STUC could see
that they were often allied with their large Scottish organizations in opposition to Conservative policy. A devolved parliament offered the prospect of a
more stable environment in which Scotland would be autonomous to pursue goals that the unions often shared with their organizations (or could at
least negotiate with less acrimony). The other was local government, represented in the large representative body Cosla (Convention of Scottish Local
Authorities). Local government was, on one hand, the school and power base
for many Labour politicians. On the other hand, it was also a large interest
group including non-Labour politicians. Its misfortunes at the hands of the
Conservatives, with clashes over utilities, development, and finance but especially reorganization, made it an active supporter of devolution while Cosla's
influence—and its members' influence—in Labour helped snuff out
antidevolutionist sentiment in the party. Both groups ended up playing large
roles in the SCC; even the numbers they sent bore that out.

Labour's devolutionists had an extra card to play that allowed them to
argue that this was the appropriate time to solidify a devolutionist preference.
A 1988 by-election in the poverty-stricken postindustrial Glasgow seat of
Govan, one of Labour's safest, was taken by left-nationalist firebrand Jim
Sillars in an upset equivalent to the 1967 Hamilton by-election. Sillars was
hardly a reassuring figure for regional organizations—his career had led him
from Labour, through a breakaway left party, to the SNP and fame as the

originator of the slogan "independence in Europe." Just as with Hamilton or other SNP upsets, this made it seem imperative to find a Labour response. As with Hamilton, it was worrying for Labour because it meant the SNP had again escaped its rural redoubts and might invade Labour's western industrial heartlands. Labour's devolutionists could make an argument not only that the Labour social coalition was coming to support devolution, but also that there was a need to take a devolutionist position right then, before the SNP did more damage. The SNP, meanwhile, mysteriously lost momentum; more by-elections in equally troubled Glasgow Central and Paisley that year were comfortable Labour victories. Thus, while the Govan victory helped Labour devolutionists and contributes to a full explanation of the timing of Labour's participation in the SCC, it does not wholly explain the party's preference or its strength. It can be argued that the SCC made Labour Scottish enough to win again; it can equally be argued that the voters in unhappy areas like Govan and Paisley were largely unaware of the niceties of constitutional change.

The result was that, by 1994, when Tony Blair was elected Labour Party leader, a commitment to Scottish devolution was inevitable. "Tony had to do it," said one Labour politician from Scotland in 2001. "If you had held a free vote anytime, a secret ballot in the Scottish [Parliamentary Labour Party] you would not have had a majority for devolution, but none of them could admit it in public," commented a former Blair government minister in 2002. No Labour leader could avoid supporting it, and vocal Labour opposition to devolution was confined to party mavericks such as Tam Dalyell MP, a habitual rebel and leader of the 1979 opposition to devolution. This time there was no oxygen among regional organizations for antidevolutionist sympathy within Labour. Blair, cautious as always, determined that there would be a referendum (as against only legislation) and that it would ask both if there should be a parliament and if it should have its tax-varying powers. This created a storm—the Scottish party, forging ahead of its English leader, was outraged even if Blair's tactic immunized the party against charges of breaking up the union and raising taxes. The Scottish Labour executive, in a nice reversal of the 1970s, locked Blair into three hours of personal debate over the decision and then only voted 16–12 to support the two-question initial referendum (Harvie and Jones 2000:172–174).

Thus, the game was won within Labour. Meanwhile, the 1992 election and John Major's 1992–1997 government solidified the regional coalition in favor of devolution. Policy change and imposed welfare pluralism continued, with efforts to semiprivatize public services, extensive use of targets to control them and reduce their autonomy, and the local government reorganization that made many enemies. The 1992 election victory of the Conservatives had been a bad shock for Labour, the SNP, and regional organizations, and gave the Conservatives another chance. The Conservatives in Scotland explicitly fought on a Unionist platform, arguing that they would save an endangered UK. Contrary to expectations, they revived a bit in Scotland and held onto their UK parliamentary majority. This gave the Conservatives another chance to reestablish their links with Scottish regional organizations. Their failure to do so is instructive. Malcolm Forsyth, the controversial former junior minister, returned as Secretary of State in 1994 with a brief to repair relations (Harvie and Jones 2000:162–169). He tried to do this through a mixture of further devolution, showy Scottish gestures, and changes to Scottish representation in Westminster. The further devolution signally included the separation of Scottish historical site administration, arts funding, and higher education funding from UK-wide bodies (as part of larger changes in those areas) while the changes to Westminster representation included reviving a Scottish Grand Committee of all Scottish MPs to consider legislation; this would travel around Scotland, holding its meetings in different places. Neither of these agendas changed the UK. The new Scottish Arts Council and similar organizations were more quangos with Conservative-appointed boards. The Scottish parliamentary delegation had a large Labour majority and so the Grand Committee had to be packed with English MPs to make up a government majority (they disliked the prospect of traveling around Scotland to that end). "We appreciate the [new Scottish Higher Education Funding Council] but be realistic—it does all the same things the government makes it do. They control it," commented a university official in 1998. "Tories Tories Tories," sighed a Scottish Office civil servant involved with arts quangos in 1998.

More to the point, neither was convincing. A densely interconnected set of Scottish regional organizations and their closely linked Labour party had just gone through, and were still going through, major policy changes they felt were driven by English Conservatives, were inimical to their interests, destabilizing, and that diminished their autonomy. The old structure of Scottish committees and administrative decentralization through quangos and the Scottish Office had proved to be no defense in the cases of law, health, local government, universities, privatization, education, trade relations, and economic policy and were proving to be no defense in the cases of public sector management and transport. The Conservatives' conviction politics, as applied to Scotland, had almost eliminated the credibility of the informal autonomy granted to Scotland and the final Forsyth ingredient, showy Scottishness, failed to restore it. Forsyth returned a Scottish national memorial—the Stone of Scone—to Edinburgh and was ridiculed for it. Hosting a party for the cast of *Braveheart* (a movie about William Wallace) while wearing a kilt did not restore his party's autonomist credibility either (Harvie and Jones 2000:169). More meaningful activities such as establishing a University of the Highlands and Islands were appreciated, but failed to convince. His participation in earlier, centrally driven policy changes (he held the health portfolio during the introduction of the internal market), along with his current participation in a Conservative government, were not forgotten. In short, he and his government lacked credibility because the central state had too often violated Scottish rules about Scottish autonomy.

Thus, the devolutionist consensus born in 1987–1992 grew under the government of John Major. There was enough policy reform to remind Scottish organizations of the threat to their autonomy (such as the inability to affect the decision to privatize their railways). There was also a credible devolutionist alternative and a devolutionist Labour Party. Not only was the Scottish press hostile, but it also had trouble finding credible Scottish advocates of Conservative policies in the regional organizations affected. The consensus, and its contribution to the image of Conservatives as anti-Scottish, undoubtedly contributed to their 1997 electoral wipeout—in the general election they won no Scottish seats at all. The election in Scotland was about "British" issues and closely coordinated by Labour's headquarters in London, but that did not matter—it would produce devolution (Denver et al. 2000:44–45). Tony Blair's government entered with a strong manifesto commitment to devolution and it would be almost the first thing that the new government did.

This account focuses on the development of the devolutionist consensus within the majority party—Labour—and among powerful social organizations. The analysis largely ignores the SNP because the SNP modified Labour strategy in these years—it was an "agenda-setter" (Newell 1998). The SNP had a goal that regional organizations would never sign up for and as a party without their alliances was unstable and destabilizing. The 1988 Govan victory helped Labour devolutionists push the debate up the agenda, but otherwise the SNP excluded itself in these years (and, in 1988, its subsequent by-election losses took the heat off Labour, even though Labour continued with devolution). As the devolutionist coalition solidified, the SNP was pursuing a very different strategy summarized in its disastrous 1992 electoral slogan "Free by '93" (a Labour leader, Donald Dewar, joked that the slogan was a good one because the SNP could use it every ten years) (P. Lynch 2002:198). The SNP's problem, as usual, was that its dependence on a mobilized activist base left it open to their shifts. The intense frustration they felt throughout the Thatcher and Major governments and the early-1990s sense, created by the fall of the Soviet bloc, that there was a "springtime of the nations" led them to support a flatly secessionist strategy. Their pragmatic new leader (and former early-1980s leftist schismatic) Alex Salmond opposed the strategy, since the SNP clearly would not be the Scottish majority party. His pragmatism was overruled by activist sentiment (P. Lynch 2002:192–200).

The SNP under Salmond moderated somewhat in time for the 1997 elections, but still argued frankly for independence. As a result, it lacked resources and the stability that comes from stable resource dependencies. Its new affiliates, such as New Scots for Independence (made up of immigrants) were strategies that, for example, answered media charges of racism rather than built institutional links on the scale of the other parties. Its membership climbed and its organization improved under Salmond, but it still was less institution-alized (linked to other institutions) than any other serious party. It at no point considered abandoning independence and thereby cut itself off from the same regional organizations that were undeniably Scottish but who preferred the moderate defenses offered by the SCC and its parties. The SNP, with its activists, and the Conservatives, with their central funding, were reliant on groups that had interests other than those of Scottish regional organizations. The result was that the SNP representation remained fairly small in the 1997 elections and the Conservatives went from very small to nonexistent.

*The Referendum, 1997*

One of the tactical lessons Labour drew from the 1979 experience was that any devolution referendum should be fast and on the principle of devolution rather than the detail. The government accordingly called a referendum almost immediately after its election. The referendum experience was short and intense—and almost wholly one-sided. There simply was no credible No coalition this time around. The full weight of Scottish regional organizations swung in favor, and the party they had helped make strong, Labour, fulfilled its side of the bargain by campaigning strongly and with almost total unity— regardless of what Members of Parliament might have thought privately.

Labour came into office on 2 May 1997 (the day after the election). The White Paper titled *Scotland's Parliament*, sketching the bill and explaining the referendum, came out in July. It would have two questions. The first would ask if the voter supported a parliament as outlined in the White Paper; the second would ask if the parliament should have the power to vary income taxes by 3% in the pound. By then Labour, the Liberal Democrats, and the SNP agreed to campaign together for a "Yes–Yes" vote in favor of an affirmative answer to both questions. Pro-devolution strategists, including moderate SNP leaders, agreed that a unified campaign would be more impressive and cost-effective. A No–No campaign counseling a No to both questions also started up (called Think Twice). Despite its best efforts, it was unable to find significant support-ers who were not implicated with the Conservative Party (when Thatcher appeared in Glasgow during the campaign to address a convention of travel agents and argued against devolution, it was generally agreed to be a public relations disaster for the No–No campaign).

What is most striking about the campaign is the weakness of the No-No camp and the strength of Yes-Yes. This reflects the switch by Scottish regional organizations such as the church, local government, public sector unions, small business, and professional organizations. In 1979, there were funds of finance, activists, infrastructure, and legitimacy for the No coalition and many of the supports that formally were committed to the Yes camp were half-hearted—the unions, Church of Scotland, pro-devolution parties, and local government, which between them had great resources, were reluctant to throw them behind the campaign and harbored many antidevolutionists. In 1997, by contrast, the church, unions, local governments, and major Scottish parties were behind devolution—the church might have fallen out of step with Scottish society in that it still was almost half composed of self-identified Conservatives (C. G. Brown 1997:165), but it still saw devolution as diminishing threats to its existence and values (K. Wright 1997). Even quietist organizations such as the association of university vice-chancellors and the Law Society had participants who lent their legitimacy and stamp of approval to devolution. The major institutional resources of the devolutionists—the complex of unions, local government, and Labour—was far better organized and more united and were tied together in a sizeable coalition that was further supported by legitimating players such as the churches, academics, professions, lawyers, small businesses, and artists. Cosla, the STUC, and major public-sector unions helped greatly with organizing, contributing organization, infrastructure, legitimacy, and the ability to get press as well as activists who were numerous and deeply embedded in Labour.

By contrast, the sustenance of the 1979 No campaign was almost gone by 1997. It had some old-style unionist figures—financiers, bankers, lawyers, aristocrats—but they were few in number and the weight of personal legitimacy (and all the weight of organizational legitimacy) went to the Yes–Yes camp. It did have money—the No campaign, Think Twice, spent £270,000 to the Yes (Scotland Forward) spending of £275,000 (Denver et al. 2000:59). The only real break came when a member of a skeptical group spoke up (see Harvie and Jones 2000:182). That group was the Edinburgh financial sector, which was worried about the prospect of irresponsible economic policy, but focused its concern only on the second question, that regarding income tax variations. It was resource-dependent on London and worried about erratic policy while its investments, and the salaries it paid, in Scotland made it wary of any tax variation that could harm its sizeable position there. "We are trying very hard to explain the devolution proposals to our members, discuss the issues and the advantages . . . they are naturally nervous . . . markets do not like risk," explained a staffer of the trade group Scottish Financial Enterprise in 1998. Thus, Bruce Patullo, the Governor of the Bank of Scotland (a large private bank whose domed building overlooking Edinburgh looks more like a parliament than a bank), gave a newspaper interview opposing tax-raising power. Labour and the Yes–Yes campaign orchestrated a public relations battering that kept the Bank of Scotland from repeating its charge and quieted any other possible recalcitrants (the press use the evocative word "monstering"). "Devolution was inevitable. I can't believe how stupid [Patullo] was to say that—he wasn't going to stop it by then" remarked an antidevolutionist financier in a 2001 interview. This was possible largely because there was so little other support for antidevolutionists (Harvie and Jones 2000:182). The Bank of Scotland appeared alone with the remains of the Conservative Party against the bulk of Scottish regional organizations. The legitimacy and institutional resources of interlocking regional organizations kept other financial groups and other centrally dependent groups from expressing any doubts they might have had.

The campaign was short and shortened first by a distracting scandal in the Renfrewshire (Paisley) Labour Party and then by the loudly mourned death of Princess Diana. The direct campaign incorporated the campaigning machines of Labour, the SNP and the Liberal Democrats as well as Cosla, the unions, many smaller voluntary sector organizations, and many professionals under a single umbrella. The umbrella organization, Yes for Scotland, blanketed Scotland with flyers and a successful canvassing operation as well as a successful set of events intended to win media attention. The 11 September 1997 vote was overwhelming and positive (Denver et al. 2000:chs. 5–7 for the results and interpretation). By the day of the referendum, the No–No advocates were drowned out by the newspapers headlines. The right-wing *Daily Mail*, an English paper that had very few readers in Scotland, advised Yes–No while the other newspapers supported Yes–Yes. On a turnout of 60.4% (probably equal to 71%, given the dated electoral register, which had been compiled for the 1997 election), 74.3% voted for a parliament and 63.5% for the tax-varying powers. No region of Scotland voted No–No, and only outlying and traditionally skeptical Dumfries and the Orkney Islands voted Yes–No by very small margins. The vote would have cleared the 40% hurdle.

## CONCLUSIONS

If the 1978 Act and 1979 referendum were hard-fought and dogged by guerrillas within Labour and absenteeism by many erstwhile supporters, the 1997 campaign was a model of unity with no serious Labour figure breaking ranks and a discredited No campaign almost bereft of serious institutional support. The year 1979 was a picture of disharmony within Scottish parties and institutions, while 1997 was dominated by a consensus and a powerful devolutionist coalition. As a result, while in 1979 devolution faced Labour rebels and relatively weak support among Labour's Scottish social allies, 1997 saw the parties greasing its skids and a massive campaign to launch devolution. What happened?

The key difference is that the Thatcher and Major governments, above all from 1987 to 1992, violated the traditional compacts between the central British state and Scottish regional organizations. Until the Conservatives arrived with their "politics of conviction," the rough bargain dating from the negotiations of the Treaty of Union had held. The British central state, endowed with almost unlimited executive power, had left Scottish organizations to their autonomy and broadly not changed their environment or relevant policies without consulting them. The government after 1979 had far less respect for this and other conventions that structured much of the British state, and when it turned its attention to public policies relevant to Scottish elites it neither pursued policies that they supported nor granted them the respect and consultation that their own stability required. They were just as brutally changed as their colleagues in England, and resented it.

Policy conflict in Scotland therefore took not just the form of disputes over policies, as it did in England, but also of disputes over whether Scottish regional organizations should be subjected to the straightforward implementation of policies designed in London. The British constitutional order said they should, and as a result regional organizations became interested in a different constitutional order. The authors of the *Claim of Right for Scotland* and the Scottish Constitutional Convention participants crystallized such a moderate, nonsecessionist, alternative that promised to insulate Scottish organizations from broader British politics and the British executive. The document, coming just as a wave of Conservative policies jolted Scottish regional organizations, became the objective of a new coalition for devolution that acted directly and brought Labour along. Even as its rival the SNP waxed and waned (sometimes within a single year), the devolutionist consensus solidified among Labour's resource dependencies. Dependent on them, Labour promoted their devolutionist allies within the party and coalesced around devolution. By 1997, there was no serious opposition to devolution—the regional organizations' enmity and the decline of Conservative bases in Scotland had left them with no MPs or good name, while the Labour Party and its Scottish regional organizational allies were free to create a new Scottish political order.

The alternative argument that devolution was, and succeeded solely as, a Labour strategem to damage the SNP has some support throughout Labour, but it remains that devolution and constitutional change were unlikely vote-winners, and Labour certainly behaved that way (Bogdanor 2001). Labour interviewees and civil servants cite the focus groups the party consulted before the 1997 election when constitutional reform, including devolution, was ranked fourteenth in importance out of fourteen options. One 2001 interviewee speculated on when Tony Blair would admit that devolution was one of his most important legacies—"probably only when he's out of office." The actual campaign in Scotland was a UK-wide campaign, run from Labour's headquarters in Westminster, and it was run on the issues that Labour's research said *did* matter to voters. John Major told voters just before the election that they had "72 hours to save the Union" and Labour shot back a day later that they had "24 hours to save the NHS" (Butler and Kavanagh 1997:111–112). If Labour had enacted devolution to spike the SNP guns, they would have discussed it more.

Meanwhile, international opportunities were not obviously propitious. Arguably, European integration gave Scotland a wider stage and the inspiring post-Soviet "springtime of the nations" both increased Scottish sentiment and desire for autonomy, but it is unclear why these arguments did not apply to independence—the coming introduction of the Euro had meanwhile further eased economic integration (since Scotland, an oil exporter, would have had a dangerously high currency on its own) and most of the nations having a post-Soviet springtime had advanced to independence and were negotiating state to state with the UK. By contrast, in Scotland something (namely, the form of regional autonomy and the institutions required to sustain it) had changed: "we could never let ourselves go through something like that again," sighed a devolutionist retired leader of a professional organization at the end of a 2001 interview about Thatcherism.

Devolution did fix that problem. It was easy to implement, as such changes go, because there was a strong consensus among interested parties that a Scottish Parliament should take responsibility for Scottish Office powers. The question now is if it will survive other challenges—to its funding, to its organization of intergovernmental relations, or to its low profile in English politics.

# Chapter Five

# Catalonia 1975–1980

## Compelling Autonomy

In November 1975, when Generalissimo Francisco Franco died, Spain was an intensely centralized dictatorship with a particular animus toward expressions of national identity and autonomy in Catalonia and the Basque Country. The coup that started the Spanish Civil War and eventually led to Franco's victory was triggered in part by Catalan autonomy, and the Franco regime's repression of Catalan identity (let alone autonomism or secessionism) had been savage. It has meant economic discrimination, harsh measures against the Catalan language, brutal secret policing, and extremely centralized public policy. Yet Catalan political forces emerged within months of Franco's death. Within five years, the new Spanish constitution recognized Catalan autonomy, the Catalan government (Generalitat) from the 1930s was recreated, and moderate nationalists had won the first elections.

The outcome for this chapter, then, is positive: Catalonia emerged in the 1980s with an elected regional government, the Generalitat, and a substantial list of powers that it could have or at least plausibly seek. The next chapter and chapter seven will discuss the politics of filling out that list of competencies. This chapter focuses on the politics of mobilizing political resources around autonomy in the tense times of the transition and the mix of negotiations, mass mobilizations, and pressure that created the Generalitat.

The strength of Catalonia's web of regional social organizations explains the Generalitat in good part because it explains the origins, organization, and weight of the Catalan demands for autonomy during the Spanish democratic transition. Catalan regional organizations could survive the repression that political forces could not (such Catalan organizational webs had survived many Spanish regimes). They provided the crucial support for a particular form of Catalan political organization, a constellation of parties that could oblige the negotiators of the transition to grant Catalonia autonomy. Their resources created a party system in Catalonia that was structurally in favor of autonomy. Via their direct pressure, the organizations that coordinated and aggregated their efforts, and the parties they influenced, Catalonia won a degree of regional autonomy overall and a statute that promised competencies in the sectors of interest to them.

Such autonomy, however, required participating in the transition in a way that would lead to Catalonia's walking the line between centralism (a powerful thread in the activities of central organizations, including political parties, the judiciary, and the state bureaucracies) and secessionist nationalism (as was so strong in the Basque Country). This led to a remarkable, and remarkably explicit, exercise in sociopolitical engineering. Catalan regional organizations' leaders and the politicians who allied with them wanted to create a Catalan political system that would aggregate resources to pursue Catalanism and autonomy, nothing more or less. To do this, Catalan organizational elites systematically and often explicitly supported political parties that would support Catalan autonomy rather than Spanish nationalism or Catalan secessionism. They thereby lopped both ends off the political spectrum.

The newborn parties, organizationally weak (except for the Communist Partit Socialista Unificat de Catalunya or PSUC, which was stronger but as a social movement tied to its activists and ill-adapted to the new democratic politics), needed alliances from those with resources. The parties' weakness created dependencies on the regional organizations. This created a political sphere that suffocated Spanish centralism and Catalan secessionism alike—the resources gained from mobilizing for either cause were small (due to the weakness of non-Catalan elites) and outweighed by the negative sanctions of crossing regional organizations. Media silence, financial problems, lack of participation in public administration, lack of help down to inability to borrow meeting halls, well-organized and financed competitors, and constant campaigns against secessionism and "Spanishism" (*espanyolisme*) awaited those who tried to organize for a cause other than Catalan autonomy. The density of Catalan elite interconnections undoubtedly facilitated this narrowing process by improving coordination and information flows, but above all the efforts to guarantee autonomy were the consequences of their frustration with and domination by the central state's elites under Franco. The upshot of this narrowing process was that Catalan political forces were throughout the transition unified ideologically on the question of autonomy, autonomy at least in the spheres where there were Catalan organizations. Their internal political competition was thus not for the right to define goals; it was to become the main negotiators on behalf of Catalonia. The partisan conflicts were to determine what party or political force would be able to muster the resources of Catalonia to oblige other transition players to grant it autonomy.

This chapter focuses on the broad processes of consensus formation — the creation of the "Catalanist consensus" in favor of policy autonomy — and the mobilization of Catalan resources that would oblige the transition leaders to grant Catalonia that autonomy. It analyzes the processes that allowed Catalan politicians to mobilize resources that could not be ignored at the center. The resources came with the specific support by regional organizations for autonomy. It worked; the Spanish constitution and the Catalan Statute of Autonomy both grant Catalonia autonomy to manage public services on its own. An alliance was possible between regional organizational resources and Catalan politicians on the condition that the politicians won autonomy for regional organizations. The key process argument behind this thesis is that Catalan autonomists drew upon the resources of Catalan regional organizations, using their support to grow at the price of agreeing with them about autonomy and stability. This made the key parties resource dependent on regional organizations, and eventually created a party system geared to providing autonomy in their own image. Chapter seven will discuss this, policy sector by policy sector.

## PRELUDE: WHAT DID SURVIVE FRANCO

The first efforts at democratic party organization took place under late Francoism, when Catalan society was politically demobilized and disorganized by the authoritarian Spanish regime. The quintessentially authoritarian Franco regime had had prized quiescence rather than any sort of mobilization or participation (Linz 1970, 1975), but was particularly concerned about preventing any assertion of Catalan social or political activity. The main resources available, apart from those built by painstaking and dangerous clandestine collective action, were strong Catalan regional organizations such as business and professional organizations that were intact, often thriving, and distinct from their Madrid-based peers. In Catalonia, the 1970s transition saw not a weakening of those regional organizations in business, the professions, and the civic society of Barcelona, but the weakening of the state as the Francoist dictatorship ended. Modern Catalan politics was born as regional organizational elites and aspiring politicians of the late 1970s set to work constructing governments and political power bases. The basis on which they developed their preferences and campaigns for autonomy was the distinct, sizeable, and interconnected organizational infrastructure of Catalonia. Apart from old and closely connected elite families (see Cullell and Farràs 2001), the density of regional interconnection was visible in organizations designed specifically to improve intra-elite communication and mobilize elites for Catalan success. The most prominent, and explicitly autonomist and Catalanist, was the Cercle d'Economia, an elite society of Catalanist business, academic, professional, and political leaders founded under Franco by an eminent historian, Jaume Vicens i Vives, in an explicit effort to recreate the progressive, autonomist leadership that had been in the vanguard of Catalan development, culture, and autonomist nationalism in the nineteenth century (Vicens i Vives and Llorens 1958, Muñoz i Lloret 1997). "Either you were not Catalan, or you were not important, if you were not a member," commented a Barcelona lawyer and publisher in a 2000 interview. "Of course we had a catalanist mission," added a Cercle officer in 2000; "the Cercle was created to advance Catalan interests, like in the nineteenth century when businessmen led."

It was not obvious that Catalan society was stable. Like the rest of Spain, Catalonia underwent rapid economic growth and urbanization in the 1960s and 1970s. While these were processes that had shaped Catalan society since it began its industrialization in the mid-nineteenth century, they were nevertheless dramatic. Catalonia led Spain's growth (Castells and Parellada 1998). A number of social changes came with this industrialization. The rapid demographic and economic changes of the 1960s and 1970s broke up older networks of solidarity that had made Barcelona's workers famous (Balfour 1989:41–61). A consumer society arose from the poverty of the immediate postwar years while work in Europe raised horizons. The result was a pair of macrosociological changes for which the Spanish democratic transition is well known. First, the affluent society of the 1970s was a poor cultural fit for the antique pseudofascist Catholic ideology of the dictatorship. Second, the increasing pluralism of the society's elites meant that the possibility of arranging compromises without liberal democracy steadily decreased (Carr and Fusi 1979; Gunther, Montero, and Botella 2004).

Within this context, the overwhelming change in the Catalan social structure of the postwar years was mass immigration from other parts of Spain: 1.4 million "immigrants" arrived between 1950 and the peak of the "immigrant" population in 1970, during which Catalonia's total population grew from 3.24 to 5.12 million. The immigrants came from most areas of Spain but above all from Andalucia, arriving at an average rate of 72,000 a year (Sancho i Valverde and Ros i Navarro 1998:92,110). The change was particularly marked in Barcelona city and province. In 1962, just under a third of the inhabitants of Barcelona were from outside Catalonia (Candel 1964:156). That same year more Andalucians arrived than Catalans were born (Candel 1985:107). By 1975, these (uniformly Spanish-speaking) "immigrants" made up an estimated quarter of the population of Catalonia. The influx looked to many like it would destroy Catalan identity, or create a social divide between Catalans and "immigrants." Such a divide seemed especially plausible as the Catalan-born workers were generally better educated and many small businesses were Catalan-owned while "immigrants" were overwhelming industrial proletarians concentrated in dense and often disagreeable Barcelona suburbs or nearby industrial towns such as Cornellà, Sabadell, and Sant Feliu.

This fear for Catalonia was worsened by the linguistic and social policies of the regime, which systematically repressed Catalan identity and the Catalan language (Benet 1978). Catalan nationalists worried that the influx, combined with the official repression of the language and culture, would mean the death of Catalonia as a community (Colomer 1986). Francesc Candel, the essayist who coined the term "the other Catalans" for these immigrants, summarized Catalan nationalist fears with a reference to a sign in the working-class neighborhood of Torrassa, in the industrial Baix Llobregat just outside Barcelona, that declared "Catalonia stops here. Murcia begins here." "It's not possible to blame them at all for their fidelity to Castilian [Spanish]," wrote Candel of the postwar immigrants in his famous book; "they found themselves in a hispanicized [castellanitzada] Barcelona . . . the prewar immigrants had it in their favor that they noted Catalonia much more, all around them" (Candel 1964:15,87). This meant that Catalan autonomists would face two problems: on the one hand, they had to mobilize resources such that they could oblige the transition to give Catalonia autonomy; on the other hand, they had to incorporate a large part of their population into a Catalan project if their autonomy was not to be challenged and the society severely fractured (Greer 2006a).

What were the organizational bases of the Catalan autonomist consensus? First, there was a large segment of Catalan small and medium businesses, many of them run by Catalans, which depended on local Catalan banks and suffered from Madrid's control of planning, finance, labor relations, infrastructure, and regulation. Small, often export-oriented businesses with supplier networks in Catalonia and no capacity to move, they were strong supporters of a Catalan autonomous government. Larger businesses had in many cases become dependent on the state—above all the tariff-dependent textile industry—but there was a large group of Catalan light industrial and service industries that shared the frustration of smaller businesses and their dependence on the Catalan regional economy or labor market (Sánchez 1998; Cabana 1998, 2000). Second, the workers were minimally organized, although, as the transition progressed, two unions came to dominate the industrial workforce (there were smaller professional ones). These were CCOO, or Workers Commissions, the large Communist-linked union that had been most active in the clandestine resistance, and the rapidly growing Socialist UGT. The CCOO and the Communists (Partit

Socialista Unificat de Catalunya) were closely linked and CCOO was the most important aggregator and mobilizer of workers during the transition; UGT's growth would come as the transition progressed (Gabriel et al. 1989; Molinero, Tébar, and Ysàs 1993).

Third, Barcelona was the only city outside Madrid where organizations in "civil society" were large and prosperous enough to sustain careers in science, academia, arts, and the professions at the highest levels. The regime attempted to control these groups through peak organizations (professional colleges, unions, universities) with state-selected leaders; the problem was that these appointed executives were often frustrated within. As soon as the regime began to relax its grip, Catalanist (and often Communist) slates took control of, among others, the two big universities, the College of Physicians, the College of Law (Barcelona's bar), and most of the Barcelona newspapers. Recalling his victorious slate at the College of Physicians, a PSUC leader commented in 2000 that "we used the networks we built in the big hospitals . . . the administration of the big hospitals were often sympathetic, and often our activists were the best doctors because they were in the new [medical residency program] . . . it surprised us that we had so much support from the leaders."

Many of these professional activists, in 2000–2001 interviews, reflected on the joy of finally getting to pursue ideas and policies, in fields from museum administration to elderly care home planning, they had worked out years ago but had been kept from implementing.[1] "We had just been managing a few museums, now we started to debate how to build truly popular museums, how to make the people come," remarked a museum administrator in 2001; "the idea was to make a new museum, one that is the focus of the community, that shares its spirit." "We had real debates about how to structure a health system, looking at international models, especially the French and British," noted a doctor who had been a College of Physicians officer then. "We have a tradition of educational innovation that Franco had suffocated. We wanted to develop our ideas . . . without a [picture of the dictator hanging on the wall]," explained an educational official of those years. Thus, there was a powerful set of organizations that had suffered from centralism and were willing to support autonomy. In a potentially divided society (with 45% of the population Spanish-speaking and at least possibly anti-Catalanist) and a risky democratic transition, these organizations would provide the bulwark of Catalonia's inclusive, autonomist politics.

## MOBILIZING FOR AUTONOMY

The transition began in some murk, but Catalan regional organizations and political campaigns, the latter based in elites and employees of the former, worked to establish their own and Catalonia's autonomy. In light of the success of the Spanish transition to democracy, it is worth remembering that it was hardly a given what would happen. When Franco died on 20 November 1975, ending years of decline culminating in a month-long deathwatch, it was not at all clear that Spain would be a democracy, that it would remain whole, that it would grant autonomy to its component nations or that it would retain a similar state structure. (Useful accounts of the transition are in Sobrequés and Riera 1982; Tusell 1999; Aracil and Segura 2000:11–66 and especially Preston 1990). In 1974–1975, the regime was alternately paralyzed and unpredictably violent in the face of serious economic slowdown and major increases in the amount and geographic spread of social conflict. Workers' movements and union activity across Spain spread geographically from historic centers of Barcelona, Madrid, Asturias, and the Basque Country to previously docile areas such as Aragon, Valencia, and Andalucia (Molinero and Ysàs 1998). The regime floundered under the government of Arias Navarro, which was unable to impel any significant change. Social conflict increased in this era in the clash between those who wanted reform (within the regime) and those who wanted "rupture" (Soto 1996). The number of strikes increased dramatically. After seven months of increasing tension and political blockage, Arias Navarro resigned in July 1976 and the king selected a new and largely unknown Francoist leader, Adolfo Suárez.

In Catalonia, there was already an organized, broad-front Catalan political organization whose backbone was the Catalan Communist PSUC but which included figures from much of the Catalan political spectrum. This was the Assemblea de Catalunya, a gathering of clandestine leaders headed by filmmaker Pere Portabella; it included representatives of clandestine parties and unions as well as professional, academic, cultural, and media leaders. It had already set three minimal demands for any regime: that it grant democratic liberties, that it release political prisoners in an amnesty, and that it grant at least the equivalent of the 1932 Statute of Autonomy for Catalonia. It now sought to muster its forces in favor of autonomy to put pressure on the regime not to forget Catalonia. Its 111 members were memorably arrested and jailed; when they were waiting in a police building to hear their fates, Portabella learned that all would be sent to the Model prison for a trial. As he was hustled past some others, he called out "Fantastic, tots al Model!"—"Fantastic, all of us to the Model." In 2001, another Assemblea leader was irritated by that—"of course it's not fantastic to be arrested when you are running a political movement." I repeated this to a third leader who sighed and explained that "the problem was that it was everybody. It was architects, priests, authors, journalists, academics . . . it would have been a spectacle! They could never have tried us all." Meanwhile the arrests were further solidifying connections in what is today a good part of the Catalan leadership. "Many of us had our political ideas changed by our [cellmates]; it's important still to know who we shared cells with," commented one arrestee, sitting in a bar in 2001.

The Assemblea greeted the Suárez government with a giant demonstration on 11 September 1976, the Catalan national holiday (moved by the police to inaccessible Sant Boí as a challenge to the organizers). It was a great success, with tens of thousands of participants flying the Catalan flag (Batista and Playà 1991). This demonstration was a symbolic watershed for two reasons: first, it was an impressive show of the strength and organization of Catalan sentiment, with consequent positive effects on morale and integration within Catalonia; second, it made it clear that the regime would need to negotiate Catalan autonomy to make the transition continue, since there were clearly well-organized and popular Catalanist forces organizing such displays.

Suárez meanwhile had made it clear that there would be a transition. He won general admiration with his Political Reform Law of 1976, a remarkable political feat in which he persuaded the Francoist legislature (*Cortes*) to dissolve itself and permit free elections. What followed was a remarkable period in which parties organized and sought legalization (not necessarily in that order) while social groups both organized to meet the transition and began to increase the pressure for their goals—thus, union activity and strikes skyrocketed, as well as the less palatable activities such as violence from the extreme left and the Basque nationalists of ETA (Castro Moral 1994; Fusi 1996:447).

Catalan leaders were participants in the transition for the same reason as unions, military, Communists, and political leadership: leaving them out would be too dangerous (Köhler 2000; Greer 2006a). There was a set of mobilized forces in Catalonia, expressing themselves in nationalist demonstrations, clandestine organizations, and political parties, and winning significant popular support. As with the other participants, this power could either shore up a settlement or scuttle it: if Catalonia erupted in civil discontent, it would be a threat to the transition in the same way mass strikes or shaky military support would threaten it (the smaller and less organized Basque Country, with its problems, was one of the major threats to a stable transition). Thus, transition leaders in Madrid needed Catalan leaders who could claim to represent and either control or predict the responses of Catalan social forces: a Catalan leadership that could explain what elites, clandestine organizations, and the populace would accept, and then could claim the ability to make them accept the outcome (Gunther, Montero, and Botella 2004:111–115). The first openings marked the start of a period of intense political maneuvering within Catalonia and between Catalonia and Madrid, with Madrid seeking the most "moderate" Catalan leaders who could still claim mass support, and Catalan leaders working to develop the best claim to negotiate with Madrid and the best positions from which to do it. This dynamic, present from the start of the Transition (and, in subterranean contacts, before the Transition), meant that the ability to mobilize resources in Catalonia was the key differentiator of the politicians.

The positions of the Assemblea de Catalunya and its political sibling CCFP (Coordinating Council of Political Forces, a group of the party leaders) marked out the irreducible basis for any politician and any set of negotiating positions. There was no regional support—legitimacy—for political leaders or elites outside the platform (ideological and organizational) of the twin organizations (to understand the two organizations, Caminal Badia 1998a:118, 1998b:49). Pacted between all the political and social organized forces, and with roots sunk deep into regional organizations and their employees, the Assemblea and CCFP's other members had the capacity to discredit a leader who blatantly broke ranks from the autonomist, Catalanist consensus as they formulated it. Even as the two organizations began to disintegrate under the stress of political rivalry, their political formulations remained untouchable. This meant that while the formal and informal institutions of Catalan politics were very fluid, the basic configuration of coalitions was solid (i.e., regional organizations in favor of autonomy) and this coalition was actively working to reinforce the autonomist dimension of politics.

The first actor to step forward as an interlocutor of the Madrid government was Jordi Pujol (Crexell 1982; Ferrer et al. 1984; Lorés 1985). Pujol was a nationalist who had spent time in jail for his nationalist agitation, and elements in the military clearly saw nonstate nationalism as the most important threat of the transition. The Franco regime had been harassing him and his bank for years. Nevertheless, he was still a Catholic, and a banker, and thus less worrisome than the PSUC activists, PSUC allies, and socialists who made up most of the rest of the Catalan political leadership. "Of course [the central government] preferred him. He was a banker, a businessman, they could negotiate with him," explained an advisor. Thus, for example, the *aperturista* Fraga had built relationships with Pujol years earlier in order to find out the opinions of the Catalan elites he identified as the bases for moderate reformism. This included an extraordinary 1972 away weekend of regime liberals, Pujol, and some other important Catalans developed to improve links and trust (Comissió Organitzadora XXV Aniversari Trobada de Lluçanes 1997). "He had the best team . . . he was the one who could do things," explained Fraga's Barcelona representative, who had set up a "Club Agora" in Barcelona to build such links between Fraga and Catalan elites.[2] Pujol had further advantages, as his webs of contacts extended into Catalan regional elites and he could promise to bring along or represent businesses, elements of the church, professions, and other parts of the regional elite much better than the PSUC whose insurgent activities and CCOO links had often led it into direct clashes with them for control over their own factories, professional organizations, and charitable institutions. The Catalan left also recognized this: Pujol could both bring along segments of Catalan elites that the PSUC could not, and he would make a more plausible interlocutor for the regime than they could be themselves. Meanwhile, both the PSUC and Socialists were betting on a Spain-wide rupture, and thus worked together with their Spanish homologues in these negotiations. Thus, Pujol stepped forward as the best available representative of Catalonia: an individual who could assemble a political coalition that would pacify Catalonia, but not too radical.

The actual ascent of Pujol came about through the formation of an group representing the opposition called the Commission of Nine (Arroyo and Valls 1997:45–46). In such a statewide body, Pujol could carve out a role as the representative of Catalonia, and he did. The left, which also had a good claim to Catalanism, opted to pursue Spain-wide goals, leaving Pujol as both the clearest spokesperson for Catalonia and the most credible autonomist political leader within Catalonia (for those suspicious of the left, of Spain, or of both). This meant he started to win the key support of the most regionalist Catalan organizations away from the left. "It was Pujol or the Marxists," commented a lawyer active in the Cercle d'Economia then, in a 2001 interview. His rivals were the Socialists, making a non-Communist, left autonomist appeal and the statewide Unión del Centro Democratico-UCD, making a Spain-wide appeal for democracy with a commitment to autonomy (and centralist resource dependencies that were clearly visible and would undo that commitment). "Of course they preferred a Catholic banker, a shopkeeper [botiguer]," complained an academic leader aligned with the Socialists.

## THE FORMULA FOR COALESCING REGIONALISM: 1977 AND OPERATION TARRADELLAS

The 1977 elections marked a turning point because they provided an index of political strength, while the events of the previous year had created a need for somebody to negotiate for Catalonia. The resources mobilized in Catalonia by the various coordinated parties of the CCFP, organizations of the Assemblea, and nationalists meant that the central government had to find a way to negotiate with them. This meant that the group that could show the greatest strength in the first elections would be in a strong position to speak for Catalonia, now that the high degree of coordinated mobilization had made it imperative to negotiate Catalonia's future.

The 1977 election results presented Suárez with two problems. First, any strategy based on statist parties winning a majority became impossible. Parties demanding the restoration of pre-Francoist Catalan autonomy won

Table 5.1   Vote Percentages by Party in Catalonia, 1977–1980

| Party* | 1977 (General) | 1979 (General) | 1980 (Generalitat) |
|---|---|---|---|
| AP (AP-CC, Alianza Popular— Convivencia Catalana) | 3.5 | 3.5 | 2.4 |
| UCD (CC-UCD, Centre Català— UCD) | 17.0 | 19.0 | 10.6 |
| UDC (UCDCC, Unió del Centre I la Democràcia Cristiana) | 5.6 ↘ | — | — |
| CDC (CDC-PCD, CDC—Pacte Democràtic per Catalunya) | 17.0 ↘ | — | — |
| CiU (merger of CDC and UDC lists) | — | 16.1 | 27.7 |
| ERC (in 1977, Esquerra de Catalunya) | 4.6 | 4.1 | 8.9 |
| PSC | 28.7 | 29.2 | 22.3 |
| PSUC | 18.4 | 17.1 | 18.7 |
| PSA | 2.6 | — | — |

*The name I use for the party is the core organization, discussed in the text and in bold here; in parentheses are any other names under which the party ran, usually reflecting a short-lived coalition.

*Source:* Baras and Matas Dalmases (1998:214, 223).

three-quarters of the vote. This was the consequence of the far superior resources (media attention, logistical support, finance, activists, endorsements, participation in public forums, and joint activities) they could mobilize from activists and organizational alliances. The Socialistes de Catalunya (the future Socialist Party of Catalonia, or PSC), PSUC, Pujol's Convérgencia Democràtica de Catalunya, CDC, ERC's coalition, and Unió-CC, a Christian Democratic Alliance including Unió Democràtica de Catalunya (UDC), and their leaders, all were part of the formal consensus of the Assemblea de

Catalunya and the CCFP: they demanded democracy, amnesty, and the 1932 statute. Those demands functioned like the plans of the Scottish Constitutional Convention—as a rallying point and baseline rather than a driver of their own—but in the context of transition Catalonia that rallying was extremely important. Second, his Catalan interlocutor turned out to not be so representative or powerful after all; Pujol's party Convergència did not do well. The election results caused a serious problem for any strategy based on using Jordi Pujol as the voice of Catalonia. The Socialists and PSUC had both beaten Pujol's party, and he was tied with Suárez's own UCD. Suárez needed a new strategy that would respond to the fact that his existing Catalan interlocutor clearly lacked predominance within Catalonia.

The Socialists effectively handed him the answer. Along with Tarradellas's own party, ERC, the Socialists had called seriously and repeatedly for the restoration of the Generalitat and Josep Tarradellas, its exiled president. A group of leaders with academic, professional (especially law), journalistic, and business bases had already been at work, meeting in one member's offices in Barcelona's Winterthur Insurance building, trying to organize a campaign to bring back Tarradellas (see also Bricall 2003). Their most memorable victory was a large public petition "signed by people who mattered . . . the political leaders wanted to forget about Tarradellas and . . . divide the cake. We made it clear that Tarrdellas was still Catalonia's leader for many of us." For all his appeal to Socialists, older leftists, and unaligned Barcelona elites, Tarradellas was a difficult choice for Suárez; allowing him to return would look like "rupture" rather than reform, as it would send the signal that the pre-Francoist Republic had any legitimacy. That would destabilize the transition by worrying Francoist elites. Nevertheless, the option began to look better to Suárez when the alternative was either a Socialist or a Communist. One Tarradellas associate and organizer of the Winterthur campaign reported that Suárez had said only the PSC put any effort into lobbying for the return of the aged Tarradellas.

Suárez, after contacts through intermediaries, met secretly with Tarradellas in Madrid in late June 1977 (Arroyo and Valls 1997; Tarradellas 1999). The two agreed that Tarradellas could return to head a provisionally restored Generalitat, or Catalan autonomous government. They made the stakes and positions clear to each other, according to Preston (2005:409): Suárez reminded Tarradellas not to "forget that I am the head of the government of a country of 36 million inhabitants, and you are head of the Generalitat that lost the Civil War." Tarradellas replied that Suárez should not forget that "a head of government incapable of resolving the Catalan problem puts the monarchy in danger."

Suárez and Tarradellas agreed a deal: Tarradellas would head a restored Generalitat, and the new elected deputies of the four Catalan provinces would make up his legislature, from which he could form a government. The decree restoring the Generalitat—the only decree of the transition that legitimated a Second Republic institution—was published 29 September. On 18 October, another royal decree named Tarradellas the president. The separation appears to have been intentional, to placate regime hard-liners and "reformists." The regime could still maintain the fiction that it had created a government, called the Generalitat, and then decided that the best person to head it was the person then heading a government in exile called the Generalitat. Centralist elites were to be thereby mollified.

Tarradellas returned to Catalonia on 22 October 1977. From the balcony of the provincial Deputation, soon again to be the Palace of the Generalitat, he proclaimed "Ja sóc aquí," or "I am here," taking possession of the home of the medieval and Second Republic government building in a symbolic recuperation of Catalan autonomy. Tarradellas formed a government of consensus. It had a minister from each major party, with the party leaders added as ministers without portfolio. (As a result, the PSUC became the best-placed Communist Party in Western Europe—no other Communist party held office in such a large unit. Business elites accordingly worried.) Only the vaguely anti-Catalan Andalucian Socialist Party (PSA) and Alianza Popular (AP), of the far right, were excluded on grounds of insufficient Catalanism.

Tarradellas was the focus of consensus Catalanism; unsurprisingly, his main activities were in policy areas where the most mobilized resources were and thus where he would face the most allies and the least resistance. The first, explicitly provisional, Generalitat thus embarked on the same strategy it would use for twenty years of "fishing with a basket"—that is, grabbing control over policy areas where the primary actors were existing regional webs of organizations that desired autonomy and would thus readily be trapped. "We grabbed everything we could. That meant we had to understand what we could grab," as a Pujol ally and former civil servant commented of those and subsequent years in a 2001 interview.

The Tarradellas government therefore pursued two main policies during its tenure. First, the government decided on the future of pre-university education, which every major Catalan political organization agreed would be part of a Catalan government. Specifically, it decided that education would be predominantly in Catalan in all schools, rather than leaving the choice to parents or having the language in the schools reflect that of the community. Establishing this precedent, a case of the Catalanist consensus in action, created the single most powerful mechanism for extending it downward from the level of organizational elites and political leaders. It was possible because most of the educational organizations were regionalist or opportunistic and willing to accept changes that looked inevitable and might make an ally of the new government. Thus, individuals and organizations representing the municipal schools (generally partial to or organized by the then-Catalanist unions CCOO and UGT) and private schools (filled with the children of Catalan elites) were relatively positive about developing a Catalan educational policy, especially if they could control most of it. The church was divided but willing to be friendly, and CiU promised to leave its schools alone—that is, to guarantee its autonomy and stability in return for some Catalan. Meanwhile, a key aspect of the Catalanist consensus was language, and education was clearly vital to language policy. Thus, an educational policy focused on language could be a bid to make friends as much as a regulatory imposition.

Second, it began innovative work on health, designing a "Health Map of Catalonia" showing the spatial distribution of resources and needs (Generalitat de Catalunya 1980). The consultation process, led by Ramón Espasa, a young PSUC surgeon who had helped take over the peak-level medical organization the College of Medicine before becoming a deputy and provisional minister, allowed ordinary people across Catalonia, only one election into the transition, to meet elected officials of the Catalan government asking their opinions. The map, still proudly cited by Catalan health officials and observers, was a largely successful effort to demonstrate the superiority of the autonomous Catalan government by linking its agenda with those of thinkers and practitioners, and users, in the health system. "It was a sensation," remembered Espasa in an interview, "to have a Catalan government asking people, asking professionals, what they wanted." The map reflected discussions in pre-transition Catalonia among health elites and the PSUC's numerous doctors. This, in turn, reflected the existence of a web of Catalan organizations in health. The Catalan health system was older than that of most of Spain, focused on municipal, trust, and public hospitals around Barcelona. It had its own College of Medicine (which returned a PSUC leadership under Espasa in the 1970s) and hierarchy with the major Barcelona teaching hospitals most important. These high-status professionals resented the centralism and lack of autonomy that resulted from direct employment by, or contracts with, the Francoist regime as well as the policy designs and funding they found inadequate. In the ferment of the transition years, many of them developed alternative ideas for the health system (Gol i Gurina et al. 1978). These were leftists, but they existed in a distinctive organizational milieu—different leftist ideas developed in a different medical set of regional organizations.

They were thus strongly supportive of organizational autonomy from Madrid, and their younger physicians were well organized (as social groups went) by the PSUC, which had found the new American system of medical residents in teaching hospitals to provide excellent recruiting grounds. This meant that, on the one hand, the College of Physicians was flatly in favor of autonomy for Catalonia (and left-wing policies), while clinical leaders of high-profile institutions such as the big hospitals (Vall d'Hebron, Sant Pau) threw themselves into debating new systems and let the PSUC organize their workforces. The map's method and conclusions were the first case of what would become a common pattern, in which the Catalan government would hand over policy to the leaders of regional organizations in a given field, and in return they would supply a coherent policy design that was distinctively Catalan and often did work better than the anachronistic Spanish state institutions while suiting them well. Thus, the Tarradellas government won over two of the sectors with the strongest regional organizations and divergence from the rest of Spain, two sectors in which Catalonia's very divergence lay in its dense regional organizations. The pattern would repeat until the Generalitat was filled out.

## THE CONSTITUTION 1977–1980

The provisional Generalitat demonstrated that the Catalan political forces were able to muster the resources that were necessary to win a degree of temporary autonomy, even if it required risking the opposition of some right-wing centralist forces. Its activities demonstrated that the easiest fields of political activity were those in which there were ready Catalan networks of organizations and few or no centralist organizations. Its existence added further to the resources mustered for Catalan autonomy. This played into a second set of negotiations starting at the time, negotiations around the permanent Spanish constitution. In this period, the object of most political activity was the new Constitution while the number of actors continued to increase—the process of decentralization introduced new autonomous lobbies while the military and other centralists began to worry and threaten.

Shortly after the formation of the Provisional Generalitat, the deputies in Madrid had to begin work on the Constitution—the 1977 Cortes really only had a remit to design and approve a democratic Constitution for submission to the population in a referendum. The Cortes selected a panel of senior politicians, most of them with university law backgrounds, to draft the Constitution. Originally the plan was for the drafters to all come from the two largest parties: the UCD and the Spanish Socialist Workers' Party PSOE, and a representative of the Spanish Communist PCE/PSUC. However, there was a strong consensus that the Constitution, to be successful, had to be pacted. The logic was expressed in an influential book by University of Barcelona law professors Jordi Solé Tura, later a drafter, and Eliseo Aja, which argued that every previous Constitution had failed because it was written and imposed by the victors in a civil struggle and thus was seen by the losers as illegitimate (Solé Tura and Aja 1977). Thus, participation was expanded and modified to include potential opponents (Solé Tura 1999:401). It included Fraga at the Communists' behest, so that the extreme-right would be brought in rather than form an opposition to the Constitution around him. Then, to reflect the capacity of the nationalists in the Basque Country and Catalonia to damage the progress of the Constitution, the PSOE ceded a place. The Basque Nationalist Party had very bad relations with Suárez, and Pujol very good relations, so the joint seat for nationalists went to Pujol's close associate and lawyer Miquel Roca. There was another Catalan on the committee, Solé Tura sitting for the PCE/PSUC, but he spoke for the Communists rather than for "Catalonia." Again, Pujol's detachment from other forces and dominance in the center-right nationalist space meant he could speak for Catalonia in a way the left could not (for an account of the writing, see Solé Tura 1986).

Meanwhile, Suárez was growing increasingly fond of the "pre-autonomies" strategy to deal with territorial dissent in Spain (Aja 1999:46–50). At first, it was a response to regional mobilization that was enough to force the region into the negotiations. He suggested it to the Basques, but the Basque "pre-autonomy" failed to gain the support of the Basque Nationalist Party and became a political football. He then applied it in Galicia and began to experiment with it in Valencia. Observing this, other Spanish deputies developed an interest in having pre-autonomies, and formed themselves into groups by region, the better to control some government resources and bulk up their own bases within government, society, and their parties. Some pre-autonomies reflected traditional regions, such as Andalucia and Aragon. By 1978, the town halls and deputies of Galicia, the Basque Country, Aragon, Andalucia, Extremadura, and the two Castilles had all voted to constitute autonomous communities. Even the Spanish heartland began to split, with León considering its own autonomy and Castille itself dividing. In April and October 1979, Cantabria and La Rioja, previously thought integral parts of Castille, opted for autonomy (Fusi 1996:459).

This changed the dynamic of Spanish politics significantly, and in a direction not welcomed by the Catalan and Basque nationalists. Namely, it created the possibility that Spain would be a state of many autonomous governments with diverging levels of national self-consciousness, rather than a state of four autonomous nationalities (Spaniards, Catalans, Basques, and Galicians). Catalan and other nationalists preferred the latter because they resented and thought politically dangerous the equivalence of Catalonia or the Basque Country with Cantabria or Murcia that might turn into an argument for Catalonia's competencies to equal lowly Murcia's (Catalan organizational elites seemed less bothered, as Murcia's autonomy was irrelevant to theirs). Much more threatening, however, was that the "fiebre autonómico," the fever for autonomy, increasingly worried centralist elites in the military, police, and state bureaucracies. Worried military and coercive organisations in the central state increased the ever-present risk of a coup. This risk, more disturbing to leaders of the transition than the risk of offending Catalans, caused the UCD and political elites in Spain to backpedal on autonomy. Thus, the ability of Catalonia to gain powers when there was an increasing centralist swing to uniformity became the test of Catalonia's ability to mobilize resources to extract autonomy.

The shift to uniformity, reflecting the worries of centralists, took its most potent form in the actions of the UCD, Suárez's state party. It was the main party of the Spanish state elites (being built primarily out of high-level state servants in Madrid and the provinces); it was bidding successfully for opportunistic support as the party constructing a polyarchy that would assure them stable environments and internal autonomy (Huneeus 1985; Hopkin 1999). It appears to have been content with the multiplication of weak autonomous governments, since they would employ its politicians while not threatening the actual organization of the state in most areas. On the other hand, its power base was the state itself and those dealing with the state. The result was that the party submitted one highly devolutionist—almost federal—draft of the relevant sections.

The discussions leaked. The centralist right orchestrated a campaign involving AP, the right-wing press, and pressure on UCD leaders from within state bureaucracies, and UCD withdrew its proposal in favor of one that placed greater central limits on the autonomous communities and reduced their influence on the central state. This involved hints, personally conveyed from the military and paramilitary police, that the draft was too decentralized and offensive to the armed forces, as well as a noisy campaign led by the rightist newspaper ABC—"it was an extraordinary media campaign, so strong," remembered a legal advisor to the PSOE drafters "the UCD was scared and withdrew the draft." Keeping autonomous communities under tutelage and limiting their influence on the state would protect the civil service and law, reduce possible variation in regulations and other instability, and please elites in the military and coercive apparatus who were highly sensitive to any prospect of Spain breaking up. The alternative increased the ever-present chances of a coup. "We had to be careful about how far we pushed autonomy . . . you saw what happened when the army worried about the *proceso autonómico*," remembered a PSUC leader in 2001.

The result was an odd compromise of a state structure in which the regional state was imposed on the previous Napoleonic state structure (Solé Tura 1986) and the autonomous communities were licensed to try to extract powers from the existing levels of government. The Constitution was strongly geared toward devolving autonomy downward, but did not give a significant role to autonomous communities (or any other level of territorial government) in state politics; it was, in Stepan's terms, minimally demos-constraining because it scarcely allowed the autonomous communities to restrain the central state (Stepan 2001:340–341). The Senate became a territorial upper house, but its electoral circumscriptions were mostly set not at the level of the regions but at the level of the provinces. Not only did this rule have strongly majoritarian effects, it also meant that the territorial upper house did not represent the autonomous communities, the major arenas and actors of territorial politics, or much at all (Russell 2000). This was a deliberate demand of the UCD after its swing to centralism. The result was that there was no institutional mechanism to forestall or resolve clashes between the central state and the autonomous communities save recourse to the Constitutional Tribunal.

Legally, the ensuing territorial organization of the state was a minimally invasive implantation of a new level of government. It just superimposed regions on provinces and handed them some central state powers and administration. The central state's elites supported the maintenance of the existing administrative structure, which they dominated; their rebuff to the UCD, to "their" party's plans for decentralization, made that clear. The activists for the autonomous communities (i.e., the Catalan and Basque elites and the pro-autonomist currents of Spanish politicians in the parties) wanted an opportunity to create new administrations on the regional level ("after *fer país* we wanted to move to *fer política*," explained a Pujol ally, citing a common phrase). The result was that the regional administrations were created, and awarded powers, but the territorial infrastructure of the central state remained intact. This shaped the debate afterward: there could be no frontal attack on the state structure, Spain-wide civil service corps would remain intact, and autonomous communities would not be able to shape their territorial organization as they pleased. Autonomy—in the very specific sense of the room to administer itself—was what Catalonia had won and kept.

This meant that conflicts over the powers of autonomous communities would be channeled into debates over competencies. The Constitution sought to balance citizenship rights and the interests of the central state with the autonomy of the autonomous communities through a system of majority (as against plurality) laws, known, depending on constitutional type and function, as organic and framework laws (*leyes orgánicas* and *leyes de base*). These are specified in the Constitution, and are laws of special importance governing constitutional aspects of state organization, such as the law covering the organization of the judiciary, the statutes of autonomy of the different regions, the laws organizing the universities, and the laws governing health provision. Of these, the base laws are those that cover competencies shared between the state and another level of government. In them, the state lays down the bases of the system, outlining its chief characteristics and certain floors beneath which autonomous communities cannot descend. The broad extent of this system (Aja 1999:108) means that there is constant friction over the border between the central state's right to set minimal requirements and coordinate through the laws and the autonomous communities' autonomy.

## THE STATUTE

The passage of the Constitution narrowed the possible options and reduced the number of contestants in Catalan politics while the need to negotiate a statute of autonomy obliged Catalan elites to continue to work together to maximize their bargaining power. Catalan politicians wanted to negotiate a complete statute before taking it to Madrid. They remembered the Second Republic precedent, when Catalonia passed a referendum demanding extensive autonomy, but found its autonomy much restricted when the law was written in Madrid (Gerpe Landín 1977; de Riquer 1996:480). The statute began with a meeting of politically prominent Catalan jurists in the resort town of Sau. There, led by the Constitution drafters Solé Tura and Roca, they began by taking an inverse draft of the Constitution's list of state powers ("we called it the mirror method," commented Solé Tura in a 2001 interview). Every power not turned over to the central state, the draft statute attributed to Catalonia (Sobrequés and Riera 1982). In the case of some autonomous communities, the statutes differed from the lists in the Constitution—in the less powerful autonomous communities—because the statute specified which powers they would actually have. Catalonia, by contrast, seized the moment to take the highest level of competencies offered in the Constitution, and thus had a relatively uneventful period of negotiation (for the formal powers of Catalonia, see Table 2.1).

Thus, what did not happen during the negotiations of the statute is more important than what did. The statute codified the powers already fairly clearly offered in the Constitution, sealing the agreements in the Constitution. It shared with the Constitution the allocation of powers on paper. It specified the institutional form of Catalonia, with a "provisional" electoral system that turned out to be highly majoritarian and overrepresented rural voters by setting provinces as the circumscriptions (which helped rural parties, above all CDC).[3] Its interpretive ambiguities are those of the Constitution, namely, confusion about frontiers between state oversight and administrative devolution and broad allocations of powers that would later be debated in endless bureaucratic struggles. It did make Catalan an official language of Catalonia, along with Spanish—the Generalitat would promote Catalan, and had legal cover to do so, but could not tread upon the right to speak Spanish. The Catalan nationalist opponents to the Constitution, who had campaigned against the Constitution and lost heavily, threw in the towel by not fighting the statute. They were weak, deprived of oxygen of support from regional organizations and dependent, according to leader Jordi Carbonell, "on despondent activists who saw the Constitution as both the real problem and a *fait accompli*." As Carbonell realized, the political forces that had been able to draw on preexisting organizations had won that support by supporting stability and autonomy, and they had shaped the negotiations all along. "There were no nationalists. There were bankers presenting themselves as nationalists, there were Communists presenting themselves as nationalists. There were no nationalists in the transition . . . we were excluded, we had nothing . . . at least we voted against the constitution," he complained in 2001.

## THE 1980 ELECTIONS

The result of the statute's passage into law was the creation of the Parlement of Catalonia and the first elections. At this point, the parties' focus shifted from winning autonomy by aggregating forces to winning the election by aggregarting their own particular coalitions. This introduced other splits, with the resources of regional organizations coming with new and irreconcilable prices. This time the split was between business and more left-wing groups, and the reason was a campaign by regional, opportunistic, and centralist businesses alike to prevent the likely victory of the left. This campaign would be the last push to establish CiU in the center of the Catalan political structure as it was the largest clearly Catalanist party that was also pro-business and could attract the support of businesses. The other Catalanist parties were too left (PSUC and the Socialists) or too weak.

The dominant feature of this campaign, which came on a high tide of Catalanist sentiment, was a fierce campaign led by the employers' organizations (Foment de Treball and the Barcelona Chamber of Commerce) and organized by fixers associated with AP. The prospect that worried regional and opportunistic businesses alike was that of a left victory—a victory of the PSUC (still thought possible) or of the PSC in coalition with the PSUC. In an unstable Spanish political and economic environment that seemed to be moving leftward, there was widespread concern among businesses. In Catalonia, it focused on the prospect that Catalonia might become the largest Communist-run government in the West (and the particular prospect of government by the PSUC and its CCOO ally was particularly disturbing). "We could not let Catalonia have a Communist government . . . the most developed part of Spain could not have a Marxist government, and we told the people not to do it . . . we applied all the best political techniques, advertisement, meetings with the press," explained a leader of the campaign.

"We had the best funds and organization because the president of Foment was behind us," he continued. The well-organized employers' organizations, led by Foment de Treball, threw massive funds behind a campaign to stop the left (Serrano 1997) (Foment was at the time also organizing Spanish business groups into an overall, right-wing, business organization, the Spanish Confederation of Business Organizations, CEOE). The campaign included large-scale media spending (including buying space for a mini-newspaper inside each day's *Vanguardia*), informal efforts to influence journalists, and political actions such as leafleting. ERC denies the persistent rumors that it received direct financial assistance (in order to supply a non-Communist, left alternative to the PSC and PSUC). CDC formed a permanent coalition (joint lists) with the small Unió Democratica de Catalunya, thereby gaining some Christian Democratic legitimacy as CiU. The PSUC, overconfident and overestimating the utility of its numerous canvassers, and the PSC, overconfident and riven internally over its Catalanism and links with Spanish Socialists, scarcely responded. There is little doubt that the campaign influenced the election outcomes, as the PSUC and PSC spent months undergoing a well-planned media and publicity battering. In a campaign in which media dominated, far beyond the experiences of many observers, the non-Communist parties did well enough to prevent a majority of the PSUC and PSC. The PSC turned down Pujol's offer of a coalition, and Pujol was voted into office as a minority administration supported by ERC and the UCD. The power of business elites had been displayed in a particularly forceful and scarcely concealed manner, adding the direct efforts of Foment and the Chamber of Commerce to the existing regional support for nonstatewide parties that could guarantee them autonomy rather than submergence into a statewide organization.

## CONCLUSION: NEGOTIATING CATALONIA'S AUTONOMY

This chapter has explained how the preferences of regional institutional organizations were reflected through the development of the Catalan political system to win an autonomous government responsible for the environment of those organizations. Catalonia's regional organizations, an old, dense, and distinctive web, had survived Francoism because they were the texture of social life and political economy in Catalonia. This meant that there was a pool of resources available to defend their autonomy and build a more stable environment for them. Clandestine activity before Franco was dangerous, but based in such organizations (unions, professions, universities) where it had an elective affinity with younger professionals and leaders not scarred by the civil war. Each of these offered slack resources such as basic infrastructure and social networks as well as legitimacy that made them more difficult to attack. With the transition, the political forces based in these organizations grew and the organizations themselves began to lobby. Whether directly, through the representations of professional organizations and business lobbies, or indirectly, through autonomist political parties of all stripes, they shaped an autonomist politics that excluded centralist and nationalist extremes. This unity, in turn, allowed Catalonia to organize coherently and establish both a place at the table and representatives.

The eventual outcome of the formal negotiations of the Transition was a Catalan government with primary responsibility for policy areas in which there were webs of regional organizations. This outcome was possible because regional organizations could apply their own explicitly political pressure (such as the demonstration in Sant Boí) and quiet lobbying (as happened over the constitutional drafts and in health and education). In addition to their own direct efforts, however, regional organizations were the dominant sources of resources for the fledgling political parties of Catalonia. If the parties were to mobilize successfully, it would have to be on autonomist planks. Otherwise they would not win the resources and their ability to ally with other elites or to mobilize activists would not be enough. As a result of this resource constraint and pre-transition efforts by the same groups to establish the consensus, politics was about which major, autonomist, Catalan political forces would represent Catalonia in Madrid and how. The answer eventually was the consensus candidate Tarradellas, whose provisional Generalitat, like the formal one in the Constitution and the statute, would win its powers based on the existence of potential regional allies in each policy sector and the absence of centralist organizations.

The actual shape of Catalan self-government in 1980 most closely reflected the preferences of Catalan regional organizations because the Catalan parties that created the Generalitat were shaped by their ability to draw resources from regional organizations. Whether it was the PSUC inhabiting medical residency programs and universities or Pujol networking with the Cercle d'Economia and nationalist publishers, the Catalan leaders of the transition were the ones who had best mobilized the resources of these organizations—directly through the organizational elites support or indirectly as beneficiaries of widespread discontent in the organizations themselves. As a result, in 1980, Catalonia regained its self-government on the back of popular mobilization that was already converging toward the set of elite pacts and divisions of responsibility that it would become, and neither Catalan nationalism nor the PSUC and Communists had been a threat—Catalan nationalism had been largely coopted by the elite-friendly CiU and the left had been harnessed to the moderate autonomist project by its own leaders, who were increasingly occupied defending their party against the PSOE central leadership. These electoral resources integrated into parties and the system then entered an era in which the politics of devolution would focus on competencies and policy. Both the shape of Catalan self-government as established on paper during the transition, and the shape of the Catalan party system (autonomist, nonsecessionist, and Catalanist) were products of regional organizations' strength in Catalonia and according ability to shape politics by lending or withholding resources. Even the parties that depended on central organizations such as the banks, the PSOE, or the employers' organization CEOE that Foment had founded, AP, UCD, and PSC, had to win Catalan regional organizations' support or fade away. The result of this hard work was that, both formally and informally, Catalonia had an autonomy-oriented political system in 1980. Its parties would seek autonomy; the question became what they could accomplish.

The political opportunity structure certainly affected this period—Spain changed from being an authoritarian to a democratic regime. While this part of the third wave of democratization (Huntington 1991) might respond to larger global shifts, it is hard to see how any of the arguments identified in new regionalist literature explain the outcome. Spain was not part of the EU and it is hard to find any evidence that the world economy motivated Catalan autonomists. The opportunities to be grasped in the transition years had much more to do with establishing autonomy within democracy than with seeking new forms of regionalism.

Analyses based on the activity of nationalist parties would be only superficially correct in explaining the Generalitat. Throughout this crucial transition period, groups other than Catalan nationalists made key decisions. The PSUC first unified the autonomist opposition before Franco's death; the PSC dominated Catalonia and negotiated Operation Tarradellas with the UCD. The Constitutional drafting panel included only one nationalist, Pujol's ally Roca, and his lack of staff support compared to the others (and the weakness of his party relative to the big all-Spanish parties) limited his effectiveness. CiU benefited when it took the 1980 Generalitat elections, but if any parties deserve the laurel for being the prime advocates of autonomy, they are the PSUC and the Socialists.

# Chapter Six

# Catalonia 1980–2000

The Constitution and Catalonia's Statute of Autonomy superimposed the Generalitat on the Spanish state, gave it form, and granted it the right to intervene in many policy fields. That meant that in 1980 it had a Health Map but no health system, an educational policy but no schools. The positive outcome of juridical regionalization now led to contestation over real power and transfers of competencies. The two decades after 1980 created a regional government with real, as well as paper, competencies.

As soon as the Generalitat was elected, with Jordi Pujol at the head (supported by the ERC and UCD), it faced the new challenges of organizational institutionalization and intergovernmental conflict in a consolidating democracy. On the one hand, central state organizations began to recover their own balance and resist any efforts by regional governments to change the structure of the state—elite state bureaucrats resisted losing powers, while their allies (i.e., groups with resource dependencies on those state organizations) also began to overtly resist regionalization. On the other hand, this fightback began just as the regional governments, including the Generalitat, had to begin to extract the real funds, responsibilities, powers, people, and infrastructure—needed to exercise their new autonomous competencies. The result on the level of high politics was a series of bitter contests (up to and including a coup attempt), while on the level of public policy the result was trench warfare in policy fields as different governments attempted to mobilize coalitions to support them (chapter eight extends the analysis of this dynamic).

The conflict through the 1980s created a distribution of government powers that were by 2000 relatively stable. Two interviewees described CiU's strategy in these two decades with an idiomatic Catalan expression: "fishing with a basket." Literally, this means identifying the densest, most accessible shoals of fish and dunking a basket in the water to catch a large number of them, rather than seeking out a particular fish with more elaborate equipment and greater risk—the English equivalent is "grabbing the low-hanging fruit." Politically, this meant that CiU had been campaigning for competencies in fields such as health or education where they could identify a coalition of regional organizations that would support Catalan autonomy in that policy field. CiU offered these groups autonomy over their policy sphere (i.e., to make them the dominant players in the policy field) and in return they supported CiU directly (with donations, manpower, legitimacy, information, and cooperation) and indirectly (by supporting the transfer, and then by supplying distinctive policy ideas to CiU).

This strategy produced a steady flow of competencies and allowed CiU to squeeze more radical nationalists; the implicit promise was that the Generalitat would win powers (and the EU erode the central state) until Catalonia was "sovereign." CiU became the avatar of the Catalanist consensus, and other parties that stepped out of the CiU-dominated consensus found the same weight of regional organizations that crushed them during the transition (thus, ERC's secessionism and the Partido Popular's Spanish nationalism would implode in the 1990s). The coalitional strategy worked— CiU gave regional organizations the autonomy they wanted as well as political support. The problem was that this coalitional strategy, born of CiU's resource dependencies, progressively helped stabilize the distribution of competencies between different levels of government. CiU, with a nationalist wing that supported further destabilization as a way station to independence, became progressively more restive as new competencies dried up. The result was a gathering crisis of Catalan nationalist politics toward 2000, when the strategies born of the 1980 conjuncture had ceased to produce the new competencies that nationalists wanted, but had satisfied regional organizations that now only wanted stability. In 2003, it would end with CiU losing the Generalitat to a PSC-ERC-IC-V (Communist-Green) coalition. This chapter traces the politics, analyzing the mutual affiliation of CiU and the regional organizations of the Catalanist consensus and the failures of other parties to win that support (the PSC for being unreliably autonomist due to its Spanish dependencies, and the others for being too destabilizing). The outcome of CiU's elective affinities with the regional organizations of Catalonia was a government capable of marshaling the coalition to ride out and resist the revindications of central elites (which ranged from organic laws and legal challenges to a coup staged by one fringe).

## THE HIGH AND LOW POLITICS OF DEVOLUTION

This chapter analyzes the high politics. This means examining the efforts of the Generalitat, CiU, and Catalan organizations to carve out a sphere of autonomy. It also means examining the resistance of the central state and its resource-dependent allies to regionalization, their strategies (ranging from dubious fraud investigations to parliamentary votes), and their changing relations as the limits. Just as in the transition, the ability of the Catalan leaders to aggregate and direct Catalan political resources was crucial in explaining their ability to negotiate or compel a given outcome, and now they faced the challenge of doing it against resistance. CiU did this by allying with Catalan regional organizations to win autonomy for them via the Generalitat while using the constant increase in competencies to rally nationalists who would otherwise support more secessionist parties (such as ERC). This depended on CiU's ability to make credible promises that it would deliver autonomy, and for most of this period it could. It also could make promises to others. It briefly tried to create a center-right party for the whole of Spain. However, its regional organizational allies controlled key resources and their autonomy was what it supplied in return—it failed when it experimented with the idea of creating a Spanish sister party.

The twenty years after 1980 divide into three periods based on the particular configuration of parties. The first period is 1980–1984, when CiU was consolidating itself as the key regionalist party and ally of regional organizations in their desire for autonomy. The second period runs from 1984 to 1992, when CiU and the PSOE leadership in Madrid polarized territorial politics between the central state on one side and CiU's combination of autonomists and nationalists on the other. Caught in the middle, the PSC was in serious trouble in these years. The source of its organization and initial funding, the PSOE, also ruined its credibility as a Catalan party by pursuing Pujol in a self-defeating series of attacks on CiU and the Generalitat's autonomy. The third period runs from 1993 to 2000, when CiU, on one hand, won considerable power in the Spanish government by aiding minority parties but, on the other, saw its coalition of nationalists and regional organizations under stress since regional organizations were uninterested in much more autonomy while nationalists were.

*1980–1984: A Centralist Backlash and the Response*

The first problem Pujol's new government faced was the gathering response of centralist organizations that saw their powers and environmental stability under serious threat. This was not wholly a response to Catalonia; it was equally or more due to the fact that the process of regionalization had spread beyond the "three historic nations." Political leaders of the rest of Spain appeared to be starting to bid for autonomy—an autonomy that would start to dismember centralist organizations. It was bad enough for a convinced Spanish nationalist to see Catalonia take over education—the blow was cushioned by the long tradition of Catalan differentiation. To have Andalucia and Valencia also bid for important powers, however, threatened a genuine dismemberment of the state apparatus (and, many rightists thought, of the state). The worry spread to the PSOE; a former minister, in a September 2000 Madrid interview, explained that "after the Andalucia vote we had to slow down the process, control it. Otherwise there would be a crisis, otherwise the transition would be in danger"; he specified the danger first as the danger to a coherent state, and only secondarily that of a coup. Centralist and mostly right-wing organizations, above all the military, police (and *guardia civil*), judiciary, and elite state bureaucrats began to work out how to stabilize autonomy at a low level that would not threaten them. In this effort leaders of Spain-wide parties, worried by a parallel disintegration of their own organizations, and centralist elites (above all in industry and finance), long linked with the central state, willingly joined.

What caused this sense of crisis that would end by threatening the transition? The original process of devolution was generally expected to stabilize with Catalonia, the Basque Country and Galicia at the highest level of autonomy, and with the others at lower levels. The Constitution reflected this assumption, offering two major routes to autonomy. One route, through article 151, was the "fast route" via a referendum to a high level of competencies. A second, the article 143 "slow route," went through central state legislation and would let the state set the more limited autonomous competencies. Andalucia, however, provoked a crisis when in February 1979 the political elites of its "pre-autonomy" successfully called an article 151 referendum on a level of autonomy equal to that of the "three historic nations"— and won. This meant that Andalucia could negotiate extensive powers. This introduced a serious worry among central elites that the process would get out of the control of the deal-making elites at the center who had until then been steering the Transition. The effect of this vote on the UCD was marked. In the runup to the referendum, the Suárez government, under pressure from state elites and business, suffered an internal crisis and the pro-autonomy minister responsible for the process resigned in favor of harder-line Martín Villa. The UCD flipped in the last weeks before the referendum, counseling abstention (it had previously approved). The referendum nonetheless passed, and Villa began to canvass experts on a strategy for regaining control by creating homogenous autonomous communities across Spain, under similar tutelage and with similar powers and relationships to the state (Fusi 1996:458–459).

The military was among the organizations disturbed by decentralization. A long-running breakdown in military and paramilitary police coherence led finally to a coup attempt in 1981. The coup failed, with the military mostly remaining loyal (Agüero 1995). Part of the reason was that King Juan Carlos

spent much of the night on the telephone with military commanders, request-
ing their loyalty and promises to stay in barracks (Preston 2005). He also, that
night, found himself listening to their concerns. A paramount concern of the
(loyal) military was that the *proceso autonómico*, with no obvious endpoint in
sight, was threatening the unity of Spain. Thus, after the coup was settled, the
king spoke with leaders of the PSOE and UCD and told them that the military
felt the *proceso autonómico* was damaging the unity of Spain it was determined
to preserve, and that the party leaders, many of whom were already worried,
should take action to stabilize the process. Otherwise, the threat of more coups
and right-wing subversion remained (Boix Angelats 1997). Soon after came the
Organic Law of Harmonization of the Proceso Autonómico, known by its
initials, LOAPA, and the "autonomous pacts" designed to set the competencies
of the "slow route" autonomous communities.

The exact relationship between LOAPA, the coup, and the commission of experts is still debated, but there is little doubt that the law was
intended to truly, firmly stabilize the state structure and lay down the bases
for a state with homogenous regional governments. This reflected the interests of the central state's elites—military and bureaucratic—who were worried that the unity of the state and of their organizations was under. It was
in the interest of the top politicians in the PSOE and UCD leaderships.
Their party organizations were still relatively fragile and they had no interest
in letting their regional tiers continue to threaten to seize power from the
center, and by extension from the party and state leaders.

The UCD's problem was local party barons, who still controlled frag-
ments of the disintegrating Francoist single party and union organization,
and who could see the autonomous communities as ways to preserve their
status (Gunther, Sani, and Shabad 1988:140–145). Indeed, as the UCD
began to crack up (the Andaluz reverse was the first crisis of its self-destruction),
its elites began to adopt increasingly regionalist stances as a strategy to diver-
sify their political bases. The coherence of the UCD and the extent of
regionalist pressure in Castilian Spain would begin to vary inversely
(Sepúlveda 1996). The PSOE's problem was that its incorporation of regional Socialist federations was still weak, and if they had governments with
greater power they might undo the centralizing work of the party leadership
and either win more autonomy or take over the central party—just as the
PSC's Catalanists wanted to do (Gunther, Sani, and Shabad 1988:159–164).
It also reflected the interests of opportunistic groups who were worried by the
degree of environmental disturbance—the state had been regionalizing since
1977, and with the Andalucian referendum the centrifugal tendencies appeared to be gaining strength.

The two parties' leaders signed an accord on 31 July, five months after
the coup attempt, agreeing to form a united front that would have the votes

and social support necessary to pass organic laws redirecting the devolution process. This was the process that came to be known as "café para todos" or the Spanish neologism "reconducción" (of the process), and which had first been mooted by Martín Villa in 1980 (Boix Angelats 1997:261). It meant establishing a similar level of competencies for all the autonomous communities ("harmonizing" them) and the principle that such competencies were the central state's to allocate: if one was to have coffee, all would have coffee. It led to a number of pacts that began to stabilize the system (Rebollo 2000). LOAPA was agreed between the UCD and PSOE and passed in 1982, just after the PSOE won a general election (the UCD having spectacularly disintegrated; Huneeus 1985; Hopkin 1999).

However, this coalition between the central state and the central parties against the parties' regional leaders collided with a strong coalition of regional organizations and nationalist parties in Catalonia and the Basque Country—the central coalition and its law threatened their autonomy. CiU (and other nationalist and autonomist parties around Spain, and the PCE/ PSUC) saw it as a direct attack and began massive mobilizations as soon as word leaked of the two big parties' plans (Boix Angelats 1997). After it was passed, the full spectrum of non-Spanish-nationalist parties, Basque, Catalan, and Andaluz, brought it before the Constitutional Tribunal in a procedure that prevented its being enforced until it was judged. The tribunal, in August 1983, ruled that most of it was unconstitutional; fundamentally the argument was that the legislators had no competency to interpret the Constitution—only the tribunal did (Rubio Llorente 1997). Thus, a law explaining what it meant to hand over competencies of various types, and the role of the state in governing those competencies, could not be constitutional (STC 76/ 1983) (Leguina 1984). Of the goal of flattening and homologizing autonomous competencies in principle, the tribunal said nothing. This is a classic instance of a top court deciding a highly controversial case on technical grounds that allow it to avoid pronouncing on the principles at stake while retaining a role. It is also what CiU apparently hoped for. LOAPA had become so controversial that the court would avoid judging the principles of the law, or upholding them. Political mobilization had once again won Catalan autonomy, and that political mobilization was possible because of the ability of CiU and its allies (above all in the press, cultural organizations, and the educational system) to create an issue, expand conflict, and organize a protest.

At the same time, CiU lost no opportunity to highlight the PSC's unhappy stance—as part of the PSOE federation, the PSC deputies had voted for LOAPA, but in Catalonia the PSC tried to highlight its *Catalanitat*. CiU had nothing to lose by marking itself off as the anti-LOAPA leadership; the PSC, by contrast, was caught between its Catalanist, autonomist instincts and resource dependencies (in its links with, above all, parts of the educational system and the professions) and its Spanish resource dependencies on the central PSOE and on the state it ran. The vote reopened internal conflicts over the extent to which the party should be autonomous of the PSOE. The PSC was dependent on the central state and the PSOE for most of what it had achieved, but prevented by that dependence from building the linkages with regional elites and Catalanists that would give it victory in the Generalitat (Boix Angelats 1997:263). A solution would be difficult. One would be impossible as long as the center of power and resources in the party was in Madrid, and in the hands of a centralist statewide party whose strategies for undermining the liberal, Catalanist irritant Pujol would often, as in the case of LOAPA, merely polarize Catalan politics further and drag the PSC further away from credible Catalanism.

The next major episode of this PSOE-CiU conflict (and PSC humiliation) was the scandal of Banca Catalana, when the PSOE's central leadership attempted to damage the center-right CiU that was their main obstacle to power in Catalonia (Antich 1994; Missé 1997:113–134). Once again, reliance on the central party (and state) would mean the PSC would harm its own autonomist credentials and thus support. In an early-1980s banking-sector collapse, small banks across Spain perished, while the central bank concentrated on reinforcing and merging the big (mostly Basque and Northern) banks with which it had been linked for over a century (Díez Medrano 1995; Pérez 1997). One of the small casualties of the collapse was Pujol's bank, Banca Catalana. In what appears to be a political process, the central state's highly politicized financial regulators began intensive criminal investigations into accusations of malfeasance starting in 1980, took control of the bank in 1982, and filed charges in 1984. The result was another explosion of resistance, again orchestrated by CiU, with the help of its nationalist activists and its friends in parts of the regional media and the nationalist organizations it was by now funding. As a direct attack on Pujol, the nationalist leader, the outcry was ferocious. Again, CiU could present to the public a direct threat to the man who was the lynchpin of its autonomist nationalism. The case dissolved into acrimony, leaving no evidence of malfeasance by Pujol.

Again, the PSC, which had elected a more Catalanist leader after the LOAPA clash, emerged disliked by nationalists, inextricably linked to the PSOE's actions, with its leaders in the Madrid government accused of organizing the campaign, and having left the impression of being opposed to the whole course of Catalan politics and disposed to dirty tricks. The new leader, Raimon Obiols, said Banca Catalana marked the start of what he called, using a slightly melodramatic term borrowed from Italy's years of political violence, the PSC's "years of lead" (Missé 1997:329). The party's dependence on Madrid (coupled with its reliance on "immigrant" votes) and conflicts such as LOAPA and Banca Catalana made it seem a tool of the central party—a party of *sucursalistas*, or Catalans who were content to be branch offices of a Spanish organization. At the same time, its organizational implantation in local government tied it more strongly to that level of government (as against the Generalitat) and fragmented the party between different mayors (Colomé 1989).

In terms of party organization, CiU benefited from its role as the key nationalist party and the one that most reliably defended a stable autonomism. During the early 1980s, CiU completed its territorial implantation across Catalonia, running lists in nearly every city and organizing territorial party structures for both Convergència and, more slowly, Unió (Barberà 2001; Calsina i Buscà 2001). "Public office helped; they put militants in posts and the militants helped them . . . elected officials have to give over part of their salary to the party, and they reward the people who help them as well, people like the local businessmen, mutuals . . . they also tried to take over banks and *caixes*," remarked a journalist who covered those years. The coalition, like most other Spanish political forces, also penetrated the Generalitat with its appointees, in both political and civil service posts (Matas Dalmases 1995, 2001). Like other Spanish parties, Convergència and Unió had weak membership bases and low member participation. Thus, the proportion of party members remained low, and interviewees suggested that there were few members of Convergència or Unió who were not elected officials or employees of the Generalitat and CiU's local governments.

Thus, the parties with control over significant governments and elite alliances stabilized organizationally. Other parties had weaker elite alliances and weaker bases in elected governments, and passed these years badly. Without resource dependencies on outside organizations, they were weak. Equally, they were not bound by the terms of alliances with outside organizations in the way CiU and the PSC were. They therefore depended on activists and veered between policies depending on the internal struggles of their activists and without restraints from outside.

The preeminent party dependent on collective action, the PSUC, destroyed itself in what was ostensibly a debate about its response to the Soviet investigation of Afghanistan. In reality, the debate was the fruition of long-developing tensions within the PSUC between its red-belt cadres and its Catalanist, Catalan, middle-class leadership, exacerbated by its internal ideological diversity and its Leninist governance structure. These tensions exploded into fratricide (between the "Afghans" of the red-belt grassroots and the critics of the Catalan party leadership), and the party, disabled by infighting, collapsed in the 1982 elections (Cebrián 1997). ERC, meanwhile, continued to impress by its survival: as a liberal, Catalanist party with a strong nationalist discourse, it found it difficult to distinguish itself from its ally CiU, except in its lack of success. The result was that ERC's aging leadership, committed to an anti-left strategy in alliance with Pujol, increasingly diverged from younger nationalist groups entering the party out of dissatisfaction with the moderation of CiU and the failure of their smaller parties and movements. Meanwhile, the Spanish right had effectively no parliamentary representation due to the failure of the UCD and AP's continuing inability to implant itself in Catalonia. This failure was in good part because they still suffered the oppubrium of the Catalanist consensus. The absence of UCD, though, also eliminated any chance of a developing noncentralist right party in Spain or in Catalonia in the 1980s (Gunther, Montero, and Botella 2004).

This dynamic was assisted by the strategies of party finance and support that emerged in Catalonia and Spain after the first elections. Spanish party finances are extremely murky, in large part due to parties' use of private foundations to carry out electoral work and the minimal transparency required of parties (in Catalonia, the parties are particularly opaque about their finances, reflecting two decades of opportune failure to pass significant campaign-finance legislation). Formally, parties are financed by the state (since 1978, with a change in 1987). They receive a fixed sum per vote and per seat obtained in statewide elections (del Castillo 1989, 1990; Méndez Lago 2000:102–104; Irujo 2005). This hurts small and extraparliamentary parties, especially given the majoritarian effects of a d'Hondt system in small (provincial) circumscriptions. Parties also have informal ways of raising funds, including taking a percentage of elected officials' salaries, franking privileges, use of public media (the Catalan television stations, like television throughout Spain, were tools of the party that controlled them), and corruption.[1] These mean that parties are dependent above all on their electoral success and control of state resources of financing, both because of the public financing formula and of the potential that a government position has to raise further funds and build coalitions with elites. In Catalonia, this means an overwhelming advantage for the PSC and CiU. Government begets government.

Thus, the PSC was CiU's only real rival, and after LOAPA, Banca Catalana, and the constant court cases and struggles over specific competencies between the central government (with its PSC ministers) and Pujol, it was no surprise that in 1985 CiU won an absolute majority in the Catalan parliament. As a political party, CiU benefited from opportunities to increase its activity, profile, and electoral results. Its own agenda-setting efforts and its clashes with the Spanish central government had raised the profile of nationalism as against left–right disputes. Catalan politics had taken the form of a clash between Catalonia (represented as the Generalitat, and nationalism in general, and CiU) and Madrid (represented as Spain, the central state, the PSOE, and the PSC). More facilitation came from the support of regional elites, whose organizations, as argued later, were increasingly bound with CiU in alliances born of policymaking in the new fields—CiU was offering them the long-denied opportunity to control their own policy areas with only a light outside political touch. In addition, the process of building the Generalitat's administration had given CiU extensive resources within the government; it was even more dependent than its allies on the regional resource of the Generalitat. With all that facilitation, the party benefited and won the 1984 Catalan elections with an absolute majority, even as the rest of Spain was still seeing a PSOE tide crest (Table 6.1).

CiU and the PSOE had polarized politics in Catalonia around autonomy and centralism, to the detriment of the PSC (whose regionalist credibility was further battered) and secessionists (who joined the CiU coalition in the polarized atmosphere) and to the benefit of CiU.

## 1984–1993: SPANIARD OF THE YEAR

In 1986, CiU demonstrated its Catalan nature and consequent limits. CiU's coalition had two components and a benign ally: regional organizations, nationalist voters (and party activists), and the benign support of opportunistic organizations of a rightist bent that opposed the PSOE as a threat to business. CiU prepared for the 1986 elections by organizing a Spain-wide federation of liberal parties to dislodge the ineffective AP as the opposition to the Socialists (Antich 1994:201-220). Run by Miquel Roca (constitutional drafter and general secretary of Convergència), the project was to create a liberal party (Democratic Reformist Party, PRD) to oppose the PSOE, running outside Catalonia and filling in the center-right that fell between the Alianza Popular and the PSOE. The timing for such a party seemed propitious: after the collapse of the UCD, Suárez's successor party in the center had not taken off. AP remained too rightist, and Fraga's sizeable personal vote came along with the antipathy of a large part of the population. Business support was in play in those years (Hopkin 1999). The withdrawal of support for the UCD by the Spanish employers' federation CEOE had contributed to its collapse, but the AP seemed trapped in a rightist vote that was leaving the labile PSOE dominant (Share 1999). Thus, "Operation Roca," as the project was nicknamed, seemed like it could plausibly win business support and the voters of the center-right who were unhappy with AP and the PSOE, and it was already starting with the electoral base and resources of CiU as a contribution to the planned confederation. Big banks agreed, and paid for the adventure (Antich 1994:217). This was a bid by CiU to create its own allies in Spain and to build up its own power and reputation as a stabilizing, liberal force that would not only secede but also would work to defend capitalism in the face of the PSOE.

Table 6.1   Party Votes in Catalonia, 1980–1989

| Party | 1982 General | 1984 Catalan | 1986 General | 1988 Catalan | 1989 General |
|---|---|---|---|---|---|
| AP/PP* | 14.4 | 7.7 | 11.3 | 5.3 | 10.7 |
| CDS** | — | — | 4.1 | 3.8 | 4.3 |
| CiU | 22.2 | 46.6 | 31.8 | 45.5 | 32.7 |
| ERC | 4 | 4.4 | 2.7 | 4.1 | 2.7 |
| PSC | 45.2 | 30 | 40.6 | 29.6 | 35.5 |
| PSUC/ IC-V*** | 4.6 | 5.6 | 3.9 | 7.7 | 7.3 |
| UCD | — | — | — | — | — |

\* The AP became the Partido Popular (PP) from the 1989 results onward.
\*\* The Democratic and Social Center—a small center-right party led by Adolfo Suárez.
\*\*\* The PSUC was UEC in 1986 and became part of IC-V from 1988 onward.
Note: Results of less than 1% are omitted.
Sources: For 1982–1988, Equip de sociología electoral UAB (1990); for 1989, Pallarés (1999).

The project failed. It won not a single seat (but evidently did win the record for the most expensive failure in Spanish democratic politics, counted as money spent per vote; Antich 1994:218) . What is interesting is that CiU tried. The party, which sat with the Liberals in the European Parliament, was using a liberal self-identification increasingly often in order to present itself to businesses around Spain as a liberal defender of business and stability, and its Catalanist project as a nation-building project based in cheerleading, local economic development, and public administration rather than secession or attacks on Spanish capitalism. Likewise, Pujol went to considerable lengths to win over the Spanish royal house and persuade the king to address an audience in Catalonia in Catalan (Antich 1994:161–190). CiU was squaring the circle, for a royal address by the king in Catalan simultaneously reassured those worried about nationalist destabilization, won Catalan nationalist acceptance for the Spanish state, and looked like a victory for moderate Catalanism and Pujol personally.[2]

Operation Roca was a chapter in a larger set of such efforts by CiU to court opportunistic elites on the Spanish level. The primary goal was to stabilize CiU's environment and win the support of opportunistic organizations by promising stability and policies they would appreciate. The alliance appears to have won CiU significant financial support from them, but primarily it appears that the efforts decreased the amount of informal repression centralist organizations directed against it. For example, the powerful, highly politicized, and mostly right-wing, media and judiciary both gave it surprising latitude in these years (to the point that *ABC*, a Madrid daily and barometer of right-wing opinion, named Pujol "Spaniard of the Year" in 1984—which was probably related to the conflicts between *ABC*'s right-wing constituents and the same PSOE government that was pursuing Pujol over Banca Catalana).[3] As an organization it was clearly dependent on regional organizations, the Catalanist politics they created, and its own nationalist voters—no obvious market existed for liberals in Spain, as Operation Roca demonstrated.

In these years, much of the actual delimitation of public administration competencies was taking place in areas where the essence of transfers (of responsibilities and equipment) was already resolved. The disputes were over the limits of the state's power to set Base Laws and Organic Laws, and about Catalonia's abilities to enact legislation on the borders of state regulation. This meant that the tussles were legal, preeminently in the Constitutional tribunal where over 400 intergovernmental relations "conflict of competencies" cases were decided. Legal battles over competencies and language laws individually tended to have very low salience as issues, were relatively hard to present as threats or opportunities, and relatively difficult to influence through political mobilization. "We couldn't explain them, and we couldn't violate legality. . . . We had to work in politics because of the *espanyolisme* of the courts," explained a former Convergència minister. Pujol's confidant Lluís Prenafeta called the state a "devourer of dreams" in his personal apologia (Prenafeta 1999:171).

The direct influence of CiU on the government was often weaker than that of the PSOE in Catalonia. This combination of poor positioning in Spanish state politics and a strong position in Catalan politics meant CiU at the same time could lose many minor battles and remain hegemonic in Catalonia. It defended regional autonomy well enough, and the regional autonomy it won it effectively delegated to the organizational elites of that policy field.

A former minister explained the ideology: "Convergència does not go with any ethereal principle, or theoretical [principle]; [Catalonia is] a nation that wants autonomy in order to improve the quality of life and the status of the person. . . . In the important issues there is consensus . . . that consensus comes from recognizing the limits of the action of the public and working together. Our way of thinking is that we are integrated into civil society, we work with its energies." By working with those energies, he explained when I asked for an example, the Generalitat negotiates its language and culture policies with the groups that must implement them; for example, doctors did not want to be forced to learn Catalan and do not have to learn Catalan. When I asked why hospital porters did have to learn Catalan, he explained that they were employees of the Generalitat.

The year of the Olympic Games in Barcelona, 1992, was the apogee of both CiU and the PSOE of this era and the year of the Catalanist consensus' biggest test since the transition. Awarded to Barcelona, the Games came the same year as the 500th anniversary of 1492, minor events in Madrid, and a World's Fair in Socialist bastion (and González's hometown) Seville. Barcelona, the Generalitat, and the central state all contributed to use the opportunity to regenerate Barcelona and raise its profile and that of Spain. However, the Games were a classic case of the value of the municipal–central–state axis contained in the PSOE—Barcelona and Spain starred because they paid for it. The Generalitat ended up reaping very little extra funding and lacked the extra funds to influence decisionmaking. Instead, it concentrated on using 1992 to present Catalonia, rather than Barcelona, to the world. CiU and its youth wing staged many nationalist stunts, rigging events to highlight banners with its slogan in English "Freedom for Catalonia," taking out advertisements in the international press welcoming the Games to Catalonia, and fighting for rights such as the playing of the Catalan national anthem at the opening ceremonies (Antich 1994:271–284; Hargreaves 2000).

CiU's direct control over policy meant that it could win alliances with regional elites better than the central-municipal Socialists. The PSC did not control the power resources of most importance to regional elites and whose autonomist credibility was weakened by the centralism of the PSOE (as seen, and elicited, in constant conflicts with CiU over competencies). "We worked with the doctors, in the hospitals, and they worked with the hospital owners and the College of Physicians. And that means they made the system," remarked a Socialist-allied doctor. And its instrumental rewards and elite facilitation meant no other party attempted to dislodge it.

In 1989, this changed with a coup inside ERC (Table 6.2). Since 1980, ERC had become a "satellite" of CiU, with a leader at one point joining one of Pujol's cabinets (Caminal Badia 1998b). At a hotly contested party conference, Angel Colom led a coup and took over as party leader. At the same conference, the delegates adopted the first explicitly secessionist plank of any Catalan parliamentary political party (Santacana 1995). ERC went on to win its best votes of the democratic era in 1992, but then began to sink in polls and suffer from factional infighting. The environmental problem for ERC was that it had few elements of opportunity: it had no chance of success in the near future, especially since it sought independence and unity for not only the principality, but also the Països Catalans: Valencia, the Balearic Islands, parts of Aragon and Murcia, and North Catalonia (i.e., part of France). Neither regional organizations nor the state apparatus assisted it with resources. Thus, it suffered from bad press, received no help from the regional powers, and lost the connections to elites that its liberal leaders had built. Its militants and electorate were accordingly those who did not care—and who were often

Table 6.2   Catalan Election Results 1993–2000

| Party | 1992 Catalan | 1993 General | 1995 Catalan | 1996 General | 1999 Catalan | 2000 General |
|---|---|---|---|---|---|---|
| CiU | 46.2 | 31.7 | 40.8 | 29.5 | 37.6 | 28.6 |
| ERC | 8 | 5.1 | 9.5 | 4.2 | 8.6 | 5.6 |
| PP | 6 | 17 | 13.1 | 17.9 | 9.5 | 22.7 |
| PSC | 27.6 | 34.7 | 24.8 | 39.2 | 30.3 | 33.9 |
| IC-V | 6.5 | 7.4 | 9.7 | 7.6 | 7.5* | 3.5 |
| EUiA** | — | — | — | — | — | 2.2 |

*Won in a Barcelona province collaboration with the PSC. Another 2.5% went to IC-V in the other three provinces.

**United and Alternative Left. A schismatic group from IC-V opposed to IC-V's breaking its links with the Spanish left party Izquierda Unida. Won no seats and reintegrated into the IC-V coalition for the 2003 elections.

*Note:* Results of less than 1% are omitted.

*Sources:* For 1989-1999, Pallarés (1999); for 2000, Pallarés (2001).

volatile and disposed to protest (Marcet and Argelauget 1998). The result was that the Colom years' small victories soon faded.

Internally, ERC remained unstable as a result of this outsider, highly mobilized position. Interviewees would blame the personalities of Colom and his charismatic deputy Pilar Rahola, but the problem was structural. No external resource dependencies meant dependence on mobilized activists, which meant extremism and instability and thus no external resource dependencies. In the Catalan political system of the 1990s, ERC was less a party, or social movement organization with a substantial chance of success, than a resource for heretofore extraparliamentary forces to whom the state funding, political office, and media attention of even a maligned ERC was a tremendous attraction. Its leaders, with weak patronage powers, could not respond that there were necessary compromises with elites to maintain, and regional organizations played little part in forming its policies. As a consequence, when its votes began to decline, ERC was taken over again. The party's constitution, held over from the Second Republic, allowed (and allows) any member to come to conference and vote. This meant that Colom and Rahola could be deposed through a simple maneuver. Yet another group that had entered the party after experiments with less successful parties arranged to hold the conference far from the homes of the supporters of Colom and Rahola. The two resigned to form a new party (that would fail) rather than face their inevitable sacking when their supporters skipped the trip and the opposition, resident nearby, came out to vote (Cucurella 2000:52–53, 61–63, 130–150).

ERC orbited in a highly nationalist sector where it, itself, was the greatest prize for militants in that milieu. It became a self-reinforcing pattern: ERC, having lost the old, weak moorings to Catalan business elites, now was confined to drawing on mobilized militants rather than elite support, and this in turn meant that it was too unstable and destabilizing to attract regional organizations. It was taken over by a mixture of long-time nationalists who had been active in extraparliamentary formations since the 1970s and had adopted an agenda of appearing more stable and backgrounding their secessionist plans. This success of a stable group of activists opened the way for ERC to perform one other operation: it slowly began to absorb activists from the militant social movement Catalunya Lliure and its violent partner group Terra Lliure, in an orchestrated reaching out that led to the dissolution of the extraparliamentary groups (Renyer Alimbau 1995).

On the other flank of the Catalanist consensus, the Partido Popular also experimented with a new strategy (Caminal Badia 1998b; Cucurella 2000). The party had been unable to build a following in Catalonia, continuing to inherit the old far right of Alianza Popular even when in the rest of Spain the PP had submerged AP voters in the voters—and many militants—of the UCD. In Catalonia, this was not possible as CiU had occupied the space once held by the UCD and integrated the potential UCD elites and cadres on the center-right. The PP in Catalonia thus survived mostly through support from the state, support that increased as the PP in Spain advanced and won right-wing elite support. Under the leadership of Aleix Vidal-Quadras, the PP in Catalonia decided to break with the Catalanist consensus. It opted for language rights as a campaign platform, combined strangely with claims to have rethought *Catalanitat* (Catalanity), accusing Pujol and CiU of attacks on the rights of Castilian Spanish speakers and demanding more egalitarian treatment. This received some play from the rightist Spanish press, and also increased the PP's votes in elections (Cucurella 2000:124–125).

Regional organizations, above all the parties and press, closed ranks against the new-style PP as thoroughly and quickly they did in the case of ERC. Vidal-Quadras's attack on Catalanism as government attacked the politics of regional autonomy, the PSC, the Generalitat, ERC and IC, and of course CiU. The PP was breaking a consensus that was a barrier to entry in Catalan politics, and it raised the prospect of the long-feared mobilization of the Spanish speakers qua Spanish speakers. Given the extent to which the PSC, central state, and local government (on one side) and CiU, the Generalitat, and the other regional elites (on the other) formed a single political system, a resurgence of non-Catalanist political mobilization threatened them both. That slack resource—the alienation of Spanish speakers in the Barcelona suburbs—had to be kept slack. The result was a torrent of media abuse in Catalonia, lobbying directed against the PP center in Madrid by elites, lobbying within the PP in Catalonia against Vidal-Quadras by elites, and miscellaneous public platforms and petitions against Vidal-Quadras. It succeeded: the price of Vidal-Quadras in Catalonia was higher than the PP in Spain wished to pay, in terms of regional organizational support fore-gone, forbearance eliminated, and CiU votes abandoned. The leadership of the (centralized) PP quieted him and then forced him out. Vidal-Quadras was removed in 1999, and replaced with placeholders until Aznar's govern-ment appointed the chair of the Cercle d'Economia (Josep Piqué) as foreign minister, and parachuted him in as party chair along with selected deputies chosen for their moderation and good connections to Catalan and Spanish business. This brought networks but not support; "Piqué works for Piqué and we all know that . . . if he were acting as a Catalan, promoting Catalonia, we would know it," snapped a Cercle d'Economia officer in 2001. The PP leadership had learned that directly attacking the Catalanist consensus was interpreted as directly attacking the autonomy and environmental stability of the regional organizations that underpinned it, and reversed course by choos-ing a well-connected member of the regional elite to represent them. The fact that Madrid could so effectively restructure ("teledirect") the party, however, sent the message that it could not be trusted with Catalan au-tonomy, digging the PP yet further into its hole.

*Helping to Govern Spain: 1993–2000*

Despite the excitement of 1992 and its value for analyzing the defense of the Catalanist consensus against ERC and PP alike, 1993 was a more important year for CiU and the analysis of Catalonia's political power in Spain. It was the first year the Catalan party coalition held swing votes in the Madrid parliament after the PSOE performed poorly in the general elections (Table 6.2). CiU decided to support a minority PSOE government in a stable electoral pact in return for policy goals, most of them pertaining to regional financing. CiU remained in this position after the 1996 elections, when the Partido Popular under José María Aznar won a plurality in the lower house and formed an-other minority government, again with CiU support. Thus, CiU spent seven years with important bargaining power in the central state legislature (Gunther, Montero, and Botella 2004:189).

  CiU was a party shaped by the initial alliance that forged it, ranging across nationalist center-right organizations such as small businesses, county hospitals, lawyers, local chambers of commerce, and professionals as well as its nationalist activitists. What did it do when it could bring down a Spanish government? These years are a test of theories that rely purely on party logics as explanations of regionalization. Divergent observers, scanning European regionalization as a whole, put great emphasis on the role of nationalist parties in statewide government. The prime example is usually CiU in the mid-late 1990s when Spanish governments depended on its votes and, it is said, won significant powers (Gibbons 1999:288–289; Hooghe and Marks 2001:74; Heller 2002:681–682). What this period of Spanish reliance on Catalan votes actually did was demonstrate the limits of CiU's power and its bilateral strategy.

Measured in powers, outcomes are unimpressive, indeed less impressive than those of the conflictual 1980s. This is because CiU, as a party, is not just a strategic actor with leverage; it is also an organization, tightly bound with regional elites and constrained by them. These constraints meant that it had to value stability to the point of not being able to use the leverage that so impresses many observers. It gained one power—that of organizing the police in Catalonia (i.e., the power to provide and organize the service, not set laws). It improved the previously very poor machinery for coordination between regions and the central state in EU affairs (although coordination also depends on goodwill, a scarce commodity in Spanish intergovernmental relations) (Closa and Heywood 2004:94–98). Its other primary gain was an improved financial settlement that gave Catalonia a stable—if small (15%)—share of the Spanish income tax (IRPF) and merged transfer budgets so that the Generalitat could move funds between purposes (the income tax rate continues to be set by the state). Each successive financial settlement since 1980 had moved in that direction; this moved it further along. Meanwhile, the financial settlement still left the Generalitat with a relatively small budget and limited capacity to increase its own funding while Catalonia systematically funded the rest of Spain by contributing more income tax than it received (Vilalta i Ferrer 1998; Castells 2001).

Finance and relations with the EU are key topics in the intergovernmental relations of any European region. It is easy to make the case for paying attention to them, and to the regional organizations that often suffer from failures of EU coordination or that would prefer greater public spending (public health, education and other systems, as well as groups like construction companies that benefit from the Generalitat). There are also unknown policies blocked by CiV's position. But what were signally missing were extensive new competencies or redefinitions of existing ones. With the handover of the police, the bulk of the state's social policy bureaucracies in Catalonia had been turned over to the Generalitat: health, education, universities, culture, security, and environment. The Generalitat did not force a serious improvement in Catalonia's status measured in new state powers or even a funding formula that reflected the Catalan population.[4]

Why did a nationalist party, with the Spanish government dependent on it, produce only a transfer of police administration, some improvement in formal mechanisms of European policy integration, and a stabler share of tax revenue? The answer lies in the coalitions that the Generalitat could produce to support any bid it made for greater powers, or that it could evoke in opposition to it. "We always work by consensus. You cannot *fer país* as a fraction; we promote consensus," explained a former minister who gave examples of laws with wide support told me that "we don't look for competencies where there is no consensus—the state tries to take powers." He concluded with a common phrase: "we pacted it all."

In general, the problem was that most regional elites were satisfied with the level of autonomy the Generalitat had, and were uninterested in supporting further gains. Improving the finance and policy coordination of existing Catalan competencies was becoming a more appealing agenda. Most opportunistic groups, on the other hand, would have opposed Catalan bids for competencies over such areas as taxes or infrastructure. Those were powers that would give Catalonia the chance to alter the economic framework of Spain, making it a player they had to court and that could destabilize their institutional environments and interfere with their operations. The Generalitat already had the power to lead, cheerlead, and subsidize. That meant it could thus bid for opportunistic elites' support, but could not oblige them to change.

CiU was trapped. Part of its support came from its nationalist credentials, and those had been reinforced for over a decade by its ability to bring back new competencies. But now it could not seek greater economic or administrative powers without creating coalitions of centrally resource dependent organizations (unions and business) and the state against it, and it lacked the support of regional elites to win greater powers than the Generalitat already had. It could not seek to change political rules that worked against it because that would have cast it as a destabilizing nationalist force that would have lost it organizational support and created a regional-central coalition against it in favor of stability (such a move, given the culture and personnel of CiU, would have been truly remarkable). Thus, it achieved the devolution of the police, almost the last case of a major, visible, state-run social service with employees on the street in Catalonia, and began to set up the force.

Its policy influence—and the impact of efforts to improve the machinery of intergovernmental relations—was limited because the ability to support or withdraw support from a minority government is not a substitute for connection to the highly political bureaucracies that make and implement the details of policy. Such ability to engage in agenda-setting and technical policy debate was limited by the lack of CiU resources in the central state, where policies were written and implemented, and its general lack of information. Without allies in Madrid, it was difficult to learn what was happening in time to use parliamentary leverage to fix it—high-ranking Generalitat officials routinely had to fly to Madrid just to be given copies of government policy documents, an example of the sort of problem CiU's parliamentary delegation had difficulty fixing and that reduced its influence. "They don't tell us anything until they have written the document. Then we have a meeting in Madrid. We all sit there correcting the grammar—it's too late to change anything. I quit going. Most of us have," explained a high-level Generalitat civil servant in 2001. I asked if it was better or worse when CiU supported the government. "Worse. They were already arrogant, but then they were also worried." The formal state structure (the parliamentary role and arithmetic) gave CiU considerable power but informal procedures of policymaking and policy formulation limited its information, capacity to intervene, and ability to roll back threats to its own autonomy. And the result was that CiU acted as often as a liberal party as it did a nationalist one.

*The 2000 Elections*

Such was the position of the Generalitat when the PP won an absolute majority in the 2000 Spanish elections, ending the dependence of the Madrid government on CiU. Months later, CiU failed to win an absolute majority in Catalonia (and lost to the PSC in absolute number of votes, being saved only by the electoral system). Positions reversed and CiU became dependent on the PP to remain in government. In part this was due to the media's favorite variables, especially the tiredness of Pujol and the CiU government. After twenty years it was often portrayed as enunciating few new ideas and producing few charismatic leaders. In part, though, it reflected CiU's strategy hitting the buffers. There were few or no new competencies where it could find preexisting regional coalitions—there was no obvious place to fish. The result was that the party became progressively more torn between its nationalist activists and voters (seeking more autonomy and national self-assertion) and its regional resource dependencies (interested in stability and technical improvements in intergovernmental relations and finance). It could not please one constituency (nationalists) without destabilizing and thereby irritating another (regional organizations).

The PSC also seems to have received more elite support—or less elite opposition—due to an ideological stance it began to enunciate that promised policy improvements for the regional elites. It can be followed by tracking the Socialist interest in the idea of federalism. The PSC—and PSOE—had always had ideological tendencies to support decentralization, tendencies that ran counter to the PSOE's internal centralization (Gunther, Sani, and Shabad 1988:252–253). The PSC in the 2000 Catalan parliamentary elections positioned itself in opposition to both Madrid and CiU, arguing to Catalans and the Catalanist regional organizations that the way forward was through federal arrangements that would make the central state more responsive to the autonomous communities. It promised better coordination between Madrid and the Generalitat and less of the polarization that can come with nationalist parties. It even debated how more federal structures could improve Spanish governance. This paralleled a greater decentralization of the PSOE, since, once the party had lost the central government, the autonomous communities leaders were its most powerful politicians (Méndez Lago 2000:137–141).

This Socialist turn to talk of "federalism," which had echos of both Catalan political thought since the nineteenth centuries and more technocratic academic work on Spanish intergovernmental relations, showed promise. It responded to the fact that many of the problems facing the Generalitat now lay in the policy process—intergovernmental relations, state duties to coordinate policy, and decisionmaking in the EU. Changing the Spanish central state to admit greater Catalan input, rather than winning more areas for sole Catalan control began to look appealing.

It thus began to articulate an alternative to the CiU strategy. CiU's strategy for self-government was one of Catalonia unifying itself behind a pragmatic party that could identify areas in which greater self-government was possible and then demanding it through skilled political tactics in Madrid. That strategy worked when there were easy coalitions to build for new powers; it fell apart as such opportunities were taken one by one. For twenty years the problem had been the PSC's—that a statewide party lacked autonomist credibility. Now it was CiU's—if the problems are on the state level, what is a regional party for (Caminal Badia 1998b:220)?

## CONCLUSION

What might alternative hypotheses suggest about the development of Catalan self-government in the two decades from 1989 to 2000? A focus on international opportunities has two flaws. On the one hand, the development of Catalan powers is largely unconnected to the development of the EU or of the world economy and indeed the key powers were regionalized before Spain joined the EU. The Generalitat does what it has competencies and resources to do, and it got those competencies and resources by fighting for them in political and legal conflicts with the central state, not by opening its offices in Brussels or attending Four Motors summits with Tuscany, Rhône-Alpes, and Baden-Württemburg (see also chapter eight). It is also difficult to see how the international economy matters, given that its powers are within the public sector; the Generalitat has not been able to change the divide between the state and society. On the other hand, the process shows no signs of the EU mattering either—CiU won battles or lost them based on its ability to move quickly and muster groups to lobby alongside it in Madrid. It is not clear where macro-level changes would impinge on these processes or on CiU's electoral prospects and organization. European integration and perhaps globalization changed the Catalan economy, and the atmosphere of politics, but barely touched the coalitions and institutions that determined possible politics.

A focus on nationalist parties is accurate because CiU is one, but Catalan politics in this period show the difficulty of relying on simple models. ERC, not CiU, is the secessionist party, and its challenges were both suppressed by regional organizations and deflected by CiU with showy and insubstantial campaigns such as the "Freedom for Catalonia" sloganeering during the 1992 Olympics. In addition to the lack of evidence that defeating ERC was CiU's priority (the PSC was a much greater threat, winning as much as ten times the votes of ERC), CiU's behavior in the 1990s has hardly been that of a nationalist party bent on secession. The flow of new competencies slowed, it participated in government, and it had little to show for such responsibility. This cost it nationalist enthusiasm—when a gap opened between its institutionalized resource dependencies and its more nationalist voters, it chose the former.

So, by 2000, the Generalitat's powers were a map of regional organizations. Where there were regional organizations, there was a Catalan competency. Where there were central organizations, there was a central competency; where there were opportunistic organizations there was competition. These limitations on competencies held by the Generalitat have mostly been fixed either by legislation and judicial interpretation that could not be opposed without making antisystem claims that CiU would not make or reflect balances of power that CiU has found itself and its coalitions inadequate to change. To try to alter the shape of the Generalitat now would require destabilizing it first, and losing regional organizations, while to accept its shape would require alienating nationalists. Trapped as it was between nationalists seeking sovereignty and contented autonomist elites, it is not surprising that CiU's think tank, the Fundació Ramon Trias Fargas, began extensively funding academic studies and conferences suggesting that sovereignty and statehood are meaningless in a globalized environment, or that symbolic recognition was what Catalonia needed, while nationalist intellectuals explored ideas of "asymmetric federalism."

Symbolism and narrative are extremely important to nationalist politics, but in government they can be a poor substitute for money and power. The CiU combination of nationalism and close ties to regional organizations ceased to work when there were no more ways to identify new powers that regional organizations would want transferred. That in turn meant that there were no new powers to assuage nationalist worries about the likelihood that devolution would really continue unto independence, or even "sovereignty." The CiU coalition faltered, and finally lost office in 2004 to a PSC-ERC-IC-V alliance. The PP followed it out of office in a 2005 Spanish general election upset. That upset was caused by outrage at its misrepresentations of terrorist attacks on Madrid; the PP, following its strategy of polarizing politics between Spanish and other nationalisms, had been part of a highly destructive cycle in the Basque Country for years and had begun the same cycle when the left, including ERC, took power in Catalonia. And the upset put a new, PSOE government in power, one committed to greater regionalization and aware in practice that it owed much of its majority to Catalan votes. The new Statute of Autonomy, presented by the Catalan parlement to Madrid, passed in a vote in the Spanish parliament and an 18 June 2006 referendum at the time this book went to press in August 2006. It creates extensive new Catalan competencies within a much looser reinterpretation of the Spanish constitution and attempts to integrate Catalonia in state policy—"building in" Catalonia through mandatory consultations on policies including those relating to the EU. It was also carefully drafted by Catalan leaders (including a former Constitutional Tribunal justice) who understood the legal and administrative techniques of intergovernmental struggles and attempted to draft the new statute so as to give Catalonia a firm defense and edge in future clashes. We cannot yet determine whether it will survive the inevitable judicial clashes, bureaucratic undermining, and reactions in the rest of Spain.

The causes and consequences of this new Socialist-led chapter in Catalan, and Spanish, history are a topic for a different study. But it is worth noting that the PSC thinkers who articulated federalist ideas and a focus on improving intergovernmental finance and relations then had an opportunity to put their ideas into practice, creating a new and potentially more cooperative machinery of government to match the currently cooperative climate within the Socialist Party and winning new powers for Catalonia as well. There is a strong case that policy would work better if there were more a cooperative and integrated machinery of intergovernmental relations, machinery that reduces the autonomy of Madrid from Barcelona and vice versa. The question is whether the PSOE, and the Spanish central state, can build in Catalonia into the Spanish state effectively enough to permanently damp down all the nationalisms, including Spanish nationalism, that help sustain electoral rivals. And for one of those rivals, ERC, the question is whether it, a movement-party led by sophisticated secessionists, can handle the transition to being a party of government without falling into the same trap as CiU. What will happen to the nationalists of ERC now that they have been in office?

# Part II

# Policies

On a high political level, regionalization was a formalization of existing, distinctive, regional organization. The process of decentralization in Scotland and Catalonia, discussed in Part I, supports the argument that dense concentrations of regional organizations explain high levels of regionalization. They do it by transmitting their preferences for autonomy and stability through the parties that are dependent for resources on them. Parties (especially Labour and CiU and, to a lesser extent the PSC) that forged alliances with regional organizations benefited from the organizations' support and were obliged to defend the organizations' autonomy and stability. In the cases of contemporary Scotland and Catalonia, this eventually meant support for regionalization. The mechanism was sometimes direct lobbying or public campaigning by organizations, but more often it was the conditional attraction of their support to parties.

What, then, about the outcome? The actual competencies and powers of the regional governments, the basis of the claim in chapter one that they are surprisingly similar, is the focus here. Scotland and Catalonia, coming from two very different historic backgrounds, have very similar regional governments, and furthermore they are joined at their level of competencies by other regions of diverse histories. They are autonomous, neither independent nor undifferentiated parts of their states; they have similar lists of competencies.

Looking at the origins of their competencies—why do they have the powers that they do—both explains the similar outcomes in more detail and permits a further test of the argument I make. If the basis of the drive for regionalization is the efforts of regional organizations to establish formal support for their autonomy and environmental stability, then there should be an identifiable relationship between the presence of particular regional organizations and the presence of a regional organization. The organizations that are the basis of an autonomous regional settlement seek their own inclusion in that settlement.

The following two chapters trace the process of regionalization in Scotland and Catalonia in the policy fields of education, health, higher education, law, police, and industrial and labor policy (and, in Catalonia, language policy) up to 2000. They are parallel demonstrations of theory, in the phrase of Skopol and Somers (Skocpol and Somers 1994). The preexisting extent of regional resource dependencies explains the presence or absence of a regional competency. Furthermore, there is evidence in the process of regionalization of the policy field that the pressure came from the regional organizations within.

The policy sectors oversample on powers of regional government; by 2000, only industrial and labor policy in both, and law in Catalonia, were not regional government powers. The reason is twofold. First, the emphasis is not on the crude correlation between regional organizations and regional outcomes. The emphasis is on process-tracing. Second, it is in line with the test: if regionalization depends on the pressure exercised by regional organizations, then it should not appear in most policy areas. Most areas should have other kinds of territorial organization and not be subject to internal pressure for regionalization. The null hypothesis is no regionalization. In many policy fields there is no regionalization and no real argument about it (such as defense, diplomatic relations, and pensions). It is thus more valuable to focus on positive cases and the processes that explain them. In addition, the case of language policy in Catalonia affords a policy sector with no real equivalent in Scotland—a serious and symbolically freighted regulatory power that affects most parts of society. Looking at language policy makes it possible to see how the Generalitat established its real powers to intervene in other organizations. Its lesson is consistent with the other policy fields—the Generalitat moved furthest and fastest where there were regional organizations that wanted a language policy, and very slowly elsewhere.

The exact structure of the two chapters is different because the sequence of regionalization was different. In Scotland, the focus of chapter seven, there is a relatively clear comparison between three points. Many powers were devolved to the Scottish Office before devolution was mooted in the 1970s. The 1978 and 1998 Scotland Acts then included different lists as well. In 1978, the powers granted to the assembly were equivalent to those of the Scottish Office. Scottish regional organizations that had other relationships with the state that afforded them more autonomy and stability successfully lobbied to stay out. In 1998, more functions were devolved to the Scottish Office and there was more support for their inclusion from within the sectors; thus, the 1998 Scotland Act devolves more competencies than the 1978 Scotland Act. The collection of powers on the Scottish level and their devolution reflects the efforts of Scottish organizations to seek stability and autonomy.

Chapter eight explains the outcomes in the same policy fields in Catalonia. While Scotland began as a large regional administrative and policy machine with competencies in the Scottish Office, the Generalitat began as a shadow of a government with only a few employees and no real competencies. This meant that while politics in Scotland centered on whether or not to grant autonomy to a preexisting regional policy system, politics in Catalonia centered on the Generalitat's efforts to claw competencies and resources away from the monolithic central state. The process of regionalization in Catalonia took years and involved endless lobbying, legal battles, and bureaucratic guerrilla warfare as the Generalitat and central state tried to get control of policy areas. In these conflicts, the organizations in the policy fields themselves were crucial. They were powerful allies to CiU in its efforts to win competencies, and in return CiU largely delegated policy to them. The result was that the Generalitat won its competencies to the extent that it could muster a strong coalition with Catalan regional organizations.

# Chapter Seven

# Shaping Autonomous Scotland
## The Scotland Office and Scotland Acts

The aborted Scottish assembly of 1979 and the Scottish parliament of 1998 could scarcely be more different. The presence of strong regional organizations, and their political activity, explains regionalization overall because regional organizations and the resources that they control attract and shape political parties. In Scotland, this meant that regional organizations had sought Scottish political organization (i.e., Scottish Office control) as early as the 1880s and that there was an extensive Scottish administrative machine in place by 1978 that would have been devolved. It also meant that as the 1979–1997 Conservative governments offended Scottish organizations that had found happier accommodation outside the Scottish Office, they shifted to support their own inclusion in Scottish devolved bodies.

This chapter relates the devolution acts of 1978 and 1998 to the presence of Scotland's regional organizations, arguing that dense regional organizations explain the presence of a Scottish devolved competency. It briefly discusses the legal structure of the two acts, since that is a valuable indicator of their intent, and it makes it clear that the 1978 Scotland Act was written to constrain the Scottish assembly and the 1998 Scotland Act to facilitate the Scottish parliament. Then it analyzes the competencies in light of the structure of six public policy sectors in Scotland.[1] In pre-university education, health, higher education, law, police, and industrial policy, the outcome in 1978 and 1998 is shaped by the existence or absence of a set of regional organizations. The differences are, first, that in 1978–1979 some key regional organizations tried to maintain the status quo ante—when they related directly to the UK state and governed themselves, they opted for that. This

option became untenable during the Conservative governments of 1979–
1997, and as a result they shifted to a preference for Scottish territorial
organization. Second, there was less enthusiasm for inclusion.

## THE ACTS THEMSELVES

It is a useful consequence of Scotland's political history that we have two
devolution Acts to compare. The structure and contents of the Scotland Act
1978 and the Scotland Act 1998 are valuable indicators of what the government was seeking to do and support my argument that a major shift took
place between the two. In 1978, the Act was about restraining a worrisome
Scottish Assembly given as a concession; in 1998, the Act was about creating
a powerful and flexible Scottish Parliament.

The Scotland Act 1978 is a strange document bearing the scars of its
parliamentary experience, including the 40% rule, a clause letting the Orkney
and Shetland islands opt out of Scotland, and the deletion of a clause saying
devolution would leave the United Kingdom united. Strikingly, it gives the
Secretary of State powers to interfere with or override legislation he or she
judges outside Scottish competency, a feature widely derided as resembling
the powers of a colonial governor. Scottish legislation could not be given to
the monarch for royal assent without the Secretary of State's agreement. This
did at least provide an extra block to Scotland's behaving in a destabilizing
manner. The areas over which Scotland would act, whether in a destabilizing manner or not, are enumerated in appended schedules. The funding
system as well as these constrained powers mimicked the old Scottish Office.

The structure of the Act here reveals the extent to which Scottish
powers were limited (Craig 1979). The list of competencies provided takes
the form of a three-part section (Bradley and Christie 1979). The first part
lists competencies of the proposed Scottish Assembly. The second part lists
competencies of the British central state. The third part is in two columns.
One provides a list of specific UK legislation in devolved subject areas that
would be devolved to Scotland for modification, acceptance, or change as
Scotland would see fit; the entries in the facing column specify the parts of
the relevant legislation that would not be devolved. This is an inflexible
system (worse than one to which Catalonia is subject) that requires specific
authorization for a devolved government to act and thus structurally creates
an asymmetry, since the central state has more financial, legal, and tactical
room to maneuver.

An example of one title in the schedule of competencies demonstrates
how unwieldy the 1978 Act was. The Scottish Assembly would have control
over lotteries and public amusements according to the first list. The lottery
example is then qualified in the third list, which specifies that one of the

included acts is the Lotteries and Amusements Act 1976 (c.32), helpfully explaining that "The matters dealt with in Parts I and II are included, except for those dealt with in sections 5 (3) (d) (ii), 6 (2) (c), 9 and 12 (5) (a). The matters dealt with in section 18 (1) and (2) are not included." The same item in the schedule also shows the inflexibility of such a specific list. It grants the Scottish Assembly specific control over, among other items, "Deer and sale of venison" and "Control of Stray Dogs." There was near universal skepticism at the time regarding the ability of the Scottish or UK politicians, or their civil servants, to interpret their powers correctly (Bradley and Christie 1979:51). Then, the specific schedules include matters in which London would legislate but Scotland would administer (land use, environment, traffic), creating scope for dysfunctional relationships and leaving key powers in Westminster (Kellas 1979:157). The likely impact would have been to give central government considerable powers to interfere with Scottish legislation and to slow the Scottish government, especially through the powers of the Secretary of State. It is a law written to avoid scaring central or regional organizations by denying Scotland crucial controls over their autonomy and environment and day-to-day tactical and political flexibility, and backing up the system by giving the UK government extensive override powers. Kellas, in a commentary on the likely workings of the proposed Scottish assembly, noted that "it is . . . somewhat paradoxical, and ultimately unsatisfactory, to be emphasising the importance of the Scottish Office after devolution. But that will be the reality of the system devised" (Kellas 1979:160).

By contrast, the 1998 Act is intelligible and clean and the Scottish Parliament less constrained and more powerful ("It's one of the most readable laws I know, and I'm proud of that," said a Scottish Labour politician involved in its drafting, in 2003). It lists reserved powers of the UK state by topic (rather than legislation) and all other powers are transferred to Scotland (this is known as a "negative list"). Thus, Scotland has a competency for health because it is not mentioned, and the Act only reserves to the UK a small number of issues related to professional qualifications and bioethics (amazingly, and almost uniquely, this means there is no UK restriction on what substate units do with their welfare state—Scotland could abolish its health service; Simeon 2003; Greer forthcoming). This reflects the changed circumstances—after the centralizing experiences of the Conservative governments, Scottish regional organizations and elites' faith in the stabilizing and autonomy-enhancing values of central state links was much diminished. The SCC called for a negative list, and Labour's will to make legislation work was such that it adopted the conclusions of the SCC and an influential 1996 think-tank report making the case for a negative list (and the referendum) (Constitution Unit 1996; Morrison 2001:43–44). In 1998, Labour created a strong Scottish parliament that could insulate Scotland from England;

this meant they placed real value on having a workable and flexible act biased toward the autonomy of the Scottish parliament rather than toward restrictions on its destabilizing potential (instructively, the reverse happened in Wales's 1998 devolution legislation, and the National Assembly for Wales does find itself legally and tactically very constrained; Rawlings 1999, 2003; Patchett 2000).

## HEALTH

Scottish health care is and was organizationally distinct and regionally organized with strong regional organizations and few strong central organizations (Woods and Carter 2003). Like Scottish education, it has a long and proud history and a strong sense of Scottishness. Aberdeen is the home of the second-oldest teaching hospital in existence and for centuries Edinburgh and Glasgow have been among the great medical research and education centers of the world. From their inception, these Scottish teaching hospitals were distinct from their English equivalents, as linked to and influenced by developments in Europe as by developments in England. The separate Scottish Royal Colleges (further subdivided between Edinburgh and Glasgow) institutionally maintained the different culture of Scottish medicine even when they converged with English and international peers and despite their unwillingness to consider themselves "parochial" Scottish institutions. Local government and voluntary foundation hospitals, meanwhile, were Scottish as the local authorities and charities that sustained them and were generally led by local members of the interlocking complex of Scottish business, professions, and church. With the creation of the NHS in 1948, the entire health system was transferred to the Scottish Office, which became responsible for the administration, planning, and budgeting of a largely self-governing service. Even as the level of political involvement in the NHS increased from the 1960s, the structure remained Scottish—political involvement in England meant the Department of Health intervening in health services and in Scotland it meant the Scottish Office. Institutionally, Scottish teaching hospitals linked to Scottish universities (a much closer link than in England) supplied the vast majority of Scottish doctors while professional organizations—especially the three Royal Colleges—informed policy implementation. The combined weight of these groups could have real impact, such as helping impede Thatcherite policy changes. Scottish Office responsibility for health in turn meant that Scottish health organizations were well placed to participate in the insider politics of the health services—their command of information, implementation, and legitimacy in the public eye meant that the civil servants and politicians consulted them. It was a "reign of professional ideas" (Hazell and Jervis 1998:44).[2]

The outcome was health's inclusion as a devolved power in 1978 and 1998; to do otherwise would be to reverse existing Scottish administrative devolution. In both acts it was included as a largely unfettered competency of the Scottish devolved body. The full powers of the Scottish Office in health would be handed over, although in 1978 some careful provisions were made to keep the new assembly from clashing with professions. In both acts the finance, organization (and, extraordinarily, existence) of the health service was devolved to be funded out of the block grant, subject only to the exclusion of some ethical issues (leaving Westminster with the hot potato of abortion) and professional regulation (which effectively stayed with the professional organizations, where they wanted it). "We wanted the health service in order to do things to fit Scottish conditions. We didn't want to fill up the Parliament's schedule with abortion," explained a Scottish Labour minister in the 1997 government. The difference was in the strength of regional health organizations support for devolution with them included. After the perceived indignities of Thatcher's health reforms, their ongoing resistance to their implementation, and the envenomed atmosphere of health policy, the Scottish health sector increasingly saw devolution as safer and more likely to produce a health system that would work in accordance with their values.

The mechanisms linking the policy sector to the outcomes changed little across time. In the 1970s, the Scottish Office still gave Scottish medical elites a sympathetic administration that respected their autonomy and environmental stability by largely letting them run the system. Apart from the explicit lobbying of Royal Colleges to be allowed to continue professional regulation at a UK level, there was little enthusiasm for the 1978 devolution project. They were devolved; the question was whether the minister would be Scottish Office or Scottish Assembly. In the 1980s and 1990s, however, acceptance of devolution switched to support. The experience of Conservative health reforms had been disruptive and diminished their autonomy and environmental stability (as well as angering many of them); thus, there was broad-based support for differentiated Scottish health policy and a devolved parliament that could defend it. In many ways, these key decisions were made in 1948 when the formative NHS legislation put health under the Scottish Office, but the effect of the Thatcherite years was to convert many professionals from a belief in their own autonomy from any politics to support for political devolution. "They wrecked the health service. It's still in crisis . . . we can't let it happen again. We have to be able to make policy for ourselves," said a health services manager in 1998.

In conclusion, Scottish health care supports the argument that complexes of strong regional organizations explain devolution. Scottish health had never been anything other than devolved. As with education, it had been devolved to Scotland long before 1978 and the question of devolution was and would remain whether it would have insider politics and UK Cabinet policies or an elected assembly with freedom to maneuver. Interviewees spoke of professionals' skepticism about devolution in 1978, despite the fact that they were both already dealing with concentrated dependency on a government they could not control—the Scottish Office—and accustomed to being left alone by any government in many fields of health policy. "We just wanted to be able to modify policy to satisfy Scottish needs, which we couldn't do when we were ministers [in the UK government] and we didn't want any of those policies like fundholding . . . we want to be able to agree, not . . . have them do things to us," explained a leading Scottish Labour politician with a health portfolio in 2002. When after devolution I made the case to professionals and policy scholars in Scotland that devolution changed NHS Scotland, I would regularly be asked if devolution actually changed Scottish health policy at all. That is how distinct the world of Scottish health has always felt.

## EDUCATION

The organization of Scottish primary and secondary (pre-university) education has long been intellectually and organizationally distinct—and a point of pride for Scotland, which for much of the early modern era boasted higher literacy rates than the rest of Britain (Davie 1961; R. D. Anderson 1995; Humes and Bryce 1999; Paterson 2003; Raffe 2006). It had strong regional organization and had to contend with no central organizations. The Scottish education sector was woven into a web of Scottish regional resource dependencies since its earliest days (despite convergence with England over time under the pressure of policy advocates and the attractive English labor market). In 1840, the Scottish Schools Inspectorate was created, and there has been Westminster legislation on Scottish education since 1870, when the central government was first becoming involved in UK education (McPherson and Raab 1988:34–35). The Scottish service adhered to different standards and methods that reinforced the remaining distinctiveness of Scottish education. By the 1970s, its basic organizational structure combined Scottish Office funding with a mixture of local authority and Scottish Office control. The Scottish Office set standards, provided the bulk of funding, and inspected schools (S. Brown 1999; Gallacher 1999; Humes 1999) and the curricula and structure remained different (Bryce and Humes 1999; Darling 1999). There was a distinct Scottish policy community (see the sociological study of these insiders at work by McPherson and Raab 1988 and the critical Humes 1986). The regular interlocutors of the Scottish Office in educational policy were the Scottish teachers' unions, the Church of Scotland and other denominations, most of them Scottish-only, that operated state schools, academics from the Scottish universities (including special Institutes of Education, not mirrored in England, that were set up by the Scottish Office to supply Scottish teachers and educational policy expertise), local governments charged with school responsibilities, and consumers organizations that, given the institutional distinctiveness of the other actors, were set up on a devolved or Scotland-only basis. The curricula were not particularly different, but the workforce tended to be Scots educated in the Scottish universities, polytechnics, and Institutes of Education. Thus, the Scottish educational sector was a set of interlocking regional organizations that were resource-dependent on each other, with funds, standards, expertise, and workforce flowing in relatively closed circuits between them within Scotland. Shielded by Barnett and the Scottish Office as well as its policy community, it was not directly dependent on London for its key inputs. Funds, oversight, students, and policy all were at least mediated by, and usually came from, the Scottish Office (Humes 1999; Mackenzie 1999). The mismatch between the institutions of Scottish and English educational systems was such that even a small amount of policy spillover was irritating—effectively, the rules of UK legislation meant that Scotland was obliged to fix what was broken in England, when it was thought broken, and rarely got an opportunity to fix what was broken in Scotland (see also McPherson and Raab 1988:394). Much of education policy since devolution has, indeed, been about rolling back various "English" policies from the pre-devolution years (Greer and Jarman 2006).

The outcome was that the already devolved competency was in lists of devolved powers in 1978 and 1998. Education was already so far devolved as to be an obvious candidate for inclusion in the 1978 Act as a devolved power, and the sector contained many of the more nationalist or devolutionist Labour activists. Effectively, the extent of Scottish regional organizational power had been such that it had always been formally isolated from Whitehall in most senses and subject to autonomous Scottish administration (barring occasional reforms to fix English problems). What changed in the 1980s was the sector's sense that the Scottish Office was an adequate defender of stability and autonomy. "We felt it was attacking our traditions . . . we value education and community more here," argued a union leader; such rhetoric, including references to the Scottish image of upward mobility by education known by the stock character raised from penury by schooling (the "lad o'parts") infused the rhetoric of unions, especially the Educational Institute of Scotland, and schools leaders. "We had to go down to the St Andrew's house and argue, and argue, and argue, and—they're civil servants, they do what they are told by the government, even if they tried to listen," reminisced a regular consultant in July 1998.

By 1998, the experience of Conservative government in Scotland had led to considerable pro-devolution sentiment, with the teachers' union a major supporter. The Educational Institute of Scotland supplied many activists to support the referendum campaign; "They were among the best," a Labour minister involved in the campaign said in 2003. Educational policy insiders were positive, "I'm looking forward to fixing all the little things we never got around to doing," noted a civil servant when I asked what devolution would do in 1998; "policy in Scotland . . . can't get worse than it has been and that's why everybody wants devolution. Part time ministers you never see . . . and they don't do things that need doing . . . and there is something to what they say about having a different culture up here. The style of the ministers was wrong," said an academic in 1998 who regularly worked with educational policymakers in the Scottish Education Department.

The case of education therefore supports the argument that interlocked regional organizations explain devolution. The pressure put on by organizations of the distinct Scottish educational system had guaranteed a high degree of autonomy. The devolution of educational policy meant its democratization rather than a change in the resource flows. Its Scottish autonomy was of long standing, and the Scottishness of this competency predated not only devolution but even the Scottish Office. By 1978, it was clearly a Scottish devolved competency since that was how the key actors had long preferred it; for education, devolution would be about changing the governance and freedom of action of a Scottish devolved policy rather than creating a new Scottish competency.

*Universities*

The university sector in Scotland is substantially regional but historically funded by the central state in a manner that respected its autonomy. It was unlike education and health in that it had a privileged financial relationship with the center that left the sector throughout the UK as almost self-governing until the 1980s. Universities of the UK, with their tradition of autonomy, formal distinction from the state (they are regarded as independent institutions in receipt of public funds), and royal charters were left alone to pursue their professional activities (Keating 2005). They have a different organizational form and degree structure from English universities (including a four-year, instead of a three-year, degree), predominantly Scottish students, and strong, very old institutions entrenched in their localities (the "ancient universities" of Aberdeen, Edinburgh, Glasgow, and St. Andrew's). Their graduates dominated other Scottish regional institutions, including education, health, and the clergy, clustered in the Scottish Office civil service, and made up the bulk of Scots with higher education. More vocational institutions were closely tied to the Scottish economy through their integration with specific labor markets (such as the Instiutes of Education with the

Scottish educational sector). The universities differed from the health and education sectors in their self-government, which was unmediated even by the Scottish Office. Scottish professors and professors in Scotland, unlike Scottish teachers or doctors, tended to cross borders. Thus, the institutions of Scottish education, above all the ancient universities, had meshed their Scottish and UK-wide aspects in a system that gave them great self-government and a structure of UK financing that effectively funded the universities throughout the UK with little oversight. Simon Jenkins, trying to explain this solicitude for universities and the Arts Council, concludes that the interest "was probably cultural. Universities and the arts were subjects in which Treasury officials had a personal interest. . . . They were thus happy to keep them close, favoured jesters at the court of public finance" (Jenkins 1995:137).

Higher education outcomes unsurprisingly varied between 1978 and 1998. In 1978, the universities had themselves written out of the Scotland Act. Their financing provided them with more autonomy and stability than either formal Scottish Office control (such as experienced by health and education) or a Scottish assembly. The structure of higher education funding was largely run by the universities themselves, and in the case of Scottish institutions this gave them liberty to combine their strong dependence on Scotland (for students, political involvement, and political support) with finance that came according to their professional priorities and gave them professional and financial autonomy from government. University administrators saw no need to decrease their autonomy by subjecting it to Scottish political control. This changed dramatically in the late 1980s. As in health, the Conservative government reshaped the university sector without consultation. The process started early, with swinging funding cuts. First, it cut back the grant to the University Grants Committee (UGC), which hastily tried to restructure grants to universities to reflect academic output; between the new criteria and the funding cuts, the immediate effect could be year-to-year budget cuts of as much as 30%. By 1981, Aberdeen, among other great UK universities, was almost bankrupt and had to be rescued. Meanwhile, government plunged deeper into university management and priorities, pressuring the independent UGC to extract more of what it wanted from universities. As Jenkins comments, "if government cuts your income each year without cutting its expectations, you not only run out of money, you run out of autonomy" (Jenkins 1995:147).

Visibly hostile to universities (beds of anti-Thatcherite sentiment), the government then in 1988 set out to enact more comprehensive reform. It switched funding responsibility to spending departments (of Education, an otherwise English department) and abolished the UGC, which had been autonomous and composed of academics. The new funding body, the Universities Funding Council (UFC), was directly under political control and set out to combine rewards for student numbers with rewards for research, as evaluated statistically (to gauge research instead of simply funding by student numbers, a large panel evaluates all the output from each department and rates it with a star system that then governs much of the grant). Its goals were ostentatiously late-Thatcherite, focusing on research of use to business. The result was a system many academics found insulting and, as with most such attempts to change professionals' incentives, proved easy to manipulate (spawning an amazing number of journals in order to supply the number of peer-reviewed articles needed to get good research ratings; this explains both the dearth of large new research monographs in Britain and the startling rise of many departments in the 1990s to a top five-star ranking). Pathologies multiplied; the reformed student finance system punished universities for admitting UK citizens and rewarded them for taking international students and running graduate degrees. This had predictable effects on top schools, which tried to avoid undergraduate courses and new degrees in such topics as British Politics that were unlikely to attract coveted non-EU students. Meanwhile, capital spending dropped along with salaries and spending per student.

Adding insult to injury, the 1988 bill abolished the distinctions between classes of institution, making them all universities (polytechnics, with four-year applied degrees, had been the property of local government; this hardly improved their standing). This pitched the old polytechnics into often hopeless competition with old universities for status and research funds. Finishing the job, the legislation abolished academic tenure. This was predictably unpopular.

By 1998, however, universities were worse off (in autonomy and stability) than they had been in 1978. Once the changes had unified polytechnics and universities, it was logical in the Scottish case to create a single higher education funding agency that could deal with the distinctive shape of its system. So, trying to win autonomist credit for this rather practical decision (Keating 2005), Secretary of State Michael Forsyth created a Scottish Higher Education Funding Council (SHEFC). This meant that higher education was now regionally funded and controlled; the problem was that further such efforts to win over Scottish organizations were denuded of credibility by the Conservatives' policymaking in other areas such as health, local government, and education. Vague efforts to make it more visibly professional and autonomous failed because the government had no credibility with professionals and had (predictably) still stacked control of the SHEFC in its own favor, the better to apply universities to its economic development strategies (Mackie 1999). The result, though, was that by 1998 Scottish higher education was in much the same situation as health or education—theoretically administratively devolved with flexibility, in practice skeptical of the willingness of the central state to recognize their claims and provide autonomy and stability.

The universities, at least in higher education policy, could respond in two ways. They could lobby directly through groups such as the Association of Vice-Chancellors Scottish subgrouping—that meant both lobbying the (Whitehall) spending department to which Scottish universities were now attached, and supporting moves such as the creation of the Scottish Higher Education Funding Council. "The problem is that we think Scottish universities are often as good and as important as Oxbridge, but the English think they are second-tier like Durham or Nottingham, or worse so we get squeezed like they do between the former [polytechnics] and Oxbridge . . . the [department of education] is just parochial like that and they think we're the provinces," said a Scottish university administrator in 1998, explaining his colleagues' support for even limited devolution of higher education funding. Second, university faculty and student leaders directly felt the impact of the educational reforms and other Conservative policies; even if an individual faculty member was unable to influence public opinion much, the Scottish universities contained many faculty members, many of whom were irritated. The result is that they both aided the construction of a devolutionist climate of opinion; this helped change Labour's incentives, and the activism gained many foot soldiers for the final referendum campaign. In this way, Thatcherite higher education policies turned the universities on multiple levels to support devolution. "The hostility to English politics is palpable," commented a largely apolitical Scottish academic in 1998.

Therefore, the experience of higher education is particularly strong support for the thesis that the timing of central state clashes with Scottish organizations explains their swing. Scottish health and education had (over a century) been under the Scottish Office and thus, in 1978, would be devolved. In 1998, they positively wanted it. Scottish universities had initially done better, with almost no political control in 1978, but the rude shock of centralization both led them to seek firmer support for their autonomy and to act as Scottish organizations.

*Law*

Law was another famous old Scottish regional institution, with strongly interconnected and regionally resource-dependent organizations and little resource dependency on the center (Meston, Sellar, and Lord Cooper 1991; R. M. White and Willock 1993). It had developed separately from English common law, and Scotland's long-standing links with France and the Low Countries had given it a strong dose of civil law thinking by the time of the Treaty of Union. The result was that Scottish legal reasoning and forms were significantly different from the common law and required translation. After 1707, the governments generally left Scottish law alone. The substance of

legislation converged, but the procedure in Scotland remained very different—and from a legal point of view, procedure *is* the law. Scottish law
maintained its own internal hierarchy of courts and final appeals were generally to a court in Edinburgh (in the rest of the UK, they were to the House
of Lords). Scottish lawyers largely regulated themselves and preserved their
different rules of procedure and legal reasoning even as the substance and
functional activity of Scottish law converged with England. The result was
a clear regional organization linked by resource dependencies within Scotland. Scottish lawyers manned Scottish courts, Scottish universities taught
Scots law, Scottish legal publishers printed the output, Scottish courts service
officials carried out procedure largely laid down by Scottish judges, and
none of them could work outside Scotland. Their skill sets diminished in use
to the extent that they got outside the Scottish legal system or when its
procedure converged with English law. Furthermore, Scottish lawyers occupied a key social position in the networks of Scottish elites—they tended to
be the charity board members, business advisors, and social figures tying
different Scottish elites together. In short, Scottish law was regional, highly
autonomous, and the keystone of many other Scottish regional organizational connections.

The outcome was that law was largely devolved in both 1978 and
1998; it was hardly closely linked to the rest of the UK. A Scottish lawyer,
the Lord Advocate, was in government alongside the Secretary of State for
Scotland to represent Scottish law. The interesting differences, however, lie
in the extent to which the 1978 Act constrains the ability of the proposed
Scottish Assembly to structure the legal system. The Assembly would not be
able to restructure key courts, legislate with respect to judicial appointments
and service, and would be constrained in its ability to make changes to
jurisdiction and procedure (Bradley and Christie 1979 c.51/ s.10, analysis of
group 21). In other words, the devolution of legal powers in 1978 excluded
the ability to change the structure of Scottish legal institutions.

The difference lay in the extent of legal enthusiasm rather than the
degree of devolution. The basic structure of the Scottish legal system is
written into the Scotland Act; this fixes the Scottish legal system and its
procedural autonomy in high-profile constitutional legislation rather than
turning it over to the Scottish parliament. Only the remuneration of judges
remains as a UK power. This preserves the autonomy of law better even than
devolution enhances the autonomy of health or education, for it entrenches
the legal system's autonomy, limits the say of the Scottish Parliament, and
also limits the influence of Westminster.

The process leading to devolution was, like universities, centered in
the organizations' response to the central government's dimunition of their
stability and autonomy. Like the universities, the Scottish lawyers in the

1970s had a highly stable and autonomous position before devolution legislation. As with their academic colleagues, they were directly dependent for their legal position on London and not even the Scottish Office, and London had left them to their own devices. Devolution offered direct political control rather than UK oversight practiced in the breach and thus 1978 excluded the powers necessary to significantly restructure the Scottish legal profession and system. They lobbied to retain this position, arguing on grounds of professional self-administration. By 1998, however, they had found that a determined UK government might defer to neither professions nor Scotland. As Scottish regional elites, they lobbied for inclusion in the devolution bill and the Law Society participated in the work of the Scottish Constitutional Convention (although the basic structure of Scottish courts remains undevolved and is now enshrined in the Scotland Act of 1998) (Scottish Constitutional Convention 1995).

Scottish law was to be devolved in 1978 in name, since the aspects of most interest to Scottish lawyers (their professional structure) remained largely isolated. Scottish law had its autonomy and stability challenged by the Conservative governments, and in 1997 Scottish lawyers were sufficiently irritated to not only support formal devolution and their inclusion, but even to send a representative to the Scottish Constitutional Convention in support of devolution. "It's the right distance from London now," concluded a Scottish lawyer in 2001. It is also a long way from the Scottish parliament.

## INDUSTRIAL/LABOR POLICY

Industrial and labor policy are instructive negative outcomes. The key aspects of industrial and labor policy are outside Scotland's grasp. Scotland effectively has powers to run development agencies, but has no say in health, safety, hiring, or other workplace regulation; in taxes relevant to business; in financial regulation; in corporation law and regulation; in key economic sectors regulated by the state such as energy and transportation. It simply does not have the levers of control governments use to regulate the economy. "Our policy isn't very intelligent," noted a remarkably blunt civil servant in 1998; "we talk about [consultant] Michael Porter stuff, clusters and synergy, but really we just pay foreign companies to employ Scots." Scotland no longer has regionally dependent businesses that would benefit from Scottish political control and fight for it; it scarcely had a regionally dependent union movement. Regionalization (let alone independence) offers to most businesses destabilization they do not want in return for regional autonomy they do not need.

Scotland does have distinctive economic groups, although many fewer economic regional elites than in the nineteenth and early twentieth centuries (witness the change in Scott and Hughes 1980). There is a substantial Edinburgh financial sector that is one of the largest in Europe, individual Scottish businesses of note (poetically, many of them based on deregulation and privatization, such as the transport company Stagecoach and the utility Scottish Power), and a complex of small and medium-sized businesses, mostly in service sectors. It also has many foreign-owned information technology plants, although these have not had the desired spinoff effects in Scottish-owned businesses. They can use the Scottish lobbying network as well as others, but only for limited purposes—above all ad hoc government intervention in their favor, while their worries about economic decline under Thatcher took the form of reluctance to support her rather than active opposition (Harvie and Jones 2000:130–132). Multiplying the divergent jurisdictions under which they trade would decrease their environmental stability, while the prospect of a Scotland split between the Labour Party and the unstable, leftward-trending SNP could be seen as a problem for their competitive position. "What, you think we wanted to live under a big Labour local authority? . . . like the idea from the '70s," exclaimed a representative of a business group in 2001. The exception, and the only pro-devolution groups, were among small businesses; for them, Westminster was hard to lobby and unconcerned, and as a result destabilized their environments. Subject to a political forum in which they could not easily participate, Scottish small business could see the virtues of a closer political forum that would allow them more say and thus more stability and autonomy (see P. Lynch 1998:96).

Meanwhile, trade union organization mimicked their negotiating partners; the UK-wide Trades Union Congress, not the STUC, was unquestionably the senior partner (Wood 1989). The unions most involved in the STUC's devolutionary work were the public sector unions whose employees directly suffered from Conservative policy. Even those unions, such as the large merged public service union UNISON, did not want separate negotiations and pay deals built into the devolved health, education, and local government sectors (given that most of Scotland has wages and a cost of living lower than the UK average, the salaries in UK-wide pay deals are quite high relative to local standards). As noted in the discussion of the devolution debates, the interest of the STUC in devolution stemmed not from its component member unions' interest in winning better pay deals, but in its conviction that the policy outcomes under devolution would be superior for its workers and values. This did not mean that it supported breaking up its UK-wide pay deals and negotiations. The STUC is made up of UK unions that supported the sorts of public policies one might expect from Scotland, but that do not support their own breakup into regional shards.

The outcome was that neither the 1978 nor the 1998 devolution acts contained meaningful provisions giving the new Scottish assembly or parliament control over the economy, and Labour was careful to point this out in 1997–1998 meetings with business. Otherwise, the long schedule of economic and financial reserved powers in the 1998 act testifies to Labour's strategy of not devolving economic powers that would incur business opposition.

By 1998, when there was an overwhelming regional coalition in favor of devolution, the political leaders of the devolutionist parties and the Scottish Constitutional Convention were going out of their way to prevent business opposition, even though polls suggested business still supported the constitutional status quo (and Think Twice, the No–No campaign, raised almost as much as Scotland Forward, much of that thought to be from a few Scottish businessmen) (P. Lynch 1998; Denver et al. 2000:59). Some of the most tightly regionally focused businesses (i.e., the small ones) participated in the SCC through the Federation of Self-Employed and Small Businesses in Scotland while other groups took observer status. In other words, businesses tightly linked into Scotland were interested, while the others at a minimum were interested in preventing devolution from being too destabilizing. Thus, business's low profile came about because they "had largely been neutralised before the campaign got going. The CBI (Scotland) had concluded after the general election that devolution would happen anyway, and that there was little to be gained, and potentially much to be lost, by attacking a popular policy deriving from a government with a huge electoral mandate" (Denver et al. 2000:68–69). "Bruce did have a rough ride . . . it was hard to speak out," said a financial business organization leader in 2001. Thus, the CBI(S) remained quiet and criticism from business, above all the governor's intervention, focused on almost the only part of it that could hurt firms with Scottish markets or those who worked for Scottish firms—namely, the tax-raising power (also P. Lynch 1998 and Harvie and Jones 2000:182). "Why should they have fought? They're perfectly happy as long as their taxes don't go up. All the laws that matter to them are the same," said a long-time Scottish journalist in 2003; I asked what explained the difference from 1979, when the proposed assembly had even fewer relevant powers, and he replied that "in 1979 they thought they could stop it."

In conclusion, this is consistent with the proposition that strong regionally dependent organizations explain devolution of a given policy sector through their political activity. Business in Scotland is fundamentally centrally dependent as it competes across the UK, often in highly government-dependent areas such as finance and transport, and must compete in the UK. This means it lobbied against inclusion of economic powers devolution because that would add a new source of instability as well as comparative disadvantage and higher taxes on businesses and their elites. It is an interesting question whether such old Scottish regional elites such as the West of Scotland industrialists would have found reason to support devolution (if nothing else to prop them up), but the key Scottish businesses by 1978 and 1998 were dependent on the central state and averse to either multiple jurisdictions or to Scotland's likely left-wing policies. So Scotland is free largely to subsidize business investment from its overall block grant.

## CONCLUSION

Perhaps the final evidence of the relationship between devolution and Scotland's distinct policy communities and institutions will come in the form of its post-devolution policy trajectories (Greer 2004; Schmuecker and Adams 2006; Keating and McEwen 2005; Greer and Jarman 2006; *Publius* 2006). In multiple policy fields the pattern is clear: Scottish policy divergence since devolution turns out to have been prefigured by Scottish implementation divergence before devolution. The same regional networks that altered the implementation of UK policy in Scotland, and resented the policies of the UK government between 1979 and 1997, came to dominate policy debate after devolution. This meant, for example, rolling back the internal market in health care—which Scotland had never implemented well. It meant reducing the reliance on testing, differentiation, and parent choice in Scotland—all policies that were poorly implemented in Scotland. It meant trying to develop better relations with local government—a far cry from the Conservatives' struggles. In other words, there were preexisting Scottish regional organizations and policy communities with policy preferences ready to spring into action once Scottish policymaking was loosed from UK politics.

Both devolution acts basically replace the Secretary of State for Scotland's functions as head of the Scottish Office with a form of democratic oversight—the Scottish assembly would have been, and the Scottish parliament is, a novel form of democratic oversight for a Whitehall department. The difference in the acts reflects the enthusiasm of their political drafters and the extent of devolution established in Scotland as a response to regional organizations. The 1978 act is inflexible and limiting; the 1998 is flexible and intelligible. In 1978, some such regional organizations, enjoying informal autonomy under the administrative devolution of the consultative, quasicorporatist Scottish Office, resisted inclusion in devolution. Strong regional organizations with little oversight, such as universities, resisted inclusion because a Scottish assembly offered them environmental destabilization and a possible loss of autonomy relative to their position. Regional organizations in education and health, already practically run from Edinburgh, were included, but were almost the only significant powers. By 1998, the experience of centralizing, destabilizing Conservative governments had swung the ones that had stayed out and the structure of the legislation changed. It now included them with few strings attached (Greer forthcoming). The autonomous Scottish government would insulate them from the central state, taking on the costs of dealing with the central state and leaving regional organizations free or freer to dominate their newly fortified Scottish policy communities.

# Chapter Eight

# Constructing Catalonia

## Policy Sectors and the Politics of Competencies

The Generalitat in 1980 had to hew its every employee, building, competency and bureaucratic branch office out of a centralized Jacobin state that had just spent four decades trying to remove any trace of Catalan distinctiveness. By 2000, it was hard to find visible traces of the Spanish state on the streets of Barcelona; despite the importance of the Spanish central state in issues such as taxation and social security, the aspects of government that put civil servants on the street were overwhelmingly now Catalan. How did CiU do it? It did it with extensive facilitation from regional organizations because it supplied the stable autonomy they sought. This fits in with the broad argument that the dense, strong regional organizations of Scotland and Catalonia explain their autonomy because of their own strength and major regional parties' dependence on them.

The more detailed answer lies in the network of alliances between regional elites and the Generalitat that the CiU built up over the years. The currency was policymaking. These alliances involved the exchange of policy for support, creating links with regional elites by subcontracting policy to them and giving them both their own organizations' autonomy and often their policy reform ideas. This took advantage of the fact that in Spain the regional governments were created before their administrations. The Generalitat had the opportunity to demonstrate its nationalist credentials by winning new powers year after year, and forge its elite alliances by giving the existing regional elites control over its new policy agendas. They then concluded that CiU was the vehicle best suited to provide them with the (regional) autonomy and stability that they sought.

The formula, analyzed further in this section, can be stated crudely: CiU's Generalitat won control over policy areas from the central state and to some extent from local government. Its approach was to create policy networks centered on itself, populated by the elites of that sector, and then effectively subcontract policy in that area to the elites. This gave elites considerable autonomy and tied them to the Generalitat and the political party within it. The CiU-elite coalition itself was reinforced by its control over appointments, allowing it to place a substantial number of members and sympathizers in the Generalitat's apparatus. The party could also win the support of nationalist militants and elites. The nationalist support came from the constant transfers of power to Catalonia, the controversies over them, and periodic conflicts between the Generalitat and others that were articulated by CiU as conflicts between Catalonia and others. Center-right voters and opportunistic elites were both built into the coalition by CiU's deliberate self-positioning as a liberal party with a pro-business, pro-competition consensus agenda that contrasted with the agenda of the Spanish and Catalan left (and at times right). The policy result was that the Generalitat used the powers it had to administer resources in policies that were a combination of its own nation-building agenda and the preferences and ideas of the regional elites with whom it formed alliances; if there was a preexisting elite, they dominated policy formation.

The policies in Table 8.1 show the relationship between the presence of regional organizations and the Generalitat's competencies. The variance—in police, research, universities, and industrial policy—suggests that the density of regional organizations, rather than other factors, explains the competencies of the Generalitat. The logic is that the presence of regional organizations created a demand for autonomous, predictable policy, and CiU could win their support by trying to fulfill that demand.

Table 8.1   Regional Organizations and Competencies

| Policy Area | Prevailing Organizational Structure, 1980 | Outcome (Primary Responsible Government), 2000 |
|---|---|---|
| Health | Regional | Generalitat |
| Universities | Regional | Generalitat |
| Law | Central | Central state |
| Education (pre-university) | Regional | Generalitat |
| Language policy | Regional | Generalitat |
| Industrial policy | Opportunistic/central (varies by sector) | Central state |

## HEALTH

The resource dependencies of the Catalan health system have been pronouncedly regional since its inception, and it was one of the first powers regionalized. The Catalan health system had an unusual form: due to Catalonia's precocious (for Spain) industrial development, it already had an extensive infrastructure of municipal, university, private, and mutual hospitals when the Francoist state began to construct its network of state hospitals as part of its social welfare programs. The state in Catalonia thus built fewer of its own hospitals and maintained capacity by contracting with existing hospitals. This meant that there was already a network of interlinked Catalan institutions—hospitals, professional colleges, municipal health organizations, mutual assistance funds, and university education—that existed autonomously of Madrid. The health system was written into the Constitution and the Statute as one of the powers available to the most advanced autonomous communities, and Catalonia rapidly took advantage of it (Gallego 1998). "We knew we could have a great impact in health, we knew we had people who wanted to do things," explained a PSUC leader of the provisional Generalitat; a CiU health advisor from the 1980s echoed him: "they wanted us to take over . . . [people in the health sector] wanted to do things better and we wanted to show that we could." In 1983, the health responsibilities of the former social security system were transferred to Catalonia, bringing the state organization that ran several very large hospitals, the entire primary care system, and some ancillary services as well as the budget that had previously been used to contract for private services. "We were fishing with a basket . . . walking along grabbing everything we could get," explained a former high-level civil servant of the Generalitat in 2001.

Winning control of these competencies was relatively easy in principle, as the government did not resist significant transfers of infrastructure or legal responsibilities and the base law governing health came relatively late. When it finally came, it bowed to the strides made by several autonomous communities including Catalonia and the center of gravity of the health system at the level of the autonomous communities, allowing them the option of joining a larger state-run system (most did join). Catalonia simply opted out and constructed its own system within the obligation to provide care universally and for free. Most legal conflicts centered on the allocation of public health responsibilities and professional competence, which led to most professional matters being adjudicated by the Spain-level organizations (Abbad et al. 1992).

Catalan health policy had two goals: to upgrade the quality of the system by following the policy ideas of the pre-transition debates about health policy, and to do it by pacting the changes and policies with existing elites— that is, hospital owners. The quality agenda meant that Catalonia pioneered (in Spain) the accreditation of hospitals, designating some as full hospitals and downgrading the rest into well-funded care homes. Meanwhile, the system's evolving shape came through debates with existing regional health organizations rather than the more assertive policy the PSOE would pursue in Spain (Guillén and Cabiedes 1998; Gallego 2001). Health policy evolved through discussions with existing hospital owners, leading to a progressive rationalization of contracts and subsidies to improve quality.

At the same time, both thanks to the interests of its rural constituents and the intellectual influence of (and deficiencies revealed by) the Health Map, the Generalitat began to construct a network of "county hospitals," basic facilities with maternity and emergency facilities in historically underserved rural Catalonia. With one exception, this took the form of modernizing and subsidizing existing facilities, binding them more tightly to the state through contracts while building them up—thereby winning local support and giving the Generalitat a new cohort of allies in both the health system and on the ground. CiU wins much of its support and has most of its municipal governments in the rural areas the hospitals served, so the result was positive for the party. "The people notice it, and they understand that we did it, and the doctors appreciate it. There is nobody who wants to always go to Barcelona," said a provincial Unió politician of the new hospitals. Poor quality hospitals were converted to palliative care.

Primary care was an even more pronounced case of pacting the design of the system with existing professional groups. The system was known to be inefficient; it placed excessive demands on the hospital system since it depended on doctors working very short hours in state-run facilities and then making most of their income in private practice. As a result, doctors, through the College of Physicians of Barcelona, resisted any efforts to lengthen hours, for that would reduce their private incomes ("We are very proud of the role we played in the transition, but this country now is a democracy and we must represent doctors," explained a college representative, telling me about the insurance services, supplies purchasing service, and restaurant the college operated in 2001 as well as its lobbying to stop changes in medical hours). Because many patients did not have the money or inclination to buy private services, they wound up either getting inadequate treatment with too much pharmaceutical prescribing in the state-run facilities, or going to hospital emergency rooms for problems that a family doctor could treat. Nevertheless, longer hours for family doctors is a goal that the Generalitat had pursued mainly in the breach, in large part thanks to the influence of the private–sector-dominated medical colleges. "So now primary care is better for the poor because the doctors and the medical services here—everywhere—are concentrated where the rich and middle classes live, so there is less resistance from the medical profession to improving primary care in poorer areas," explained a medical academic and consultant to the Generalitat.

The system was finally formalized in a 1989 law that spun off the Generalitat-owned hospitals and the whole primary care system into a huge organization called the Catalan Health Institute (ICS). This move allowed the state's new purchasing body (the Catalan Health Service, SCS) to buy health care from the ICS or from any other provider. Like its equivalents in other systems such as Britain, this was expected to improve quality and cut costs. Like its equivalents in other systems, the links between the purchasers and providers meant that the system instead began to create yet more dependence of nonstate hospitals on the Generalitat, creating a class of clients strengthened by the Generalitat's efforts to solve its primary care problems by handing primary care over to private and nonprofit hospital companies (Equip ESTUDIS 1997). I asked an ICS official what guided the handovers; the initial response was "it's random, completely random," later modified to "they hand them out where there is a big hospital that wants them" and qualified by an offer to send along some statistical evidence that ICS services were just as good.

Hospitals that began to fail increasingly appealed to the Generalitat, which would become a partner in return for a minority on the board. Most interviewees interpreted such a development as an unqualified victory for the hospitals. They had now diversified their funding beyond SCS purchasing and secured their futures (see Gallego 1998). The only major attempt to interfere with the structure of the system was an effort to take municipal hospitals out of the direct control of Socialist-dominated town halls, one that eventually led to a solution in which the town halls usually created foundations to run their hospitals, with Generalitat and municipal subvention and divided overall control ("we couldn't afford them anyway," explained a Barcelona Socialist politician).

Catalonia won control of health services relatively easily. The theme of health policy has been to partner with the existing forces in the system: after twenty years of health policy, much of it innovative (such as the internal market and the accreditation procedures), the striking result is the extent to which the players in 1980 were the players in 2000 (the same people who designed the system mostly still ran it). Policy has scarcely changed the ability of partners to bargain with each other, leaving finance in the hands of the state and provision and control of provision in the hands of the professions, with unions and hospital owners built in with autonomy over their own administration and participation in panels and groups solving problems.

The counterfactual is clear in the rest of Spain, where a Catalan minister in the PSOE government, Ernest Lluch, introduced a state-run system funded by direct taxation modeled on the United Kingdom's NHS—including the effective nationalization of hospitals and primary care (Rico et al. 2001). This was a common idea in pre-transition medical politics in Catalonia (Gol i Gurina et al. 1978). The result in Spain was a decade of violent polemics between the PSOE and the professional organizations in the rest of Spain (de Miguel in Pérez Yruela and Giner 1988; Rodríguez and de Miguel 1990). The Generalitat, focused on building alliances with its regional elites and largely impressed by the outcomes of leaving Catalan health elites to themselves, instead opted for collaboration with them. This cemented a class of donors and supporters linked to the Generalitat, Convergència, and (through the municipal foundations) the Socialists. Meanwhile, the novel Catalan model of health care became a point of pride for CiU. In Catalonia, "It's all pacted. We pacted it all," said an interviewee, head of a Catalan medical union, in a 2001 interview.[1] Unusually for a trades union leader, he had an oil painting of Jordi Pujol on his wall, a painted version of the photo that was in the office of the head of the ICS and the head of the Generalitat's health policy think tank.

## PRIMARY AND SECONDARY EDUCATION

Education in Catalonia, like health, has long been distinctive and regional and was another power quickly devolved. The link between the autonomous communities and the mass tiers of education was important—the educational system is very high profile; it is costly, exceeded only by health; it socializes the youth; and most important for immediate post-transition Catalan politics, it teaches languages. "We needed education. We needed it," said a member of the provisional Generalitat; others concurred in interviews. Thus, the educational system was the first policy sector to feel the effects of Catalan autonomy when the provisional Generalitat decreed that education would be bilingual, with extensive Catalan immersion as well as Castilian as a taught and sometimes teaching language. Transfer of responsibility for pre-university education came in 1981, among the first competencies. The sector the Generalitat had to take over was both complicated and regional. As with health, the Catalan educational sector had grown up precociously and based on the needs and resources of the better-off in Catalan society, and thus strongly represented independent and Catholic schools. Partially counteracting this middle- and upper-class educational focus, the City of Barcelona developed a network of public schools that was small by global standards but advanced by Spanish ones. Given that elite private schools and church schools both are nodes of elite socialization and communication, and dependent on fees, the top of the school system became structurally linked into the business and professional elites of Catalonia—their children attended and they sat on the boards. The middle range of schools tended to be Catholic and middle class and thus both dependent on the Catalan professional, white-collar and small-business sectors and on the church.

Catalan education came with many of the same legal features as health (Bonal and Rambla 2001). There were extensive disputes over competencies, because the Constitution again used a formula in which the autonomous communities were responsible for education but state organic laws set the basic conditions of education. Educators transferred from the state were state functionaries with all the accompanying rights. As a result, the state claimed rights to structure the system of education, its quality control measures, and personnel policies (and, under pressure from the civil servants' lobbies in Madrid, fought to maintain equality of pay, conditions, and staffing across the different educational services). The result was a decade of legal conflict during which the basic outlines of the policy were established: the Generalitat would have extensive administrative autonomy, especially over contracts with the public sector and the curriculum in the schools, and restricted powers over staff policy (Boix i Navarro and García Suárez 1985).

With its policies, the Generalitat pacted a two-tier system of educational provision. It is composed of a large contracted sector of primarily religious state schools, which overwhelmingly serve the Catalan middle classes, and a large (much-expanded since democratization) sector of state schools under the direct control of the Generalitat and local school councils (in Barcelona, the city government acts as an intermediate layer of administration). The organization of education is extremely complex, and the interest groups and forms of relationship with the Generalitat very fragmented. What the system does afford is autonomy to the various actors within the system: the various private schools; the professional and trades union organizations of teachers; and the public school administrators, as organized through their various representative organizations (Boix i Navarro 1992; Bonal and Rambla 2001). The Generalitat intervenes primarily through the basic curriculum and the central state primarily through its control over pay of the public school faculty. This design evolved through close consultations between the Generalitat and the sector's elites and seems to basically satisfy all players (Bonal and Rambla 2001). As with health care, this means that the regional elites are both autonomous in their own institutions. The Church is left alone to govern its schools. The resulting organization, like health care, is distinctively Catalan. It is unique primarily in its linguistic policies (which please nationalists) and in the degree of autonomy given to its elites in running the institutions, both in contracting with independent schools that in other parts of Spain were nationalized or edged out, in its better relations with the church than those of the PSOE, and in effectively subcontracting public education to the professional organizations within it (Bonal 1998).

## UNIVERSITIES

Much of the activity of universities is at least theoretically global, but as institutions they are strongly tied to their physical locations. In Spain, students' localism can be extreme; in Barcelona, administrators' folk wisdom is that students select their university by ease of transport links—if they live near the metro, they choose the University of Barcelona; if they live near the train, they choose the Autonomous University of Barcelona. In Catalonia, the grandee tradition of Southern European academia and the universities' key role in the clandestine resistance further increased the importance of universities as nodal points in the connections and careers of political and social elites. Thus, the Cercle d'Economia, the avowedly catalanist business and intellectual organization, was founded by the historian Jaume Vicens i Vives and is still run out of faculty offices at the University of Barcelona (UB). UB faculty in politics in 2001 included the nationalist econometrician Joan Hortalà, who was once ERC's one cabinet minister under CiU and campaigned for Mayor of Barcelona from the back of an elephant before running the stock market; the political scientist, Rafael Ribó, important in the PSUC and later to lead its successor party IC-V, three members of the PSC council (in political science, public finance, and economics); Jordi Solé Tura, who was the PCE/PSUC representative on the panel that drafted the constitution, and his main advisors as well as two main PSOE advisors to the constitutional drafters, including Eliseo Aja. The Universitat Autònoma de Barcelona (UAB) was almost as well connected; a substantial group of its faculty members was elected to the Catalan parliament on the Citizens for Change (CPC) list with former Barcelona Mayor Pascual Maragall in 2000; one of its most visible research institutes is the Institute d'Estudis Politics i Socials, co-financed wth the left-dominated province (*Diputació*) of Barcelona and run by Socialist intellectual Isidre Molas, who was also a senator for the PSC. The result was that the universities focused both political activity and connections into the rest of Catalan elites, giving them a strong regionalist focus as institutions.

The Constitution made responsibility for university education particularly confusing, as it guaranteed their autonomy, placed them under the autonomous communities, and then gave the central government authority to harmonize their structures and the conditions of staff and qualifications. Policy was thus set by a state organic law (substantially changed in 2001 to diminish the universities' own autonomy and internal democracy). This law gave most of the power to set conditions and standards to the central state while ceding broad power over budgetary allocations between universities and priorities in the system to the autonomous communities. The state determines the pay and conditions of the faculty, and state-run organizations form the hiring committees with fixed quotas for examiners from the university in question and from outside it. Universities' autonomy is mostly confined to establishing or running down departments, and in their decisions about physical and academic infrastructure. Informally, the universities have extensive control over their own hiring as they can dominate the committees that select the new hires. This means that universities with a political agenda can do much to create coherent profiles.

The Generalitat thus inherited the excellent, influential, overcrowded, leftist, and expensive UB and UAB—two of the handful of Spanish universities that have achieved an international profile. Its response was to focus its efforts on creating new universities. The flagship was the Universitat Pompeu Fabra (UPF), with an explicit remit to be Catalan-speaking and excellent. It was in many ways the personal creation of Enric Argullol, who was also a high-ranking legal advisor to CiU involved in seeking ways to win new competencies. Pursing the agenda of evening out Catalonia's territorial structure by building infrastructure in the (Convergència-voting) rural areas and secondary cities, it created three new universities built out of what were formerly field stations of the UAB and UB. These universities (Universitat de Lleida, Universitat de Girona, and Universitat Rovira i Virgili in Tarragona) have grave problems of underinvestment (such as not having research libraries), but have changed the landscape of the three cities in question, rewarding the residents of the (Convergència-leaning) provinces. Finally, after failing to win control of the Spanish distance-education university (UNED) in Catalonia, the Generalitat created its own university, the UOC (Open University of Catalonia), with a mission to be both innovative and in Catalan (this required a legal strategem; initially, the UOC used the legal cover of being ostensibly a charity funded by the large financial institution La Caixa, which was happy to oblige despite its usual reluctance to be drawn into visible Catalan politics).

While founding universities is expensive (in initial infrastructure and then in obligations incurred to employ and pay pensions for their staff), it was relatively common in Spain in the 1980s as autonomous communities pushed to expand the system. The Catalan difference was in part the sheer quantity of resources that went into the new universities—above all the UPF—and in their avowed missions as nation-building exercises. The new universities were primarily in the hands of a small number of influential Catalan academics whose dedication to Catalanism and Catalan identity, and status and connections within academic in Catalonia, combined with specific links to CiU (the UPF's founding rector, Enric Argullol, retired in 2001 while still heading a CiU-appointed commission to find and campaign for new powers for the Generalitat). Starting new universities, with considerable initial resources, and a mission to combine excellence with strong Catalanism and distinct intellectual profiles, had two consequences. First, it attracted academic entrepreneurs who were able to offer the Generalitat distinct products it could support; second, it created a policy community around the preoccupations of the Generalitat and its universities. "The old universities were full of Marxists, useless ones (*inutiles*)," explained a lawyer involved in CiU's higher education policy. "We do want to help the Generalitat; there isn't another university with that mission," said a policy specialist at the UPF. Other Spanish autonomous communities, by contrast, tended to put much less emphasis on creating profiles and specializations for their new provincial universities, thereby falling in with the old Madrid-centered structure of Spanish academia. This Catalan decision pleased the already-distinct Catalan academics even if the abundant resources and strong Convèrgencia links of the UPF did not. In terms of pay and conditions, however, the Generalitat never challenged the basic structure in which they were set by the central state for all systems, instead preferring to improve the salaries of academics and the quality of research support in its preferred areas, as determined by its policy preferences. The policy leaves academics alone with their autonomy (and attacks on their autonomy coming from the central state during 2001), but also rewards those most willing to work with CiU and on topics such as asymmetric federalism that were related to CiU's strategies and ideological preferences.

## LAW

Catalonia does not, strictly speaking, have a legal system; it has a few bits of its own private law and otherwise is as subject to a unified, central legal body as any other part of Spain. The legal systems of Scotland and Catalonia each bear the traces of their early modern political histories. Scotland's legal system remained autonomous in 1707 because the English were worried by geopolitics, not law. Catalonia's feudal usages, by contrast, had been an obstacle to the basic fundraising of the early modern Spanish state, were used to justify the seventeenth-century revolt of Catalan elites, and were largely revoked by the victorious Spanish Bourbons. As a result, only some aspects of civil (private, inheritance) law remained, and the existence of separate Catalan legal professions, courts, jurisdictions, and law was abruptly terminated. Nineteenth-century legal reformers, influenced by French examples and centralist politics both further standardized Spanish law, provoking campaigns by Catalan lawyers and bourgeoisie in defense of their civil law (Balcells 1996; Harty 2005; Jacobson 2005). The result was that long before Franco there was no real independent Catalan regional organization in law. Instead there were state-wide corps of prosecutors and judges (both powerful and important in civil law systems compared to the common law) and common regulation of private lawyers and notaries (famously a Catalan niche throughout Spain).

One of the conditions of the pacted transition was that major institutions were left alone. Even the military, *guardia civil*, and police were susceptible to only slow democratization since their internal hierarchies and leadership were left alone. Just as Catalonia, employers, and unions had negotiated in the transition for autonomy and stability and achieved it, these big central state institutions and wielders of coercive power negotiated for their own autonomy and stability and obtained it. The Constitution and the organic law governing the judiciary both stress that it is unified and autonomous. Thus, the judiciary remained conservative, right-wing, highly Spanish in culture, organized on a statewide level with career tracks across Spain ending in a Madrid pinnacle, and in good part self-governing. This meant that apart from the top judges of the Constitutional Tribunal (appointed by political parties and culled primarily from the ranks of liberal, highly respectable, academic grandees) the Francoist ordinary judiciary remained in place and reproduced through its decentralized near-apprenticeship system of training. There was not even a school of judicial studies until the 1990s (when one was created, in Barcelona, to improve the quality of the poorly regarded judges).

The fundamental structure of Spanish law therefore remained an intact copy of the French system, with a pyramid form culminating in the Tribunal Superior in Madrid. Some autonomous communities tried to affect law with their one legal competency, a provision of the organic law of the judical power allowing them a role in administration such as the operation of courtroom buildings and services. A series of Constitutional Tribunal decisions stopped these interventions quickly (Borrell 2001). "I still think we could get away with more," explained a Consell Consultatiu lawyer in 2001. Constitutional provisions guaranteeing the central state's responsibility for law and the unity of the judicial corps and doctrine did the rest.

As a result, Catalonia never tried hard to affect ordinary justice. The constitutional provisions were simply too strong as a result of lobbying by the judiciary (seemingly through the UCD, interviewees from the Constitutional drafting processes suggested in 2001 interviews). Judges' relations with the Generalitat also can be quite bad, with the judiciary resisting the Generalitat's efforts to make the judicial system accessible in Catalan (such as by publishing bilingually or encouraging judges to learn Catalan) and interfering with language policy on grounds that it invades constitutional rights. There is no lobby for a separate Catalan law now that the Statute of Autonomy has confirmed the long-established practice of leaving Catalan civil law intact as an option for deciding family law and inheritance cases, optional for each citizen. There was consequently in 2000 no regional organization in law (there are not even a meaningful number of specialized Catalan family lawyers; most Catalan notaries and lawyers know how to use it). This meant that there was little politically effective demand for Catalan law, save the incongruity of finding a major institution at work in Catalonia in 2000 that was Spanish-speaking, centrally organized, centralist, unified across the state and largely unreconstructed since the dictatorship. "We talk politely to them once in a while," observed a Catalan functionary. This incongruity would help explain how the Generalitat could write some regionalization of the judicial system, if not the law, into the new statute passed at the time of writing in August 2006.

## INDUSTRIAL POLICY

Neither business nor unions per se have figured in this discussion of the Generalitat's policies. Business appeared when the Generalitat courted it in research policies geared toward specialities of the Catalan economic region; unions appeared primarily defending the employment rights of their members as civil servants. The reason for this is that the policy fields under the Generalitat are (with the partial exception of language policy) almost exclusively concerned with the organization of social policy. I found this when a snowball strategy of interviews across policy fields in early 2001 failed to lead me to either an employers' organization or either of the two big union confederations (CCOO and UGT). When I realized this and found representatives of the Foment de Treball and CCOO to interview, I asked them to define their organizations. Each stressed their organization's *catalanitat*, with the Foment representative noting that it speaks well of Catalonia that it has what claims to be the oldest employers' federation in Europe and the CCOO representative saying that CCOO was "more than a union," pointing to its role in the transition and the symbolism that the shared union headquarters for Catalonia is in the former headquarters of the Francoist secret police on Via Laietana. I then asked what the main issues on their agendas were. Each replied with a list headed by pension reform and the introduction of the Euro. None of their concerns included competencies of the Generalitat. I asked what the Generalitat could do to help them and their constituents. Each responded with a mix of concerns: improving the vocational training system, matching workers with jobs, improving the university–industry link in sciences, and lobbying for infrastructure spending by Madrid. In other words, to these Catalan economic—opportunistic—elites, the Generalitat was a minor player, a provider of social services, and a possible useful territorial lobbyist. Both business and labor are organized, densely, in Catalonia, but likewise they are organized in each autonomous community (Foment was the base for the Spanish employers' federation CEOE, as it was the employers' organization that best survived the Franco years) (Molinero and Ysàs 1991; Casademunt 1998; Jordana 1998).

The course of devolution, as discussed in this and the previous chapter, seems to explain why the Generalitat cannot intervene in the economy. Superficially, it is because the Constitution, Statute, and subsequent bureaucratic politics have focused on the transfers of competencies and resources from the state. The Generalitat was fundamentally constructed by handing over the field services of the state in Catalonia to an elected Catalan body. At no point did the debate focus on giving Catalonia the powers of a state, rather than a part of a state—the powers that would allow it to either shape society (as against social policy delivery) or change the borders between individuals, the market, and the state. Only recently have autonomous communities begun to campaign for this, with Catalonia seeking some say in immigration policy, and the Basque Country lobbying for control over social security, neither with any identifiable success.

This means that almost the whole of economic policy is out of its remit: the Generalitat was effectively incapable of economic planning, determining tax policy, or using any of the major redistributive mechanisms such as pensions or unemployment. Its taxation powers are extremely limited by an organic law that bans any resource being taxed more than once; thus, the state's income, property, and value-added taxes, as well as lesser-known ones, block any significant Catalan tax-raising powers (Vilalta i Ferrer 1998) (the new statute, at the time of writing, would change tax collection and the Catalan share of taxes, but would not change tax bases much). Its efforts to change economic structures are caught in the Constitutional Tribunal's broad reading of constitutional provisions that give the state responsibility for overall economic planning (art. 149.13) and limit autonomous communities' interference with freedom of commerce and mercantile law. In addition, powers almost never attributed to substate governments such as macroeconomic management, antitrust, most regulation, and sectoral standards-setting and regulation are all in the hands of Madrid or the EU institutions. The Generalitat is left as a specialized form of democratically accountable spending department, just like the Scottish Executive.

Why has the Generalitat developed that way? Functional arguments for a distribution of powers, while common, are invalidated by the question: functional for whom? Namely, it cannot be determined that autonomous communities' own social security policy would be a bad thing without asking at a minimum whether the community for whom policy should be functional is the Catalans, the Spaniards, or some other group (Greer 2006b). A political process argument is necessary to avoid ideological biases. The answer then is implicit in the analysis of opportunistic and regional elites. Business and labor are both predominantly opportunistic elites willing to bid for and be bid by any level of government, and whose interests are not necessarily fixed to the region. Since their autonomy is not threatened by state centralization—it might be improved, if they have good relations with the central state—they have little incentive to support autonomy. That means their dominant reaction to devolution is one of concern for their environmental stability—that they need not negotiate differing regulatory, tax, or other regimes within Spain. "Money follows power and money avoids risk," a Convergència-linked business activist kept repeating in an interview. Given that harmonization of such regimes has been a dominant feature of Western European politics since at least the early 1980s, there has been little prospect of Catalonia finding a coalition to support its extending its powers over businesses. Regional organizations are already under the Generalitat's wing, and other elites prefer not to be, or prefer to have the Generalitat be one more level of government bidding to help them.

## LANGUAGE

Catalonia, unlike Scotland, has a thriving language with intense political importance (Conversi 1997). Health and education are far larger government activities than language and culture: the Department of Culture's budget has always been smaller than that of the large teaching hospital at Vall d'Hebron in Barcelona. Nevertheless, the best-known, and most polemical, most-studied, and most-maligned topic in Catalan public policy is language. This means it affords an extra way to examine policy not present in Scotland, since it is the only wide-ranging regulatory power that either has. Scotland is wholly an administrator of public policies, primarily social policy; Catalonia is the same except for this one important preoccupation and power.[2] Furthermore, there is probably no topic more important to nationalists and Catalanists than the language and its success. What, then, happened in Catalonia in the policy field in which it could change the borders between state and society, the lives of citizens, and the internal workings of other organizations?

The answer is unsurprising. The Generalitat treaded very lightly and in its usual pseudocorporatist style extended Catalan promotion primarily to areas in which there was an existing set of regional organizations open to it. The conditions for language shifts and normalization, subject of a large literature, are not the concern here; instead, I concentrate on how the Generalitat won its language powers and how it conducted the normalization and promotion of Catalan. That Catalan was regional is clear. Language was a cornerstone of the Catalanist consensus developed before and during the transition; organizations promoting Catalan were almost by definition confined to Catalonia (there were a few in Valencia, the Balearic Islands, and France); and most of the important pro-Catalan organizations, such as the newspaper *Avui*, the presses Editorials 62 and Proa/Encyclopédia Catalana, and the language and culture promotion group Ómnium Cultural were tightly linked into Catalanist consensus politics via their membership, funding, and leadership (see the interesting history of Ómnium Cultural by the nationalist, Convergència-linked journalist Faulí, 1981).

CiU arrived in office with a powerful Catalanist consensus around the need to win ground for Catalan (first "normalizing" it, by making it an accepted language in all walks of life, and then "promoting" it by trying to give it wider usage and higher status than Spanish). Reflecting the high profile of Catalan in stitching together the consensus, it was specifically recognized as a language in the Constitution and the statute at the insistence of the Catalan political forces. Most of the language protections were, at least on paper, geared to protect the right to use Castilian Spanish in any walk of life and to allow the Generalitat to promote Catalan. Nevertheless, the struggle to establish stable language policies continued for twenty years and shows no signs of abating. In part, this is due to the structure of the conflict: language conflict and policies are both conducted at the level of the individual organization, so if eight Catalan universities have eight slightly different interpretations of language laws, that can mean eight extended judicial contests followed by efforts to reconcile verdicts, to say nothing of implementation. Likewise, when a speaker of a language feels aggrieved, he or she has the right to demand judicial protection as an individual (*recurso de ampáro*). This immensely expanded standing relative to conflicts over competencies means that individual citizens can intervene by bringing cases to the courts (by contrast, standing in conflicts over competencies such as discussed in the rest of this section tends to be highly limited, mostly to relevant politicians and government bodies).

The Generalitat, for all the importance of Catalan to nationalists, began by treading extremely lightly. There were two barriers: first, the need to avoid creating popular enmity that would undermine the Catalanist consensus (the Andalucian Socialist Party, the PSA, had only just tried to organize on a vaguely anti-Catalan platform in the Barcelona suburbs and been asphyxiated by lack of resources); second, they faced the need to avoid offending elites by imposing languages on their organizations without their consent. Enmity, policymakers presumed, would stem from the imposition of Catalan as a preferred language. Thus, Catalonia did not opt to try and impose it in formal dealings, despite the theoretical advantages of doing so as a way to make it a high-status language. Interfering in the organization of elites' institutions would be treading on regional and opportunistic elites alike. It would lose some support from, for example, business, foreign investors, universities, the health care system, and others with important recruitment among non-Catalan-speakers. It is this combination of linguistic nationalism with respect for existing organizations that accounts for the particular form of Catalan language policy.

The normalization of Catalan in the 1980s has predominantly taken place within the public services. This began with the schools, where it was agreed by the provisional Generalitat that they would be bilingual with a strong emphasis on Catalan immersion. This was by far the most important intervention by the Generalitat in the school system; however, because it was part of the Catalanist consensus and came with resources and policy autonomy, the private sector and civil servants accepted it after negotiating transition periods and help. Otherwise, the goal of language policy in the 1980s was to make Catalan co-equal, moving it from the status of a language spoken at home to being a language in which one could communicate at any level (this was "normalization"). The most visible manifestation was that metro stations, street names, and signs on public buildings switched over to Catalan. The most labor-intensive manifestation was the teaching of Catalan to low-level civil servants and the translation of documents (Argelaguet 1998). However, much of the work went into making Catalan co-equal in the public services. In areas under the Generalitat's control, civil service or not, it was able to make Catalan a requirement for hiring and promotion. In other areas, preeminently the judiciary, the principle of the unity of state bodies meant that all the Generalitat could do was lobby Madrid to try and regard Catalan favorably as a factor when allocating judges to Catalonia. In some areas of the public service, such as the universities and medicine, Catalan had to be voluntary for the professionals, who combined civil service tenure, unionization, and professional organization with integrated labor markets that made it difficult to oblige them to learn a language. "We try to do it all with pedagogy. You're going to ask if it will be a lot of work—yes, it will," explained a Unió politician.

Normalization was a qualified success: it became feasible to deal with the Generalitat in Catalan or in Spanish, the streetscape became much more Catalan, and the Catalanization of public services meant that the language was more visible. One of the many important events of 1992 was the graduation of the first class of secondary school students who had been wholly educated in the postregionalization, Catalan-promoting schools system. In 1996, the Generalitat, encouraged by its progress in Catalanizing the public services, introduced a more intrusive law of Catalan promotion— intended as a step toward making Catalan the dominant language (counting the Madrid government's dependence on CiU votes as a propitious factor) (Argelaguet 1998:256). The laws themselves did have content that could disturb those seeking to choose their language with total autonomy, as they demanded that most public, official communication be preeminently in Catalan with Castilian Spanish available, but not dominant.

However, the actual form of the application was a different matter. The law was scarcely applied in its first years. Instead, through the polemics (caused more by the PP and ERC and aided by the Spanish right as a way of getting at the PSOE government that depended on CiU), the Generalitat focused on educational efforts such as pamphlets on what the law required. It worked with other agencies, for example, recruiting Òmnium Cultural to translate restaurant menus into Catalan (with same-day fax-back service), and subsidizing courses in Catalan for adults. Actual application of the law, when it began, followed the template of Catalan relations with other elites. The Generalitat systematically pacted the changes, working with peak associations to set out schedules and obligations for their members, and then did not actually allocate any effort to enforcing language changes. Thus, in the financial sector, the Generalitat negotiated agreements with the various financial trade bodies covering translation documents and publicity and strategies to encourage staff to use Catalan. It negotiated changes in official documents and practices and contracts with the College of Notaries. It negotiated changes in signs with large firms individually and with trade associations collectively. Then, these elite groups organize their members. Language policy implementation was thoroughly corporatist.

The Generalitat has the threat of actual enforcement (almost never used to date), but also its ability to pull strings to create upsurges of popular protest through its Catalan nationalist client groups—it funded the secessionist student group Nationalist Student's Block, which stages flamboyant campaigns against organizations that do not use Catalan (such as local beer Estrella Damm—"Estrella" is a Castilian Spanish word), and also the CiU-linked Òmnium Cultural. It spent (and spends) a great deal of time and effort negotiating with the multinationals of culture to secure Catalan translations of products such as Windows and blockbuster films, and part of the reason why was recently demonstrated. CiU used its contacts in Catalanist groups to raise large public protests when the first *Harry Potter* movie was released in Barcelona and not dubbed into Catalan, eventually extracting a promise from the American film company to do further *Harry Potter* films with Catalan dubbing, and to release the move on video with Catalan subtitles.

As a result, language policy has been slowed in its real effects on daily life, but has been the cause for much linking-up between the Generalitat and regional elites such as notaries, small business federations, and financial services bodies. The Generalitat, with a policy goal, enacted its goal in the sector it controlled directly (its own employees and buildings) and otherwise negotiated programs of work with elites in policy sectors that left them fairly free to design the policy and free to monitor the implementation. The result is if anything a strengthening of ties between the Generalitat and regional elites it would not otherwise be so able to cultivate (such as notaries) as well as with the regional organizations dedicated to the language.

## CONCLUSION: AUTONOMY AND NATIONALISM

The Generalitat accepted the legitimacy of the state's institutions, which in turn meant that it was unable to respond to judicial limitations on its power and autonomy. It could not do otherwise while enjoying dependencies on regional organizations. To oppose the totem of the constitution would make CiU a severely destabilizing force and turn it from an autonomist party with equally good nationalist and elite-friendly credentials into a nationalist party that would lose the support of opportunistic and regional elites. Thus, CiU could not wage rhetorical battles against the state or attempt to subvert it directly (as some Basque parties did). At the same time, when the UCD and PSOE had absolute majorities in Madrid, the CiU coalition had no effective way to make its voice heard. Thus, during the crucial years of the 1980s during which the broad outlines of the current devolution settlement were drawn, the Generalitat had no effective way to fight for greater power in given policy fields, and did not fare particularly well in the courts.

What the Generalitat could do with its search for powers was offer to effectively absorb the burden of the state's centralism (such as fighting for greater and more flexible finance and expanded policy autonomy) while handing policy formulation and implementation down to the existing sectoral elites. This won it elite support, by tying large sets of organizations more or less firmly to the Generalitat and giving them autonomy to organize themselves with only a light regulatory touch. The result was a large and consensual expansion of the Generalitat's networks and organizational alliances, a remarkably harmonious one compared to the rest of Spain, and the creation of a substantial coalition around the Generalitat. At the same time, the flow of competencies (even if clearly promised in the statute), the battles over their exact meanings, their divergence from the rest of Spain, and their explicitly Catalanist rhetoric meant that they counted as nation-building, nationalist victories. And the networks that CiU helped build and bind to itself appear likely to live on and shape Catalonia for a long time to come.

# Chapter Nine

# Will they stay or will they go?

It is hardly novel to point out that nationalism, territorial mobilization, and territorial change are major issues in modern politics. They can produce social solidarity and new political forms, for better or for worse—for Spanish outcomes or for Yugoslav outcomes. It is also hardly novel to see changes in the shape of Western states, including the rise of regional governments with increasingly important, and similar, powers. Despite the importance of the issues, though, and the intensive study of nationalism, little work has been done on the territorial outcomes. There is even less on a particular form of territorial politics that has become increasingly common and important— regionalization. Scotland and Catalonia are both important cases of strong regional governments, civic nationalism, and successful negotiation of the tensions of nationalism, territorial political conflict, and intergovernmental bargaining. They come from very different histories, yet have arrived in very similar situations. This means that their experiences can shed light on the reasons for territorial political change, the kinds of outcomes, and the stability of those outcomes.

The two regions vary on almost every variable cited in standard explanations of territorial mobilization, nationalism, and political change: political environment, economic change, relative levels of development, sectoral bases of the economy, linguistic difference, religion, religious difference, and timing of their nationalisms. What they most visibly share is nationalism and strong national identities. Yet nationalism is a slippery and multifaced concept. Even finding an indicator is hard—is nationalism to be found in public opinion surveys, nationalist parties, the writings of intellectuals and politicians, or social movements? Furthermore, it is far from clear how any of these indicators necessarily explains their outcomes. If nothing else, nationalists typically demand statehood and an obvious fact about Scotland and

Catalonia is that they are not states. Instead, they are highly autonomous administrators of the welfare state with extra competencies in a range of public policy fields such as subsidizing industrial development and promoting culture.

It is common enough to attribute the development of such strong regional governments to the presence of nationalists and nationalist parties, but that argument needs qualification. Scotland's national identity is as old as that of any nation in Europe; why did secession only became a major issue in the 1960s? How did that translate into devolution, rather than the status quo or independence? And why are strong regional governments imperfectly related to national identity? Nationalism alone asks more questions than it answers; the issue is what are the politics that explain the nationalism and the government, and how the three interrelate. Part I showed Scotland and Catalonia to be filled with examples of parties that pursued electoral strategies unsustained by their resource dependencies and suffered—the Labour devolution scheme in 1970s Scotland is the clearest case, but ERC in the early 1990s, the Conservatives during the Declaration of Perth, and the PP in the early 1990s were all snapped back from promising electoral strategies because their resource suppliers would not stand for the strategy. Not even political parties can rely on a free lunch.

## SUMMARIZING

I argued in chapter one that we need to loosen the explanatory connection between nationalism and regionalization—they come together in many cases, but the one does not fully explain the other. Some organizations, as diverse as newspapers, churches, professions, small businesses, and medical colleges, depend for resources on their regions; their finance, staff, clients, information, leadership, and legitimacy identifiably tie them to the region. These organizations, like any others, act as corporate bodies in defense and pursuit of their autonomy and environmental stability. This, crucially, need not be through direct intentional activity; if educational policy acts uniformly on professors, professors then act individually to help change the climate as well as through any public statements made by lobbying organizations that feel safe enough to make such statements. If health policy acts uniformly on doctors, their support will matter even if the medical lobbies that benefit remain quiet and move on to different demands. When they have regional resource dependencies, that means that their autonomy and stability is tightly connected with the governance of that region, and they will support stable autonomy for themselves and usually for the region as part of that. When there are enough of such organizations and their web of interrelationships and information flows is dense enough, they will exercise political power by virtue of the resource dependencies of parties on these regional organizations. The price of success in politics in the region will be dependence on those organizations' support, and that will entail support for their autonomy and stability. That does not mean that regional elites manipulate politics; it means that they prefer to lend resources to those who agree with them and that party politicians do their best to accumulate support. If regional organizations are powerful in the region, at least some party politicians will court them by offering autonomy and stability. Alternative forms of resource mobilization in the region carry higher prices—dependence on central resources or collective action puts a low ceiling on party resource mobilization. The former also incurs distrust, as the experience of the Scottish Conservatives or PP in Catalonia show. The latter condemns the party to a cycle of instability that makes it difficult to establish stable relations and ideological complicity with resource-rich organizations. This means that in areas with webs of regional organizations as strong as those of Scotland and Catalonia, the dominant party(ies) will defend regional autonomy. Dense webs of regional organizations thereby explain regional autonomy via the mechanism of parties' resource dependencies. Nationalist movement-parties, national identity, the EU, and the world political economy, while changing much of the conduct of politics, do not explain these outcomes as well as the preferences and activity of regional organizations.

Both Scotland and Catalonia have and have long had these strong webs of regional organizations. In both countries, these webs were the basis of the creation of their regional governments when they felt their autonomy and stability were threatened by Franco or Thatcher. They have similar governments because they have strong regional organizations, and the governments have similar competencies because they have similar sets of strong regional organizations.

## EXTRAPOLATING

Much of the interest in regional governments comes because of the strain that nationalist and territorial mobilization has put on state and society in many places. Regional autonomy offers the prospect of damping down ethnic conflict and secessionism, or perhaps fanning the flames. There is a lively debate around the topic, but fewer studies of the conditions of creation of regional government (such as this one). Without such studies of the *origins* of regional government, as against studies of the effects or advisability of regional government, we have an incomplete range of data and theories from which to draw conclusions. If regional government and nonsecession both are functions of regional organizations' power, then regional government might not be advisable as a remedy for conflicts when there are no regional organizations or where they are poorly incorporated into the state. Regional governments over time can create regional organizations, as most Spanish autonomous communities, the National Assembly for Wales, American states, and Canadian provinces all show, but in the short run it might amount to putting great power in the hands of groups not primarily interested in stability and autonomy.

The most interesting commonality between Scotland and Catalonia is that neither is a state despite credentials as nations second to none. I have argued that is because the dominant political forces in those regions, autonomist regional organizations, oppose independence. What, though, might lead them to secede? Per this argument, there are two routes to secession in regions with dense webs of regional organizations and nationalist movement-parties. The first is that the nationalist parties, not typically responsible for changes in territorial government, gain such strength that they can force secession. This would require that they win in a brute trial of political strength with autonomist, antisecessionist, parties supported by regional organizations and any centralist forces. It would also require that they maintain their commitment to radicalism even while in government—that they remain under the control of activists whose mobilization was around territorial revindication.

The second route to secession would be a shift in the calculus of regional organizations. They would have to see either such a threat to their own organizational bases from the central state, or so little cost to independence, that it would be beneficial. Regardless of the arguments outsiders might make about costs and benefits, it is doubtful whether regional organizations and their elites would easily come to perceive the breakup of Britain or Spain as an idea with a beneficial weighting of costs and benefits. However, some conditions might make such a change an option. First, there is the possibility of a near-existential threat to regional organizations' autonomy and environmental stability. It is difficult to imagine what might prompt such an attack on established autonomy, but it could lead them to throw their weight behind secessionism in an effort to preserve themselves. In less highly institutionalized states, this could more easily happen (arguably, organizations dependent on slavery in the American South were just such regional organizations facing a mortal threat, and they did support secession). Second, there is the possibility that secession would seem costless or nearly so. In both cases, this would require both regional organizations' sense that they could control the process, and that the central state not resist, and that secession not involve costly replacment of the central state's services. These secessions appear to have taken place in some former Communist states, where entrenched regional organizations faced a collapsing state and few risks to secession (Slovenia might be a good case of this). Nevertheless, if the central state does not vanish, it could offer opposition. Even if it offers little opposition, and it is not clear that England would object to Scottish secession, replacing the functions of the United Kingdom in Scotland could be deeply destabilizing. The appeals nationalist parties make to the EU, summarized in the SNP slogan "Independence in Europe," represent an effort to play down the costs of secession. If the EU already controls most economic and monetary policy and European human rights law governs rights, runs the argument, there would be limited instability from independence. This argument is not as clearly supported as it might seem at first— it would be difficult to become a functioning EU member after secession (Murkens et al. 2001). Nevertheless, it is the best argument nationalists have to reassure regional organizations that independence would not be too destabilizing. Likewise, slow steps toward greater powers (such as the SNP's campaigns to give the Scottish parliament more financial autonomy) are ways to try to persuade regional organizations that the costs of adding juridical statehood would not be too great or destabilizing.

So secession seems unlikely. It seems unlikely because regional organizations would not support it and would win contests over it. The first route—secession via nationalist victory—would take a social and political earthquake. It is unlikely that the SNP or ERC could win political power and muster a majority in a referendum (as high-level politicians of both parties admitted to me in 2001 interviews). The second route—regional organizations changing sides—would require that they not see independence as destabilizing and that something would threaten them enough to make them seek it. It is difficult to imagine what the UK or Spain could do to threaten them so, short of abolish the Generalitat and Scottish parliament, and it is also difficult to imagine how to persuade them that independence is anything other than destabilizing. The costs and benefits of secession (Bartkus 1999) are not so important as who bears them, and in even the most Europeanized region the *potential* costs to regional organizations in lost stability are likely to be decisive.

Scotland and Catalonia are also often cited as admirable exponents of civic nationalism, of inclusive, diverse national communities free of ethnic exclusivism and based on healthy civil societies, and the regional settlements in the two countries are widely admired as models of ethnic conflict regulation. The moderation of these politics is due to the autonomist, stabilizing influence of their regional organizations. It is easy enough to find bigots in the leaderships of all Scottish and Catalan parties, and easy enough to bring out disturbing sentiments in interviews. That is not the point (no political system is free of scarcely veiled bigotry). The point is that such sentiments cannot be uttered in public without a scandal; in 2001, Heribert Barrera, ERC's former leader, made anti-immigrant remarks, citing the American ideologue Charles Murray to argue that blacks were not as bright as native-born Catalans. He was effectively hounded from public visibility by autonomist parties and organizations including the press, the universities, unions, and party politicians (ERC did keep him in some of his posts, but two months later high-level ERC leaders in interviews were noticeably unwilling to discuss him). Barrera's comments risked opening a divide between Catalans and immigrants and touched on the divide between Catalan and Spanish speakers. Fearing a threat to the stability of Catalan politics and society in a threat to the Catalanist consensus, press, universities, parties, and professionals moved to silence him. In short, the relative ethnic peace in these highly distinctive, highly mobilized, and (in Catalonia) potentially divided societies is probably explained by the same factors as their autonomy.

The Catalanist consensus explains both the peace of Catalonia (and the sublimation of any conflict into electoral battles between the autonomist PSC, with Spanish-speaking votes and Catalan leaders, and the autonomist CiU, with Catalan votes and Catalan leaders). Catalan leaders know that they live in a potentially divided society, PSC leaders know that their party manages much of the political divide, and the result is an ingrained set of reflexes designed to preserve stability by preventing a backlash of Spanish speakers.[1]

These answers suggest that institutional design is not necessarily the most important aspect of ethnic conflict regulation. There are many studies of the institutional features of states and their impact on secession and nationalist conflict. This study suggests that more attention should be paid to social organizations outside the core state institutions. What keeps Scotland and Catalonia calm is not the good design of the British and Spanish states—it is the strength and power of regional organizations in Catalan and Scottish society. If anything, they explain many of the better design features of the UK and Spanish states. These organizations, capable of shaping regional politics and establishing regional autonomy, are also capable of quashing movement-parties that seek destabilizing policies. These large organizations, seeking the stability of their environments, pursue social stability just as they pursue regional autonomy when they further their own autonomy. In areas of Western Europe that lack large organizations that are regional, such as Northern Ireland, we see a direct confrontation between a central state and its allies and social movements, and a consequent clearer choice between separatism and state nationalism.

Likewise, this study suggests that we should divert some attention from the characteristics of different populations to the study of their social organization—the organizations in their societies. Many of the macro-level explanations of regionalism, secession, and nationalism work through individual-level attributes (such as language or ethnicity), while others focus on group attributes such as proximity and a history of conflicts. Like the analyses of institutional forms of conflict regulation, these can be extremely enlightening and valuable, but they also should be complemented by examination of the organizations that structure so much of the societies. The importance and meaning of language in Catalonia, for example, is clearly shaped by the regional organizations' politics of consensus and the strategic choices they forced on political parties. Despite Catalonia's clear ethnolinguistic divide between Catalan- and Spanish speakers, the structure of regional organizations effectively obliged politicians to create a political arena in which appeals to that divide are taboo. This is a clear case of the activity of regional organizations and parties in shaping a social divide that could be something different and far worse (as it is in Catalonia's near neighbor, the Basque Country).

## GENERALIZING

There are few regions with the strong, dense webs of regional organizations found in Scotland and Catalonia, but there are many with some kind of regional or meso-level government. Here again, a focus on competencies is illuminating. Regions created from the top down, to serve central organizations, as part of party programs for democratization, or to diffuse blame, are weak and constricted. Regions with allies, regions with regional organizational complexes supporting them, are more powerful, have more and more desirable competencies, and are less constrained.

### Footprints

Who are those allies? In the two cases here, and possibly in the others, they are much more likely to be connected to the public sector. That would explain something striking about the powers of Europe's most powerful regions. Scotland and Catalonia are, like most of their peers, fundamentally autonomous administrators of the welfare state. Their core responsibilities and powers are in health, education, local government, culture, and planning. In other words, they are responsible for the areas of the modern state that have the largest territorial "footprint" — the largest number of employees, the largest physical infrastructure, and the most face-to-face contact with citizens. They are far less powerful in less bureaucratic areas of fiscal policy such as taxation and pension — those are largely still the responsibility of central states. In this they are like most other regions of Europe.

This fits with the fact that their territorial politics are often driven by the interests of professionals and organizations in the public sector. Regardless of whether we call them "civil society" or not, they are publicly funded organizations. Businesses, for all the talk of economic regionalism, are much more likely to be opportunistic, less tied to individual places, less intrinsically regional, and less strategically willing to be bound to one level of government. It is rare in any form of politics that tying oneself to a single patron is a wise strategy; diffuse sources of support are less risky and most organizations are accordingly opportunistic. But public sector organizations, necessarily tied to some level of government, are likely to develop preferences as to which one they prefer. This dynamic is particularly pronounced in Scotland, but the role of the public or publicly funded sector is important in the Catalan case as well.

Even if the history of regionalization so far has been a story of the territorial reorganization of the welfare state and its political accountability, nationalism and economic development mean that there is some room for a continuing development of territorial politics (Jeffrey 2006). The Basque Country's important role in tax collection was a model for Catalonia. Quebec, the only regional government in the rich democracies with its own pension plan, perpetually intrigues policymakers in other rich states' regions. The result is a slow push for more "fiscal freedom" (tax powers) and responsibility for taxation. Likewise, borders and immigration interest regional governments that end up funding the assimilation of and social services to immigrants. Both Scotland and Catalonia are slowly entering these fields, whether through the Scottish Executive's "fresh talent" initative, which attempts to manipulate UK immigration policy in order to attract immigrants or through new tax and immigration structures in the new Catalan statute of autonomy under consideration at the time of writing. Born of regional governments' frustration with policy problems (such as immigrant integration in Catalonia and a declining population in Scotland), they are novel as objectives in territorial politics and in the extent to which they depend on an argument about policy: the basic policy responsibilities of the regional governments require new powers, ones shared with the regional government, if finance and powers are to be adequate to fulfilling regional (national) electorates' expectations. But insofar as there must be a solid social coalition for the development of greater regional self-government, the natural limits of a given regional government are suggested by the extent of the welfare state's footprint in the region.

*Neo-institutionalism*

When there are no strong groups of preexisting regional organizations, as in most of the French, Italian, and Spanish regions at their creation, the regional government will be highly limited. Whatever created it will not have been pressure from those interested in autonomy and stability for a region — it will not be "bottom-up" regionalism. Instead, it will as often be a recipe for very limited governments tightly controlled by the center and saddled with intractable problems like economic development and job skills training. Thus, most Spanish autonomous communities in 1980 were creatures of an unexpected chain reaction set off within the legislature—allowing deputies to form "pre-autonomies" gave them the opportunity to build personal political bases. Central elites colluded in the spread of autonomous communities, in the famous *café para todos* strategy, since that would allow the central state to contend with a large body of autonomous communities, most of which would be weak, rather than negotiating with highly mobilized Catalonia and the Basque Country. French regionalism is a response to crises of democratic legitimation. Charles de Gaulle proposed it as a way to appease the 1968 revolts and failed to regionalize or to quash 1968; regionalization in 1983 was part of a Socialist program based on decentralization and François Mitterand's governments pursued it with little enthusiasm (Schmidt 1990). It is hardly surprising that the resulting regional governments were weak, spurned by promising politicians and frozen out of the main policy areas of the state. Nobody thinks Wales would have had either of its devolution referenda if it were not for the simultaneous events in Scotland.

However, even weak regional governments show a tendency to grow. Over time, a lesson of European regionalism is that regional governments can create their own webs of regional organizations. A government, even a small one like the early French regions, can win clients and regional supporters by developing groups' dependence (A. Smith 1995; Nay 1997). The clearest case is that of the Spanish regions such as Murcia and La Rioja, which were born in the transition without regional organizational complexes. They began as fairly weak organizations, but progressively were able to buttress their position in parties and in their regional societies by creating client groups. The autonomous communities became part of regional politics and organizations became more regionally resource dependent as they came to depend for resources on the regional governments. The result was that the autonomous communities gained allies in lobbying for power, their politicians gained weight in their parties, and the autonomous communities themselves became more powerful. It took twenty years, but the autonomous communities of Spain are now at approximately the same level of competencies and show markedly different policies in addition to the predictable divergence in how much legislative activity they develop (Subirats 2006).

This is what Dupuy and Le Galès (2006) call the "neo-institutionalist" analysis of regionalization. The neo-institutionalist argument is that governments attract organizations and over time create their own complexes of regional organizations. Over time, European regions have been converging on a similar, fairly high, level of autonomy during the last decades. Regionalization starts for all manner of reasons, but creates strong governments with competencies, power, and flexibility when there are regional organizations that can compel parties to give the regions the powers to guarantee autonomy and stability. Scotland and Catalonia began with such webs of organizations; other regions have entered feedback loops in which regional governments create regional constituencies. It remains to be seen whether regionalized European states will truly finish up with such similar regional governments across the board.

In short, at any given point in time we should expect that the strength of webs of regional organizations will, via the mechanism of parties' resource dependencies, explain the strength and competencies of regional governments. This can be a dynamic process since there is nothing preventing social change and regionalization. Indeed, the changes in the international political economy could produce regional webs of organizations that then demand regional government. That would take the development of regional organizational webs through processes beyond the scope of this work: the development of resource dependencies on those organizations in one or more parties; and some form of constraint on the regional organizations that would encourage them to demand formal regional autonomy as a defense for their autonomy and environmental stability. These three steps might explain why dynamic regions are not necessarily regionalizing government, but equally could map the changes now taking place in diverse areas.

The alternative hypothesis is equally plausible. The changes occurring in the global political economy might mean that thriving, distinctive, assertive regions with their own webs of organizations will remain a rarity and become rarer. Many forms of economic activity do not require regions; for every region densely networked with small firms there is another region with few of its own elites or distinctive organizations, dependent on a few big firms and perpetually worried by footloose capital. Globalization and neoliberalism are not, after all, known for preserving local economic autonomy and nonmarket social institutions.

## THE PLACE OF TERRITORIAL POLITICS

To argue, as I do, that much of "high" territorial political change is driven by "low" politics of policy formulation and policy outcomes is to argue that there are limits to the usefulness of nationalism or territorial mobilization and grievance as explanations of territorial political change. The drive for Scottish or Catalan autonomy has been much broader than their nationalist mobilization, and cannot be explained merely by looking at national identity or nationalist party mobilization. It can also be understood as the summation of many narrower concerns that drove many different people to come to the same autonomist conclusions.

Regional politics cannot be understood without understanding the influence of regional organizations and the substantive concerns that under some circumstances can drive territorial, constitutional change. Norton Long once wrote that we should avoid assuming too much interest in politics—we often find that a banker's greatest likely interest is banking, and a doctor's likely greatest interest medicine (Long 1962:149). I have argued that big institutionalized organizations, preoccupied with banking or doctoring, try to maintain their autonomy and stability so that they can carry on doing what they would do. That includes resisting the politicians, activists, and bureaucrats who would make it harder for them to bank, doctor, or otherwise use their autonomy and stability to do what they would do. The stable autonomy and civic nationalism of Scotland and Catalonia are their successes, and the reasons they serve as models for others. And this happened that way because there are many people in both countries who do not want to participate in national politics and who will fight political battles primarily to defend their own autonomy and stability. Many people are not very interested in politics and simply want to get back to doing their jobs in tranquility.

# Notes

## CHAPTER ONE

1. This might serve Catalonia well in coping with overseas immigration now: unlike most of Spain, Catalan elites have this long tradition of thinking about and designing policy for immigrant integration, co-optation or at least political demobilization, and for avoiding backlashes among the existing population (Colomer 1986).

## CHAPTER TWO

1. I use the term "region" and its derivatives throughout, for consistency with international usage. Regionalism is also linked to nationalism and national self-assertion old and new—regional government often comes up as a solution to nationalist demands. Nevertheless, nationalism is not definitionally linked to regions: a region is a form of meso-level territorial government and regionalism is the political demand for such a regional government while nationalism and nations are separate sets of claims about identities, groups, rights, and obligations (Motyl, 1999; Greer and Derluguian, 2000). Regionalism, regional governments, nations, and nationalism often come together in conflict or complementarity, but there is no analytic gain or complement to the nations to be found in conflating a political demand (regionalism) and a political outcome (regions) with claims about identities (national identity) and political movements based on claims about identity (nationalism).

2. Often students of post-Communism.

## CHAPTER FOUR

1. Some contemporaries would refer to it as the "postern gate."

2. It is possible to overstate the interest of the autonomy provisions in the Treaty of Union in the context of early modern Europe. The documents attending the wedding of Ferdinand and Isabella, for example, also specifically stated that Castille and Aragon would remain separate (Sales 2002:21–22). The difference is more that Catalonia, unlike Scotland, would revolt to defend fiscal privileges that the declining Spanish crown badly needed, and would lose.

3. The preservation of Welsh or Gallego distinctiveness came about for almost the opposite reasons—the costs and benefits of imposing assimilation on those

poor and geographically difficult areas were never attractive enough to conquerors or assimilators for long enough.

4. Nations are, of course, constructed, historical, continent, and manipulated, and ultimately are just ideas, but so is almost everything in social life. Diverse (and London-based) theorists such as Anthony Smith (1991), George Schöpflin (2000), and Josep Llobera (1994) are among the most articulate exponents of the point that national identities are in the short and medium terms not very malleable and yet intensely important. See also Brubaker's remarks (1996:15n4).

5. There is evidence of a longer-term convergence on similar levels of regional autonomy within states regardless; this is discussed in the Conclusion.

## CHAPTER FIVE

1. This organization is a small example of the problems that regional organizations perceived; it was irritated by the Conservatives' reluctance to expend Westminster parliamentary time on a review of Scotland's badly antiquated child-welfare laws. "We had a 1930s legal system, very progressive for the 1930s but a disgrace since the 1970s compared to England . . . and they [the Government] didn't care," explained one child-welfare advocate in 2002. Parliamentary time is an exceptionally valuable commodity, and Scotland as often as not got less of it than even consensual, technical changes demanded.

## CHAPTER SIX

1. One of the interesting examples of this is the books published in those years by Edicions 62 and still in the catalogue (the imprint was run by Socialists and Communists such as Isidre Molas and Jordi Solé Tura): they often have oddly anachronistic titles, such as "The Political Party System of Catalonia" (Molas 1972) applied to a study of the 1930s Republic, and they focus on diverse aspects of society in a mixture of search for historic precedents and development of new ideas for a democratic Catalonia.

2. The premises are now the headquarters of ERC.

3. The statute actually includes a provision excluding non-sitting members of the parliament from running for president of the Generalitat (thereby excluding Tarradellas; "Hemos cargado el viejo," one PSC leader is reputed to have announced when it was approved). Political forces that had mobilized themselves primarily around democracy and autonomy (if nothing else, because those were the conditions of mass mobilization and regional alliances) were shifting more and more thoroughly to contestation between themselves to lead the new autonomous government.

## CHAPTER SEVEN

1. When, in the course of a 2005 attack on CiU, the new Socialist president of the Generalitat referred to corruption—the 3% widely said to be levied on con-

tracts—the cross-party response was to attack him for fracturing the Catalan consensus rather than to ask about the origins and desirability of any 3% rule.

2. Contrary to what is often said, this was not the first time the king had spoken Catalan in public. He had already done it, on his own initiative, at a crucial moment during the transition (Preston 2005:337).

3. They did this while participating in a well-orchestrated campaign to use sympathetic judges in the unreformed legal system to play up charges of corruption against the PSOE in what is at least a disturbing manipulation of the legal system (Maravall 2003).

4. That would happen in 2004–2005, after the Socialists took power in both Catalonia and Spain.

## CHAPTER EIGHT

1. The 1978 act was the devolution legislation passed contingent on the 1979 referendum.

2. "The rejection of negotiations at the formulation stage causes a displacement effect. The power for professions to negotiate the details of policy is reasserted at the implementation stage and this is increasingly manifest at each devolved level of government, since the powers of central government coordination are diluted." (Cairney 2002: 394).

## CHAPTER NINE

1. At which he also explained that a strike with 3% participation, one of the activities of his union, is perfectly good tactics because it gets press coverage.

2. The Scottish parliament and executive have powers pertaining to and are concerned about the fate of Gaelic, but that is more about preserving a language on the brink of extinction than about the wholly impractical goals of normalization or promotion.

# References

Abbad, N., A. Gratacós, A. Molera, A. Navarro, X. Padrós, C. Serrahima, and M. Vives. 1992. *El Desplegament autonomic de Catalunya: Departament de Treball, Sanitat, i Seguretat Social i Benestar Social.* Vol. 1. Barcelona: Generalitat de Catalunya, Institut d'Estudis Autonomics.

Agnew, J. 1995. Postscript: Federalism in the Post-Cold War Era. In *Federalism: The Multiethnic Challenge,* ed. G. Smith, 294–302. London: Longman.

Agüero, F. 1995. *Soldiers, Civilians, and Democracy.* Baltimore: Johns Hopkins University Press.

Aitken, K. 1997. *The Bairns o' Adam: The Story of the STUC.* Edinburgh: Polygon.

Aja, E. 1999. *El Estado Autónomico: Federalismo y Hechos Diferenciales.* Madrid: Alianza Editorial.

———. 2001. Spain: Nation, Nationalities, and Regions. In *Subnational Democracy in the European Union,* ed. J. Loughlin, 229–254. Oxford: Oxford University Press.

Albertí, E., E. Aja, T. Font, X. Padrós, and J. Tornos. 2000. *Manual de Dret Públic de Catalunya.* Barcelona: Institut d'Estudies Autonòmics/Marical Pons.

Alter, P. 1994. *Nationalism.* London: E. Arnold.

Amoretti, U., and Bermeo, N. eds. 2004. *Federalism and Territorial Cleavages.* Baltimore: Johns Hopkins University Press.

Anderson, B. 1991. *Imagined Communities: Reflections on the Origins and Spread of Nationalism.* 2nd ed. London: Verso.

Anderson, J. 1990. Sceptical Reflections on a Europe of the Regions: Britain, Germany, and the European Regional Development Fund. *Journal of Public Policy* 10.

Anderson, R. D. 1995. *Education and the Scottish People, 1750–1918.* Edinburgh: Edinburgh University Press.

Anguera, P. 2000. *Els precedents del catalanisme: Catalanitat i anticentralisme: 1808–1868.* Barcelona: Empúries.

Antich, J. 1994. *El Virrei.* Barcelona: Planeta.

Aracil, R., and A. Segura, eds. 2000. *Memòria de la Transició a Espanya i a Catalunya.* Barcelona: Edicions Universitat de Barcelona.

Argelaguet, J. 1998. Las políticas lingüísticas: diversidad de modelos lingüisto-escolares. In *Políticas Públicas en España: Contenidos, redes de actores, y niveles de gobierno,* ed. R. Gomà and J. Subirats, 294–316. Barcelona: Ariel.

Argullol Murgades, E. ed. 2004. *Federalismo y autonomia*. Barcelona: Ariel.

Arroyo, F., and F. Valls. 1997. Una transició peculiar. In *Memòria de Catalunya*, ed. L. Bassets, J. B. Culla, and B. de Riquer, 37–47. Madrid: El País/Taurus.

Ascherson, N. 2002. *Stone Voices: The Search for Scotland*. London: Granta.

Bajpai, K. 1997. Diversity, Democracy, and Devolution in India. In *Government Policies and Ethnic Relations in Asia and the Pacific*, ed. M. E. Brown and S. Ganguly, 33–81. Cambridge: MIT Press.

Balcells, A., ed. 1988. *El Pensament Polític Català del Segle VXIII a mitjan Segle XX*. Barcelona: Edicions 62.

———. 1996. *Catalan Nationalism: Past and Present* (Geoffrey Walker, tr.). Houndmills: Macmillan.

Balfour, S. 1989. *Dictatorship, Workers and the City: Labour in Greater Barcelona since 1939*. Oxford: Clarendon.

———. 1996. 'The Lion and the Pig': Nationalism and National Identity in Fin-de-Siècle Spain. In *Nationalism and the Nation in the Iberian Peninsula: Competing and Conflicting Identities*, ed. C. Mar-Molinero and A. Smith, 107–118. Oxford: Berg.

Balme, R. 1996. *Les Politiques du Néo-Regionalisme*. Paris: Economica.

Baras, M., and J. Matas Dalmases. 1998. El Sistema Electoral i les Eleccions a Catalunya. In *El Sistema Polític de Catalunya*, ed. M. Caminal Badia and J. Matas Dalmases, 191–229. Madrid: Tecnos.

Barberà, O. 2001. La coalició Convergència i Unió. In *El pal de paller: Convergència Democràtica de Catalunya (1974–2000)*, ed. J. B. Culla, 285–320. Barcelona: Pòrtic.

Bartkus, V. O. 1999. *The Dynamic of Secession*. Cambridge: Cambridge University Press.

Bassets, L., J. B. Culla, and B. de Riquer, eds. 1997. *Memòria de Catalunya*. Madrid: Taurus.

Batista, A., and J. Playà. 1991. *La Gran Conspiració: Crònica de l'Assemblea de Catalunya*. Barcelona: Empúries.

Beer, S. H. 1982. *Britain Against Itself*. London: Faber and Faber.

Bell, D., and A. Christie. 2002. Finance—The Barnett Formula: Nobody's Child? In *The State of the Nations 2001: The Second Year of Devolution*, ed. A. Trench, 135–152. Thoreverton: Imprint Academic.

Bendix, R. 1969. *Nation-Building and Citizenship*. Berkeley: University of California Press.

Benet, J. 1978. *Catalunya sota el franquisme. Informe sobre la persecució de la llengua i la cultura de Catalunya*. Barcelona: Blume.

Bennie, L., J. Brand, and J. Mitchell. 1997. *How Scotland Votes*. Manchester: Manchester University Press.

Bermeo, N. 2002. A New Look at Federalism: The Import of Institutions. *Journal of Democracy* 13(2):96–110.

Billig, M. 1995. *Banal Nationalism*. Thousand Oaks, CA: Sage.

Bochel, J., and D. Denver. 1981. The Local Press. In *The Referendum Experience, Scotland 1979*, ed. J. Bochel, D. Denver, and A. Macartney, 99–109. Aberdeen: Aberdeen University Press.

Bochel, J., D. Denver, and A. Macartney. 1981. The Background to the Referendum. In *The Referendum Experience, Scotland 1979*, ed. J. Bochel, D. Denver, and A. Macartney, 1–11. Aberdeen: Aberdeen University Press.

Bogdanor, V. 1979. *Devolution*. Oxford: Oxford University Press.

———. 1980. The 40 per cent rule. *Parliamentary Affairs* 33 (3):249–263.

———. 2001. Constitutional Reform. In *The Blair Effect: The Blair Government 1997–2001*, ed. A. Seldon, 139–158. London: Little, Brown.

Boix Angelats, J. 1997. Del cop d'Estat a la LOAPA. In *Memòria de Catalunya*, ed. L. Bassets, J. B. Culla, and B. de Riquer, 253–266. Madrid: El País/Taurus.

Boix i Navarro, M. 1992. *Grups d'interès i política educativa a Catalunya*. Barcelona: Edicions 62.

Boix i Navarro, M., and J. A. García Suárez. 1985. *La LODE. Anàlisi i comentaris des de Catalunya a una llei controvertida*. Barcelona: Universitat de Barcelona.

Bonal, X. 1998. La política educativa: dimensiones de un proceso de transformación (1976–1996). In *Políticas Públicas en España: Contenidos, redes de actores, y niveles de gobierno*, ed. R. Gomà and J. Subirats, 153–175. Barcelona: Ariel.

Bonal, X., and X. Rambla. 2001. La Política educativa a Catalunya: universalització, fragmentació i reproducció de les desigualitats. In *Govern i polítiques públiques a Catalunya (1980–2000): Autonomía i benestar*, ed. R. Gomà and J. Subirats, 113–135. Bellaterra: Universitat Autònoma de Barcelona.

Boone, C. 2003. Decentralization as Political Strategy in West Africa. *Comparative Political Studies* 36 (4,May):355–380.

Borras-Alomar, S., T. Christiansen, and A. Rodriguez-Pose. 1994. Towards a 'Europe of the Regions'? Visions and Reality from a Critical Perspective. *Regional Politics and Policy* 4 (2):1–27.

Borrell, J. 2001. El Poder Judicial y las Comunidades Autónomas. Ph.D. Dissertation, Universitat Ramon Llull, Barcelona.

Börzel, T. 2002. *States and Regions in the European Union: Institutional Adaptation in Germany and Spain*. Cambridge: Cambridge University Press.

Bourrinet, J., ed. 1997. *Le Comité des Régions de l'Union Européenne*. Paris: Economica.

Bradley, A. W., and D. J. Christie. 1979. *The Scotland Act*. Edinburgh: W. Green and Son Ltd.

Brand, J. 1978. *The National Movement in Scotland*. London: Routledge Kegan Paul.

———. 1985. Nationalism and the Noncolonial Periphery: A Discussion of Scotland and Catalonia. In *New Nationalisms of the Developed West: Toward Explanation*, ed. E. Tiryakian and R. Rogowski, 277–293. London: Allen & Unwin.

Breuilly, J. 1993. *Nationalism and the State*. 2nd ed. Chicago: University of Chicago Press.

Bricall, J. M. 2003. *Memòria d'un silenci: El govern Tarradellas (1977–1980): Una certa manera de fer política*. Barcelona: Random House Mondadori.

Brown, A. 1998. Deepening Democracy: Women and the Scottish Parliament. In *Remaking the Union: Devolution and British Politics in the 1990s*, ed. H. Elcock and M. Keating, 103–119. Portland, OR: Frank Cass.

Brown, C. G. 1997. *The Social History of Religion in Scotland since 1730.* Edinburgh: Edinburgh University Press.

Brown, G., ed. 1975. *The Red Paper on Scotland.* Edinburgh: EUSPB.

Brown, K. M. 1992. *Kingdom or Province? Scotland and the Regal Union.* London: Macmillan.

Brown, M. 1981. The Scottish Morning Press. In *The Referendum Experience, Scotland 1979,* ed. J. Bochel, D. Denver, and A. Macartney, 109–120. Aberdeen: Aberdeen University Press.

Brown, S. 1999. The Scottish Office Education and Industry Department (SOEID). In *Scottish Education,* ed. T. G. K. Bryce and W. M. Humes, 115–123. Edinburgh: Edinburgh University Press.

Brubaker, R. 1996. *Nationalism Reframed: Nationhood and the National Question in the New Europe.* Cambridge: Cambridge University Press.

Bryce, T. G. K., and W. M. Humes. 1999. Scottish Secondary Education, Philosophy and Practice. In *Scottish Education,* ed. T. G. K. Bryce and W. M. Humes, 37–49. Edinburgh: Edinburgh University Press.

Bukowski, J., S. Piattoni, and M. Smyrl. 2002. Introduction. In *Between Globalization and Local Societies: The Space for Territorial Governance,* ed. J. Bukowski, S. Piattoni, and M. Smyrl, 1–19. Lanham, MD: Rowman and Littlefield.

Bukowski, J., and S. Rajagopalan, eds. 2000. *Redistribution of Authority: A Cross-Regional Perspective.* Westport: Praeger.

Bullman, U. 1997. The Politics of the Third Level. In *The Regional Dimension of the European Union: Towards a Third Level in Europe?,* ed. C. Jeffery, 3–19. Portland, OR: Frank Cass.

Bulpitt, J. 1983. *Territory and Power in the United Kingdom: An Interpretation.* Manchester: Manchester University Press.

Burrows, N. 2000. *Devolution.* London: Sweet and Maxwell.

Butler, D., A. Adonis, and T. Travers. 1994. *Failure in British Government: The Politics of the Poll Tax.* Oxford: Oxford University Press.

Butler, D., and D. Kavanagh. 1997. *The British General Election of 1997.* Basingstoke: Macmillan.

Cabana, F. 1998. Els principals grups econòmics a Catalunya. In *La Societat Catalana,* ed. S. Giner, 483–492. Barcelona: Institut d'Estadística de Catalunya.

———. 2000. *37 anys de franquisme a Catalunya: Una visió econòmica.* Barcelona: Pòrtic.

Cairney, P. 2002. New Public Management and the Thatcher Healthcare Legacy: Enough of the theory, what about the implementation? *British Journal of Politics and International Relations* 4(3):375–398.

Calsina i Buscà, M. 2001. 25 anys d'estructura organizativa de Convergència Democràtica de Catalunya. In *El pal de paller: Convergència Democràtica de Catalunya (1974–2000),* ed. J. B. Culla i Clarà, 217–248. Barcelona: Pòrtic.

Caminal Badia, M. 1998a. Catalanisme i autogovern. In *El sistema polític de Catalunya,* ed. M. Caminal Badia and J. Matas Dalmases, 25–53. Madrid: Tecnos.

———. 1998b. *Nacionalisme i Partits Nacionals a Catalunya.* Barcelona: Empúries.

Candel, F. 1964. *Els Altres Catalans.* Barcelona: Edicions 62.

————. 1985. *Els Altres Catalans Vint Anys Després*. Barcelona: Edicions 62.

Carmichael, P. 1995. *Central-Local Government Relations in the 1980s: Glasgow and Liverpool Compared*. Aldershot: Avebury.

Carr, R. 1982. *Spain 1808–1975*. 2nd ed. Oxford: Oxford University Press.

Carr, R., and J. P. Fusi. 1979. *Spain: Dictatorship to Democracy*. London: George Allen and Unwin.

Carson, K., and H. Idzikowska. 1989. The Social Production of Scottish Policing 1795–1900. In *Policing and Prosecution in Britain 1750–1850*, ed. D. Hay and F. Snyder, 267–297. Oxford: Clarendon.

Casademunt, A. 1998. Les organizacions empresarials. In *El sistema polític de Catalunya*, ed. M. Caminal and J. Matas Dalmases, 103–121. Madrid: Tecnos.

Castells, A. 2001. Models i polítiques de finançament de la Generalitat: Pautes d'estabilitat, canvi i conflicte. In *Govern i polítiques a Catalunya (1980–2000)*, ed. R. Gomà and J. Subirats, 49–68. Barcelona: Universitat de Barcelona/Universitat Autònoma de Barcelona.

Castells, A., and M. Parellada. 1998. L'economia catalana en el context espanyol i europeu. In *La Societat Catalana*, ed. S. Giner, 493–503. Barcelona: Institut d'Estadistica de Catalunya.

Castro Moral, L. 1994. La Izquierda Radical y la Tentación de las Armas. In *El Proyecto Radical: Auge y Declive de la Izquierda Radical en España, 1964–1992*, ed. J. M. Roca, 133–154. Madrid: Los Libros de la Catarata.

Cebrián, C. 1997. *Estimat PSUC*. Barcelona: Empúries.

Checkland, S. G. 1975. *Scottish Banking: A History, 1695–1973*. Glasgow: Collins.

Closa, C., and P. Heywood. 2004. *Spain and the European Union*. Basingstoke: Palgrave Macmillan.

Cohen, F. S. 1997. Proportional versus Majoritarian Ethnic Conflict Management in Democracies. *Comparative Political Studies* 30 (5 October):607–630.

Colley, L. 2002. *Captives: Britain, Empire, and the World 1600–1850*. London: Pimlico.

Collins, R. 1999. *Macrohistory: Essays in Sociology of the Long Run*. Stanford: Stanford University Press.

Colomé, G. 1989. *El Partit dels Socialistes de Catalunya: Estructura, funcionament, i electorat 1978–1984*. Barcelona: Edicions 62.

Colomer, J. M. 1986. *Cataluña como cuestion de estado: La idea de nación en el pensamiento político catalán (1939–1979)*. Madrid: Tecnos.

Comissió Organizadora XXV Aniversari Trobada de Lluçanes. 1997. *La Trobada de Lluçanes: Anticipació a la transició*. Barcelona: NOSTRUM.

Connor, W. 1994. *Ethnonationalism: The Quest for Understanding*. Princeton: Princeton University Press.

Constitution Unit. 1996. *Scotland's Parliament: Fundamentals for a New Scotland Act*. London: The Constitution Unit.

Conversi, D. 1997. *The Basques, the Catalans, and Spain: Alternative Routes to Nationalist Mobilization*. London: Hurst.

————. 2000. Autonomous Communities and the Ethnic Settlement in Spain. In *Autonomy and Ethnicity: Negotiating Competing Claims in Multi-Ethnic States*, ed. Y. Ghai, 122–144. Cambridge: Cambridge University Press.

Cornell, S. E. 2002. Autonomy as a Source of Ethnic Conflict: Caucasian Conflicts in Theoretical Perspective. *World Politics* 54(2):245–276.

Cox, R. H., and E. G. Frankland. 1999. The Federal State and the Breakup of Czechoslovakia. *Publius* 25 (1 Winter):71–88.

Craig, C. 1979. The Powers of the Scottish Assembly and Its Executive. In *Scotland: The Framework for Change*, ed. D. I. MacKay, 47–67. Edinburgh: Paul Harris.

Crewe, I., and A. King. 1995. *SDP: The Birth, Life, and Death of the Social Democratic Party.* Oxford: Oxford University Press.

Crexell, J. 1982. *Els fets del Palau i el Consell de guerra a Jordi Pujol.* Barcelona: Edicions La Magrana.

Cucurella, S. 2000. *Catalunya 2000: Situació política.* Barcelona: Pòrtic.

Cullell, P. and A. Farràs 2001. *L'Oasi Català.* Barcelona: Planeta.

Cunningham, G. 1989. Burns Night Massacre. *The Spectator* (18 January).

Dahl, R. A. 1967. The City in the Future of Democracy. *American Political Science Review* 61(4):953–970.

Dalyell, T. 1977. *Devolution: The End of Britain?* London: Cape.

Dardanelli, P. 2005. *Between Two Unions: Europeanisation and Scottish Devolution.* Manchester: Manchester University Press.

Darling, J. 1999. Scottish Primary Education, Philosophy and Practice. In *Scottish Education*, ed. T. G. K. Bryce and W. M. Humes, 27–36. Edinburgh: Edinburgh University Press.

Davie, G. 1961. *The Democratic Intellect: Scotland and Her Universities in the Nineteenth Century.* Edinburgh: Edinburgh University Press.

del Castillo, P. 1989. Financing of Spanish Political Parties. In *Comparative Political Finance in the 1980s*, ed. H. A. Alexander. Cambridge: Cambridge University Press.

———. 1990. La financiación de los Partidos en España. *Revista de Derecho Político* 22:149–175.

Denver, D., J. Mitchell, C. Pattie, and H. Bochel. 2000. *Scotland Decides: The Devolution Issue and the Scottish Referendum.* London: Frank Cass.

de Riquer, B. 1996. La Configuración del sistema autonómico. El caso de Cataluña. In *Historia de la transición 1975–1986*, ed. J. Tusell and A. Soto, 465–492. Madrid: Alianza.

Devine, T. M. 1999. *The Scottish Nation: 1700–2000.* London: Allan Lane/Penguin.

———. 2003. *Scotland's Empire 1600–1815.* Harmondsworth: Penguin.

de Winter, L. 1998. Conclusion: A Comparative Analysis of the Electoral, Office, and Policy Success of Ethnoregionalist Parties. In *Regionalist Parties in Europe*, ed. L. de Winter and H. Türsan, 204–247. London: Routledge.

Díez Medrano, J. 1995. *Divided Nations: Class, Politics, and Nationalism in the Basque Country and Catalonia.* Ithaca: Cornell University Press.

Döring, H. 2000. Ambiguous Centralism and Occasional 'Federalism by Stealth'—Great Britain. In *Public Policy and Federalism*, ed. D. Braun, 177–204. Aldershot: Ashgate.

Drucker, H. M., and N. Drucker, eds. 1978. *The Scottish Government Yearbook 1979.* Edinburgh: Paul Harris.

Dupuy, C., and Le Galès, P. 2006. The Impact of Regional Governments. In *Territory, Democracy and Justice: Regionalism and Federalism in Western Democracies*, ed. S. L. Greer, 116–138. Basingstoke: Palgrave Macmillan.

Dyer, M. 1981. Aberdeen and the Grampian Region. In *The Referendum Experience, Scotland 1979*, ed. J. Bochel, D. Denver, and A. Macartney, 56–65. Aberdeen: Aberdeen University Press.

Eisenstadt, S. N., and S. Rokkan. 1973. *Building States and Nations*. Beverly Hills: Sage.

Elliott, J. H. 1963. *The Revolt of the Catalans: A Study in the Decline of Spain (1598–1640)*. Cambridge: Cambridge University Press.

Equip de sociología electoral UAB. 1990. *Atlas Electoral de Catalunya 1982–1988*. Barcelona: Fundació Jaume Bofill.

Equip ESTUDIS. 1997. *Les tendències de l'evolució de la sanitat de Catalunya*. Barcelona: Editorial Mediterrània.

Ertman, T. 1997. *Birth of the Leviathan: Building States and Regimes in Medieval and Early Modern Europe*. Cambridge: Cambridge University Press.

Faulí, J. 1981. Omnium Cultural 1961–1981: Vint anys de cultura catalana difícil. Ph.D. Dissertation, University of Barcelona.

Ferrer, J., R. Galí, M. Ibàñez Escolet, E. Jordi, A. Manent, J. Solé i Sabaté, J. Faulí. 1984. *Jordi Pujol: Un Polític per a un poble*. Barcelona: Edicions 62.

Finlay, R. J. 1994. *Independent and Free: Scottish Politics and the Origins of the Scottish National Party 1918–1945*. Edinburgh: John Donald.

Flora, P., S. Kuhnle, and D. Urwin, eds. 1999. *State Formation, Nation-Building and Mass Politics in Europe: The Theory of Stein Rokkan*. Oxford: Oxford University Press.

Forsyth, M. 1989. Introduction. In *Federalism and Nationalism*, ed. M. Forsyth, 1–11. Leicester: Leicester University Press.

Fry, M. 1987. *Patronage and Principle: A Political History of Modern Scotland*. Aberdeen: Aberdeen University Press.

Fusi, J. P. 1996. El desarrollo autonómico. In *Historia de la transición*, ed. J. Tusell and A. Soto, 444–464. Madrid: Alianza.

Gabriel, P., C. Molinero, G. Ramos, J. Serrallonga, and Ysàs. 1989. *Commisions Obreres de Catalunya 1964–1989*. Barcelona: Empúries.

Gallacher, N. 1999. The Scottish Inspectorate and Their Operations. In *Scottish Education*, ed. T. G. K. Bryce and W. M. Humes, 136–141. Edinburgh: Edinburgh University Press.

Gallego, R. 1998. New Public Management Reforms in the Catalan Public Health Sector, 1985–1995: Institutional choices, transactions costs, and policy change. Ph.D. Dissertation, London School of Economics and Political Science.

———. 2001. La política sanitària catalana: la construcció d'un sistema universal de provisió pluralista. In *Govern i polítiques públiques a Catalunya (1980–2000): Autonomia i benestar*, ed. R. Gomà and J. Subirats, 137–158. Vol. 2. Bellaterra: Universitat Autonoma de Barcelona.

García Espuche, A. 1998. *Un Siglo Decisivo: Barcelona y Cataluña, 1550–1640*. Madrid: Alianza Editorial.

Garman, C., S. Haggard, and E. Willis. 2001. Fiscal Decentralization: A Political Theory with Latin American Cases. *World Politics* 53 (January):205–236.

Gellner, E. 1983. *Nations and Nationalism*. Ithaca: Cornell University Press.

Generalitat de Catalunya. 1980. *La Sanitat a Catalunya: Anàlisi i Propostes del Departament de Sanitat i Assistència Social*. Barcelona: Servei Central de Publicacions de la Generalitat de Catalunya—Departament de la Presidència.

Gerber, E., and K. Kollman. 2004. Introduction: Authority Migration: Defining an Emerging Research Agenda. *PS* 37(3):397–400.

Gerpe Landín, M. 1977. *L'estatut d'Autonomía de Catalunya i l'Estat integral*. Barcelona: Península.

Gibbons, J. 1999. Spain: A Semi-federal State? In *The Politics of Multinational States*, ed. D. MacIver, 271–297. Houndmills, Basingstoke: Macmillan.

Giner, S. 1980. *The Social Structure of Catalonia*. Sheffield: Anglo-Catalan Society.

Gobetti, D. 1996. La Lega: Regularities and Innovation in Italian Politics. *Politics and Society* 24 (1):57–82.

Gol i Gurina, J., J. M. de Miguel, J. Reventós, A. Segura, and F. Soler Sabarís. 1978. *La Sanitat als Països Catalans*. Barcelona: Edicions 62.

González Casanova, J. A. 1974. *Federalisme i Autonomia a Catalunya (1868–1938): Documents*. Barcelona: Curial.

———. 1986. El cambio inacabable (1975–1985). Barcelona: Anthropos.

———. 1988. Las Propuestas Históricas del Autogobierno Catalan en el Estado Español. In *Federalismo y Estado de las Autonomías*, ed. Various, 9–25. Barcelona: Planeta.

Gorski, P. S. 2000. An Early Modernist Critique of Modernist Theories of Nationalism. *American Journal of Sociology* 105 (5 March):1428–1468.

Gourevitch, P. 1980. *Paris and the Provinces: The Politics of Local Government Reform in France*. London: George Allen and Unwin.

———. 1986. *Politics in Hard Times: Comparative Responses to International Economic Crises*. Ithaca: Cornell University Press.

Granell, F., V. Pou i Serradell, M-A Sánchez Férriz, eds. 2002. *Catalunya dins la Unió Europea*. Barcelona: Edicions 62.

Greenwood, J. 2003. *Interest Representation in the European Union*. Basingstoke: Palgrave Macmillan.

Grau i Creus, M. 2000a. The Effects of Institutions and Political Parties upon Federalism: The Channeling and Integration of the Comunidades Autónomas within the Central-level Policy Process in Spain (1983–1996). Ph.D. Dissertation, European University Institute, Florence.

———. 2000b. Spain: Incomplete Federalism. In *Federalism and Political Performance*, ed. U. Wachendorfer-Schmidt, 58–77. London: Routledge.

Greer, S. L. 2004. *Territorial Politics and Health Policy*. Manchester: Manchester University Press.

———. 2005. Becoming European: Devolution, Europe and Health Policy Making. In *The Dynamics of Devolution: The State of the Nations 2005*, ed. A. Trench, 201–224. Exeter: Imprint Academic.

———. 2006a. Demanding Only Autonomy: Catalonia in the Spanish Democratic Transition. www.deepblue.lib.umich.edu.

————. 2006b. Conclusion: Territorial Politics Today. In *Territory, Democracy and Justice: Regionalism and Federalism in Western Democracies*, ed. S. L. Greer, 257–274. Basingstoke: Palgrave Macmillan.

————. 2006c. A Very English Institution. In *The English Question*, ed. R. Hazell, 194–219. Manchester: Manchester University Press.

————. forthcoming. The Fragile Divergence Machine: Citizenship, Policy Divergence, and Intergovernmental Relations. In *Devolution and Power in the United Kingdom*, ed. A. Trench. Manchester: Manchester University Press.

Greer, S. L., and G. M. Derluguian. 2000. Macroconcepts. *International Politics* 37 (4).

Greer, S. L., and H. Jarman. 2006. *Devolution and Policy Models*. www.deepblue.lib.umich.edu

Guiberneau, M. 1995. Spain: A Federation in the Making? In *Federalism: The Multiethnic Challenge*, ed. G. Smith, 239–254. London: Longman.

————. 1999. *Nations without states*. Oxford: Polity.

Guillén, A., and L. Cabiedes. 1998. La política sanitaria: Análisis y perspectivas del Sistema Nacional de Salud. In *Políticas Públicas en España: Contenidos, redes de actores y niveles de gobierno*, ed. R. Gomà and J. Subirats, 176–199. Barcelona: Ariel.

Gunther, R., and J. Hopkin. 2002. A Crisis of Institutionalization: The Collapse of the UCD in Spain. In *Political Parties: Old Concepts and New Challenges*, ed. R. Gunther, J. R. Montero, and J. J. Linz, 191–230. Oxford: Oxford University Press.

Gunther, R., J. R. Montero, and J. Botella. 2004. *Democracy in Modern Spain*. New Haven: Yale University Press.

Gunther, R., G. Sani, and G. Shabad. 1988. *Spain After Franco: The Making of a Competitive Party System*. Berkeley: University of California Press.

Hall, P. 1986. *Governing the Economy: The Politics of State Intervention in Britain and France*. Oxford: Oxford University Press.

————. 1992. The Movement from Keynesianism to Monetarism: Institutional Analysis and British Economic Policy in the 1970s. In *Structuring Politics: Historical Institutionalism in Comparative Analysis*, ed. S. Steinmo, K. Thelen, and F. Longstreth, 90–113. Cambridge: Cambridge University Press.

Hanham, H. J. 1965. The Creation of the Scottish Office, 1881–7. *Juridical Review*: 205–244.

————. 1969. *Scottish Nationalism*. London: Faber & Faber.

Hargreaves, J. 2000. *Freedom for Catalonia? Catalan Nationalism, Spanish Identity, and the Barcelona Olympic Games*. Cambridge: Cambridge University Press.

Harris, J. 1983. The Transition to High Politics in English Social Policy 1880–1914. In *High and Low Politics in Modern Britain*, ed. M. Bentley and J. Stevenson, 58–79. Oxford: Oxford University Press.

Harrison, B. 1996. *The Transformation of British Politics, 1860–1995*. Oxford: Oxford University Press.

Harty, S. 2001. The Institutional Foundations of Substate National Movements. *Comparative Politics* 33 (2 January):191–210.

————. 2005. Lawyers, Codification, and the Origins of Catalan Nationalism, 1881–1901. *Law and History Review* 20(2):349–384.

Harvie, C. 1992. In the Time of the Breaking of Nations. *Scottish Affairs* (1 Autumn):78–87.

———. 1993. *No Gods and Precious Few Heroes: Scotland since 1914.* 2nd ed. Ednburgh: Edinburgh University Press.

———. 1994. *The Rise of Regional Europe.* London: Routledge.

Harvie, C., and P. Jones. 2000. *The Road to Home Rule: Images of Scotland's Cause.* Edinburgh: Polygon at Edinburgh University Press.

Harvie, C., and I. Wood, eds. 1989. *Forward! Labour Politics in Scotland, 1888–1988.* Edinburgh: Polygon.

Hastings, A. 1997. *The Construction of Nationhood: Ethnicity, Religion, and Nationalism.* Cambridge: Cambridge University Press.

Hazell, R. 2000. Introduction: The First Year of Devolution. In *The State and the Nations: The First Year of Devolution in the United Kingdom,* ed. R. Hazell, 1–12. Thoreverton: Imprint Academic.

Hazell, R., and P. Jervis. 1998. *Devolution and Health.* London: The Nuffield Trust.

Heald, D., and A. McLeod. 2002. Beyond Barnett? Financing Devolution. In *Devolution in Practice: Public Policy Differences Within the UK,* ed. J. Adams and P. Robinson, 147–175. London: Institute for Public Policy Research.

Hechter, M. 1975. *Internal Colonialism: The Celtic Fringe in British National Development, 1536–1966.* Berkeley: University of California Press.

———. 1999[1975]. *Internal Colonialism: The Celtic Fringe in British National Development.* New Brunswick, NJ: Transaction.

———. 2000. *Containing Nationalism.* Oxford: Oxford University Press.

Heller, W. 2002. Regional Parties and National Parties in Europe: Spain's *Estado de las Autonomías. Comparative Political Studies* 35(6):657–685.

Hennessy, P. 1989. *Whitehall.* London: Fontana.

Hobsbawm, E. 1990. *Nations and Nationalism since 1780: Programme, Myth, Reality.* 2nd ed. Cambridge: Cambridge University Press.

Hocking, B. 1997. Regionalism: An International Relations Perspective. In *The Political Economy of Regionalism,* ed. M. Keating and J. Loughlin, 90–111. London: Frank Cass.

Holliday, I. 1992. Scottish Limits to Thatcherism. *Political Quarterly* 63 (4):448–459.

Hooghe, L., ed. 1996. *Cohesion Policy and European Integration: Building Multi-Level Governance.* Oxford: Oxford University Press.

Hooghe, L., and M. Keating. 1994. The Politics of European Union Regional Policy. *Journal of European Public Policy* 1 (3):367–393.

Hooghe, L., and G. Marks. 2001. *Multi-level Governance and European Integration.* Lanham, MD: Rowman and Littlefield.

Hopkin, J. 1999. *Party Formation and Democratic Transition in Spain: The Creation and Collapse of the Union of the Democratic Centre.* Houndmills, Basingstoke: Macmillan.

Horowitz, D. D. 2002. Constitutional Design: Proposals Versus Process. In *The Architecture of Democracy: Constitutional Design, Conflict Management, and Democracy,* ed. A. Reynolds, 15–36. Oxford: Oxford University Press.

House of Lords Select Committee on the Constitution. 2002. *Devolution: Inter-Institutional Relations in the United Kingdom.* London: HMSO.

Humes, W. M. 1986. *The Leadership Class in Scottish Education*. Edinburgh: John Donald.

———. 1999. Policy Making in Scottish Education. In *Scottish Education*, ed. T. G. K. Bryce and W. M. Humes, 73–82. Edinburgh: Edinburgh University Press.

Humes, W. M., and T. G. K. Bryce. 1999. The Distinctiveness of Scottish Education. In *Scottish Education*, ed. T. G. K. Bryce and W. M. Humes, 102–114. Edinburgh: Edinburgh University Press.

Huneeus, C. 1985. *La UCD y la transición a la democracia en España*. Madrid: Siglo Veintiuno/CIS.

Huntington, S. P. 1991. *The Third Wave: Democratization in the Late Twentieth Century*. Norman: University of Oklahoma Press.

Hutchison, I. G. C. 1986. *A Political History of Scotland, 1832–1924*. Edinburgh: John Donald.

———. 2000. Legislative and Executive Autonomy in Modern Scotland. In *The Challenge to Westminster: Sovereignty, Devolution and Independence*, ed. H. T. Dickinson and M. Lynch, 133–142. Edinburgh: John Donald.

———. 2001. *Scottish Politics in the Twentieth Century*. Houndmills, Basingstoke: Palgrave.

Ignatieff, M. 1996. Nationalism and Toleration. In *Europe's New Nationalism: States and Minorities in Conflict*, eds. R. Caplan and J. Feffer, 213–232. Oxford: Oxford University Press.

Irujo, J. M. 2005. La caja negra de los partidos. *El País* 18 April, 17–18.

Jacobson, S. 2005. Law and Nationalism in Nineteenth-Century Europe: The Case of Catalonia in Comparative Perspective. *Law and History Review* 20(2).

Jeffery, C. 1997a. Conclusions: Sub-National Authorities and 'European Domestic Policy.' In *The Regional Dimension of the European Union: Towards a Third Level in Europe?*, ed. C. Jeffery, 204–219. Portland, OR: Frank Cass.

———. 1997b. Regional Information Offices in Brussels and Multi-Level Governance in the EU: A UK-German Comparison. In *The Regional Dimension in the European Union: Towards a Third Level in Europe?*, ed. C. Jeffery, 183–203. Portland, OR: Frank Cass.

———. 2002. Editorial. *Regional and Federal Studies* 12(1)v–vii.

———. 2005. Devolution and the European Union: Trajectories and Futures. In *The Dynamics of Devolution: The State of the Nations 2005*, ed. A Trench, 179–199. Exeter: Imprint Academic.

———. 2006. Devolution and Social Citizenship: Which Society, Whose Citizenship? In *Territory, Democracy and Justice: Regionalism and Federalism in Western Democracies*, ed. S. L. Greer, 67–91. Basingstoke: Palgrave Macmillan.

Jenkins, S. 1995. *Accountable to None: The Tory Nationalization of Britain*. Harmondsworth: Penguin.

Jepperson, R. L. 1991. Institutions, Institutional Effects, and Institutionalism. In *The New Institutionalism in Organizational Analysis*, ed. W. W. Powell and P. J. DiMaggio, 143–163. Chicago: University of Chicago Press.

Jones, B. and M. Keating, ed. 1995. *The European Union and The Regions*. Oxford: Oxford University Press.

Jones, G. W. 1995. The Downfall of Margaret Thatcher. In *Prime Minister, Cabinet, and Core Executive*, ed. R. A. W. Rhodes and P. Dunleavy, 87–107. Basingstoke: Macmillan.

Jordan, G. 1979. *The Committee Stage of the Scotland and Wales Bill (1976–77)*. Edinburgh: University of Edinburgh Department of Politics (Waverley Papers series, #1).

Jordana, J. 1998. Sindicalisme i política. In *El sistema polític de Catalunya*, ed. M. Caminal and J. Matas Dalmases, 123–141. Madrid: Tecnos.

Jusdanis, G. 2001. *The Necessary Nation*. Princeton: Princeton University Press.

Kavanagh, D. 1990. *Thatcherism and British Politics: The End of Consensus?* 2nd ed. Oxford: Oxford University Press.

Keating, M. 1992. Spain: Peripheral Nationalism and State Response. In *The Politics of Ethnic Conflict Regulation*, ed. B. O'Leary and J. McGarry, 204–225. London: Routledge.

———. 1996. *Nations against the State: The New Politics of Nationalism in Quebec, Catalonia, and Scotland*. New York: St. Martin's Press.

———. 1998. *The New Regionalism in Western Europe: Territorial Restructuring and Political Change*. Cheltenham: Edward Elgar.

———. 2001. *Plurinational Democracy: Stateless Nations in a Post-Sovereignty Era*. Oxford: Oxford University Press.

———. 2005. Higher Education in Scotland and England after Devolution. *Regional and Federal Studies* 15(4): 423–435.

Keating, M., and D. Bleiman. 1979. *Labour and Scottish Nationalism*. London: Macmillan.

Keating, M., and B. Jones. 1995. Nations, Regions, and Europe: The UK Experience. In *The European Union and the Regions*, ed. B. Jones and M. Keating, 89–114. Oxford: Oxford University Press.

Keating, M. and McEwen, N. eds. 2005. Devolution and Public Policy: A Comparative Perspective. *Regional and Federal Studies* 15(4).

Kellas, J. 1979. The Policy Process. In *Scotland: The Framework for Change*, ed. D. I. MacKay, 15–163. Edinburgh: Paul Harris.

———. 1989. *The Scottish Political System*. 4th ed. Cambridge: Cambridge University Press.

Kemp, A. 1993. *The Hollow Drum: Scotland Since the War*. Edinburgh: Mainstream.

Kerr, J. 1977. The Failure of the Scotland and Wales Bill: No will, no way. In *Scottish Government Yearbook 1978*, ed. H. M. Drucker and M. G. Clarke, 113–119. Edinburgh: Paul Harris.

Köhler, H.-D. 2000. *El Movimeniento Sindical en España: Transición Democrática, Regionalismo, Modernización Económica*. Madrid: Fundamentos.

Kohn, H. 1945. *The Idea of Nationalism: A Study of its Origins and Backgrounds*. London: Macmillan.

Kumar, K. 2003. *The Making of English National Identity*. Cambridge: Cambridge University Press.

Lange, N. 1998. Business Interests in Regionalist Conflicts: Changing Opportunity Structures through European Integration? *Regional and Federal Studies* 8 (3):1–30.

Lapidoth, R. 1996. *Autonomy: Flexible Solutions to Ethnic Conflicts*. Washington, D.C.: United States Institute of Peace.

Lee, C. H. 1995. *Scotland and the United Kingdom: The Economy and the Union in the Twentieth Century*. Manchester: Manchester University Press.

Leff, C. S. 1999. Democratization and Disintegration in Multinational States: The Breakup of the Communist Federations. *World Politics* 51(2):205–235.

Le Galès, P., and C. Lequesne, eds. 1998. *Regions in Europe*. London: Routledge.

Leguina, J. 1984. *Escritos sobre autonomías territoriales*. Madrid: Tecnos.

Levack, B. P., ed. 1987. *The Formation of the British State: England, Scotland, and the Union, 1603–1707*. Oxford: Clarendon.

Lieven, D., and J. McGarry. 1992. Ethnic Conflict in the Soviet Union and Its Successor States. In *The Politics of Ethnic Conflict Regulation*, ed. B. O'Leary and J. McGarry, 62–81. London: Routledge.

Lijphart, A. 1977. *Democracy in Plural Societies: A Comparative Exploration*. New Haven: Yale University Press.

Linz, J. J. 1970. An Authoritarian Regime: Spain. In *Mass Politics*, ed. E. Allardt and S. Rokkan. New York: Free Press.

———. 1975. Totalitarian and Authoritarian Regimes. In *Handbook of Political Science*, ed. F. I. Greenstein and N. W. Polsby, 175–411. Reading: Addison-Wesley.

Linz, J., and A. Stepan. 1992. Political Identities and Electoral Sequences: Spain, the Soviet Union, and Yugoslavia. *Daedalus*:123–139.

Logan, J. R., and H. L. Molotch. 1987. *Urban Fortunes: The Political Economy of Place*. Berkeley: University of California Press.

Long, N. E. 1962. The Local Community as an Ecology of Games. In *The Polity*, ed. C. Press, 139–155. Chicago: Rand McNally.

López-Casanovas, G. 2003. La descentralización sanitaria. Lecciones desde la experiencia española. In *Federalismo y políticas de salud: Descentralización y relaciones intergubermentales desde una perspectiva comparada*, ed. C. Auclair and C. Gadsden, 112–137. Ottawa/Mexico City: Forum of Federations/ Instituto nacional para el federalismo y el desarrollo municipal.

Lorés, J. 1985. *La Transició a Catalunya (1977–1984): El Pujolisme i els altres*. Barcelona: Empúries.

Loughlin, J. 1997. Representing Regions in Europe: The Committee of the Regions. In *The Regional Dimension in the European Union: Towards a Third Level in Europe?*, ed. C. Jeffery, 147–165. Portland, OR: Frank Cass.

Loughlin, M. 2000. The Restructuring of Central-Local Government Relations. In *The Changing Constitution*. 4th ed., ed. J. Jowell and D. Oliver, 137–166. Oxford: Oxford University Press.

Loyer, B., and J. L. Villanova. 1999. Etats et souverainetés en Europe: l'exemple catalan. *Hérodote* 95 (4e tr.):21–33.

Lynch, M. 1991. *Scotland: A New History*. London: Pimlico.

Lynch, P. 1996. *Minority Nationalism and European Integration*. Cardiff: University of Wales Press.

———. 1998. Reactive Capital: The Scottish Business Community and Devolution. In *Remaking the Union: Devolution and British Politics in the 1990s*, ed. H. Elcock and M. Keating, 86–102. London: Frank Cass.

―――. 2002. SNP: The History of the Scottish National Party. Cardiff: Welsh Academic Press.

Macartney, A. 1981. The Protagonists. In The Referendum Experience, Scotland 1979, ed. J. Bochel, D. Denver, and A. Macartney, 12–42. Aberdeen: Aberdeen University Press.

MacInnes, J. 2004. Catalonia is not Scotland. Scottish Affairs 47(Spring):135–155.

Mackenzie, M. L. 1999. The Politics of Scottish Education. In Scottish Education, ed. T. G. K. Bryce and W. M. Humes, 83–92. Edinburgh: Edinburgh University Press.

Mackie, D. 1999. The Work of the Scottish Higher Education Funding Council (SHEFC). In Scottish Education, ed. T. G. K. Bryce and W. M. Humes, 124–135. Edinburgh: Edinburgh University Press.

Maltby, W. 2002. The Reign of Charles V. Basingtoke: Palgrave.

Manor, J. 1999. The Political Economy of Decentralization. Washington, D.C.: World Bank.

Maravall, J M. 2003. The Rule of Law as a Political Weapon. In Democracy and the Rule of Law, eds. J. M. Maravall and A. Przeworski, 261–302. Cambridge: Cambridge University Press.

Marcet, J. 1984. Convèrgencia Democratica de Catalunya: El partit i el movement polític. Barcelona: Edicions 62.

Marcet, J., and J. Argelauget. 1998. Nationalist Parties in Catalonia. In Regionalist Parties in Europe, ed. L. de Winter and H. Türsan, 70–86. London: Routledge.

March, J. G., and J. P. Olsen. 1989. Rediscovering Institutions: The Organizational Basis of Politics. New York: Free Press.

Marfany, J.-L. 1996. La Cultura del Catalanisme. 2nd ed. Barcelona: Empúries.

Marks, G., L. Hooghe, and K. Blank. 1996a. European Integration from the 1980s: State-Centric v. Multi-Level Governance. Journal of Common Market Studies 34(3):341–378.

Marks, G., J. Salk, L. Ray, and F. Nielsen. 1996b. Conflict, Cracks, and Competencies: Regional Mobilization in the European Union. Comparative Political Studies 29(2):164–193.

Marr, A. 1995. The Battle for Scotland. London: Penguin.

Matas Dalmases, J. 1995. Els Alts Càrrecs: Política i Administració a la Generalitat de Catalunya. Barcelona: Escola de Administració Pública de Catalunya.

―――. 2001. Convergència Democràtica de Catalunya, partit de govern. In El pal de paller: Convergència Democràtica de Catalunya (1974–2000), ed. J. B. Culla i Clara, 99–126. Barcelona: Pòrtic.

McCrae, M. 2003. The National Health Service in Scotland: Origins and Ideals, 1900–1950. East Linton: Tuckwell.

McCrone, D. 1992. Understanding Scotland: The Sociology of a Stateless Nation. London: Routledge.

McGarry, J., and B. O'Leary. 1993. Introduction: The Macro-Political Regulation of Ethnic Conflict. In The Politics of Ethnic Conflict Regulation: Case Studies of Protracted Ethnic Conflicts, ed. J. McGarry and B. O'Leary, 1–40. London: Routledge.

McLean, I. 2004. Scottish Labour and British Politics. In *The Scottish Labour Party: History, Institutions and Ideas*, ed. G. Hassan, 146–158. Edinburgh: Edinburgh University Press.

McLean, I., and McMillan, A. 2005. *State of the Union*. Oxford: Oxford University Press.

McPherson, A., and C. D. Raab. 1988. *Governing Education: A Sociology of Policy since 1945*. Edinburgh: Edinburgh University Press.

McRoberts, K. 2001. *Catalonia: Nation Building Without a State*. Toronto: Oxford University Press.

Meguid, B. M. 2002. Stability in the Face of Change: A Dynamic Model of Mainstream Party Response to Rising Parties in Western Europe. Ph.D. Dissertation, Harvard University, Cambridge, MA.

Méndez Lago, M. 2000. *La estrategia organizativa del Partido Socialista Obrero Español (1975–1996)*. Madrid: Siglo Veintiuno/CIS.

Meston, M. C., W. D. H. Sellar, and Lord Cooper. 1991. *The Scottish Legal Tradition*. 2nd ed. Edinburgh: The Saltire Society.

Midwinter, A., M. Keating, and J. Mitchell. 1991. *Politics and Public Policy in Scotland*. Houndmills: Macmillan.

Missé, A. 1997. El Cas Banca Catalana. In *Memòria de Catalunya*, ed. L. Bassets, J. Culla, and B. de Riquer, 327–341. Madrid: El País/Taurus.

Mitchell, J. 1990. *Conservatives and the Union: A Study of Conservative Party Attitudes to Scotland*. Edinburgh: Edinburgh University Press.

———. 1996. *Strategies for Self-Government: The Campaigns for a Scottish Parliament*. Edinburgh: Polygon.

———. 2003. *Governing Scotland*. Basingstoke: Palgrave Macmillan.

———. forthcoming. Unity of Government, Political Equality and Diverse Institutions: The UK Territorial Constitution in Historic Perspective. In *Devolution and Power in the United Kingdom*, ed. A. Trench. Manchester: Manchester University Press.

Mitchneck, B. A., S. L. Solnick and K. Stoner-Weiss. 2001. Federalization. In *Fragmented Space in the Russian Federation*, eds. B. A. Ruble, J. Koehn, and N. E. Popson, 123–156. Baltimore: Johns Hopkins University Press.

Mitra, S. K. 2000. The Nation, State, and Federal Process in India. In *Federalism and Political Performance*, ed. U. Wachendorfer-Schmidt, 40–57. London: Routledge.

Molas, I. 1972. *El Sistem de partits politics a Catalunya (1931–36)*. Barcelona: Edicions 62.

Molinero, C., J. Tébar, and P. Ysàs. 1993. Comisiones Obreras de Cataluña: De movimiento sociopolítico a confederación sindical. In *Historia de Comisiones Obreras (1958–1988)*, ed. D. Ruiz, 69–110. Madrid: Siglo Veintiuno.

Molinero, C., and P. Ysàs. 1991. *Els industrials catalans durant el franquisme*. Vic: Eumo.

———. 1998. *Productores disciplinados y minorías subversivas: Clase obrera y conflictividad laboral en la España franquista*. Madrid: Siglo Veintiuno.

Moore, C., and S. Booth. 1989. *Managing Competition: Meso-Corporatism, Pluralism, and the Negotiated Order in Scotland*. Oxford: Clarendon.

Morata, F. 1995. Spanish Regions in the European Community. In *The European Union and the Regions*, ed. B. Jones and M. Keating, 115–134. Oxford: Oxford University Press.

Moreno, L. 1986. *Decentralization in Britain and Spain: The Cases of Scotland and Catalonia*. Ph.D. thesis. Edinburgh: University of Edinburgh.

———. 1988. Scotland and Catalonia: The Path to Home Rule. In *The Scottish Government Yearbook*, ed. D. McCrone and A. Brown, 166–181. Edinburgh: Unit for the Study of Government in Scotland.

———. 1997. *La federalización de España: Poder político y territorio*. Madrid: Alianza Editorial.

———. 2002. Decentralization in Spain. *Regional Studies* 36 (4):399–408.

Morrill, J. 1996. Three Stuart Kingdoms, 1603–1689. In *The Oxford Illustrated History of Tudor and Stuart Britain*, ed. J. Morrill, 74–90. Oxford: Oxford University Press.

Morrison, J. 2001. *Reforming Britain: New Labour, New Constitution?* London: Reuters.

Morton, G. 1999. *Unionist Nationalism: Governing Urban Scotland, 1830–1860*. East Linton: Tuckwell.

Motyl, A. 1999. *Revolutions, Nations, Empires: Conceptual Limits and Theoretical Possibilities*. New York: Columbia University Press.

Mullin, R. 1981. Edinburgh's Silence. In *The Referendum Experience: Scotland 1979*, ed. J. Bochel, D. Denver, and A. Macartney, 86–92. Aberdeen: Aberdeen University Press.

Muñoz i Lloret, J. M. 1997. *Jaume Vicens i Vives, 1910–1960: Una biografía intelectual*. Barcelona: Edicions 62.

Murkens, J. et al. 2001. *Scottish Independence: A Practical Guide*. Edinburgh: Edinburgh University Press/The Constitution Unit.

Murphy, A. 1995. Belgium's Regional Divergence: Along the Road to Federation. In *Federalism: The Multiethnic Challenge*, ed. G. Smith, 73–100. London: Longman.

Nairn, T. 1981. *The Break-up of Britain*. 2nd ed. London: New Left Books.

Naughtie, J. 1979. The Scotland Bill in the House of Commons. In *Scottish Government Yearbook 1979*, ed. H. Drucker and N. Drucker. Edinburgh: Unit for the Study of Government in Scotland.

———. 1980. The Year at Westminster; The Scotland Act Brings Down the Government. In *Scottish Government Yearbook 1980*, ed. H. Drucker and N. Drucker. Edinburgh: Unit for the Study of Government in Scotland.

Nay, O. 1997. *La Région, Une Institution: La représentation, le pouvoir, et la règle dans l'espace régional*. Paris: L'Harmattan.

Negriér, E. and B. Jouve, eds. 1998. *Que gouvernent les régions d'Europe? Échanges politiques et mobilizations régionales*. Paris: L'Harmattan.

Newell, J. L. 1998. The Scottish National Party. In *Regionalist Parties in Europe*, ed. L. de Winter and H. Türsan, 105–124. London: Routledge.

Nottingham, C., ed. 2000. *The NHS in Scotland: The Legacy of the Past and the Prospect of the Future*. Aldershot: Ashgate.

Núñez, X-M. 2005. Regions, Nations and Nationalities: On the Process of Territorial Identity-Building During Spain's Democratic Transition and Consolidation. In *Spanish and Latin American Transitions to Democracy*, eds. C. Waisman and R. Rein, 55–79. Brighton: Sussex Academic Press.

Nuñez, C. E., and G. Tortella. 2005. Economic Development and the Problems of National State Formation: The Case of Spain. In *Nation, State, and the Economy in History*, eds. A. Teichova and H. Matis, 113–131. Cambridge: Cambridge University Press.

Oates, E. F. 1999. An Essay on Fiscal Federalism. *Journal of Economic Literature* 37:1120–1149.

Ohmae, K. 1995. *The End of the Nation State: The Rise of Regional Economies*. New York: Free Press.

O'Leary, B. 2003. What States Can Do With Nations: An Iron Law of Nationalism and Federation? In *The Nation-State in Question*, ed. T. V. Paul, G. J. Ikenberry, and J. A. Hall, 51–78. Princeton: Princeton University Press.

Ómnium Cultural, ed. 1998. *Catalunya i Espanya: Una relació econòmica i fiscal a revisar*. Barcelona: Proa.

O'Neill, K. 2003. Decentralization as an Electoral Strategy. *Comparative Political Studies* 36 (9 November):1068–1091.

Ortuño Anoya, P. 2002. *European Socialists and Spain: The Transition to Democracy, 1959–77*. Basingstoke: Pagrave Macmillan.

Other, A. N. 1999. The Federal State and the Breakup of Czechoslovakia: An Institutional Analysis. *Publius* 25 (1 Winter):71–88.

Page, E. C. 1977. Michael Hechter's Internal Colonialism Thesis: Some Theoretical and Methodological Problems. Glasgow: Strathclyde Center for Studies of Public Policy.

Pallarés, F., ed. 1999. *Eleccions i comportament electoral a Catalunya 1989–1999*. Barcelona: Mediterrània.

———. 2001. Annex: Les Eleccions Generals de Març del 2000 a Catalunya. Una Perspectiva Evolutiva. In *Eleccions i comportament electoral a Catalunya 1989–1999*. 2nd ed., ed. F. Pallarés, Annex. Barcelona: Mediterrània.

Panebianco, A. 1988. *Political Parties: Organization and Power*. Cambridge: Cambridge University Press.

Paquin, S. 2001. *La Revanche des Petites Nations: Le Quebec, L'Ecosse, et la Catalogne face à la Mondilisation*. Montreal: VLB.

Patchett, K. 2000. The New Welsh Constitution: The Government of Wales Act 1998. In *The Road to the National Assembly*, ed. J. B. Jones and D. Balsom, 229–264. Cardiff: University of Wales Press.

Paterson, L. 1994. *The Autonomy of Modern Scotland*. Edinburgh: Edinburgh University Press.

———. 1998. Scottish Home Rule: Radical Break or Pragmatic Adjustment? In *Remaking the Union: Devolution and British Politics in the 1990s*, ed. H. Elcock and M. Keating, 53–67. London: Frank Cass.

———. 2003. *Scottish Education in the Twentieth Century*. Edinburgh: Edinburgh University Press.

Payne, S. G. 2000. Catalan and Basque Nationalism: Contrasting Patterns. In *Ethnic Challenges to the Modern Nation State*, ed. S. Ben-Ami, Y. Peled, and A. Spektorowski, 95–107. Houndmills, Basingstoke: Macmillan.

Pempel, T. J. 1990. Introduction. Uncommon Democracies: The One-Party Dominant Regimes. In *Uncommon Democracies: The One-Party Dominant Regimes*, ed. T. J. Pempel, 1–31. Ithaca: Cornell University Press.

Pérez, S. 1997. *Banking on Privilege: The Politics of Spanish Financial Reform*. Ithaca: Cornell University Press.

Perez Yruela, M., and S. Giner, eds. 1988. *El Corporatismo en España*. Barcelona: Ariel.

Pollitt, C. 1993. *Managerialism and the Public Services*. 2nd ed. Oxford: Blackwell.

Popovski, V. 1995. Yugoslavia: Politics, Federation, Nation. In *Federalism: The Multi-Ethnic Challenge*, ed. G. Smith, 180–207. London: Longman.

Posen, B. R. 1993. The Security Dilemma and Ethnic Conflict. *Survival* 35(1): 27–47.

Prats i Català, J. 1988. Una reflexión sobre las alternativas planteadas al centralismo español y su significación política diversa. In *Federalismo y Estado de las Autonomías*, ed. Various, 51–74. Barcelona: Planeta.

Prenafeta, Ll. 1999. *L'Home del silenci*. Barcelona: Planeta.

Preston, P. 1990. *The Triumph of Democracy in Spain*. London: Routledge.

———. 2005. *Juan Carlos: Steering Spain from Dictatorship to Democracy*. London: HarperCollins Perennial.

Przeworski, A., and H. Teune. 1970. *The Logic of Comparative Social Inquiry*. New York: Wiley.

*Publius*. 2006. Special issue on devolution in the United Kingdom, 36(1 Winter).

Raffe, David. 2006. Devolution and Divergence in Education Policy. In *Devolution in Practice 2006: Public Policy Differences within the UK*, eds. K. Schmuecker and J. Adams, 52–70. Newcastle: IPPR.

Ragin, C. 1987. *The Comparative Method: Moving Beyond Qualitative and Quantitative Strategies*. Berkeley: University of California Press.

Ragin, C., D. Berg-Schlosser, and G. de Meur. 1996. Political Methodology: Qualitiative Methods. In *A New Handbook of Political Science*, ed. R. E. Goodin and H.-D. Klingemann, 749–768. Oxford: Oxford University Press.

Rao, N. 1996. *Towards Welfare Pluralism: Public Services in a Time of Change*. Aldershot: Dartmouth.

Rawlings, R. 1999. The New Model Wales. *Journal of Law and Society* 25:461–509.

———. 2003. Towards a Parliament: Three Faces of the National Assembly for Wales. In *Contemporary Wales*, ed. R. Wyn Jones. Vol. 15. Cardiff: University of Wales Press. O'Donnell Lecture, University of Wales.

Rebollo, L. M. 2000. Estudio Preliminar. In *Constitución Española*, ed. L. M. Rebollo, 13–48. Elcano, Navarra: Arandazi Editorial.

Renyer Alimbau, J. 1995. *Catalunya, qüestió d'estat: Vint-i-cinc anys d'independentisme català (1968–1993)*. Tarragona: Edicions El Medòl.

Rhodes, R. A. W. 1981. *Control and Power in Central-Local Government Relations*. Westmead: Gower/Social Sciences Research Council.

Richardson, J. J. 2000. Government, Interest Groups and Policy Change. *Political Studies* 48:1006–1025.

Rico, A., M. Balaguer, and P. González Alvarez. 2001. The Spanish State and the Medical Profession in Primary Health Care: Doctors, Veto Points and Reform Attempts. In *Success and Failure in Public Governance*, eds. M. Bovens, P. 't Hart, and B. G. Peters, 238–258. Cheltenham: Edward Elgar.

Risk, C. J. 1977. Devolution: The Commercial Community's Fears. In *Scottish Government Yearbook 1978*, ed. H. M. Drucker and M. D. Clarke, 120–128. Edinburgh: Paul Harris.

Robertson, D. S. 1998. Scotland's New Towns: A Modernist Experiment in State Corporatism. In *Scottish Power Centres from the Early Middle Ages to the Twentieth Century*, ed. S. Foster, A. Macinnes, and R. Macinnes, 210–239. Glasgow: Cruithne Press/University of Glasgow Postgraduate School of Scottish Studies.

Robles Egea, A., ed. 1996. *Política en penumbra: Patronazgo y clientelismo político en la España contemporànea*. Madrid: Siglo Veintiuno.

Rodríguez, J. A., and J. M. de Miguel. 1990. *Salud y Poder*. Madrid: Centro de Investigaciones Sociológicas/Siglo Veintiuno.

Roeder, P. G. 1991. Soviet Federalism and Ethnic Mobilization. *World Politics* 43 (2):197–232.

Rokkan, S., and D. W. Urwin, eds. 1982. *The Politics of Territorial Identity: Studies in European Regionalism*. Beverly Hills: Sage.

Rokkan, S., and D. Urwin. eds. 1983. *Economy, Territory, Identity: Politics of West European Peripheries*. London: Sage.

Rothchild, D., and D. A. Lake. Containing Fear: The Management of Transnational Ethnic Conflict. In *The International Diffusion of Ethnic Conflict: Fear, Diffusion, and Escalation*, eds. D. A. Lake and D. Rothchild, 205–226. Princeton: Princeton University Press.

Royal Commission on the Constitution (Kilbrandon Commission). 1973. *Report of the Royal Commission on the Constitution, 1969–73, With Evidence*. London: HMSO.

Rubio Llorente, F. 1997. L'enfonsament de la LOAPA. In *Memòria de Catalunya*, ed. L. Bassets, J. Culla, and B. de Riquer, 273–275. Madrid: El País/Taurus.

Russell, M. 2000. *Reforming the House of Lords: Lessons from Abroad*. Oxford: Oxford University Press.

Saideman, S. M., D. J. Lanoue, M. Carpenni, and S. Stanton. 2002. Democratization, Political Institutions, and Ethnic Conflict: A Pooled Time-Series Analysis. *Comparative Political Studies* 35 (1 February):103–129.

Sales, N. 2002. *Els segles de la decadencia (segles XVI–XVIII)*. 2nd ed. Barcelona: Edicions 62.

Sánchez, J.-E. 1998. L'Estructura empresarial i productiva de Catalunya. In *La Societat Catalana*, ed. S. Giner, 535–552. Barcelona: Institut d'Estadística de Catalunya.

Sancho i Valverde, S., and C. Ros i Navarro. 1998. La població de Catalunya en perspectiva històrica. In *La Societat Catalana*, ed. S. Giner, 91–112. Barcelona: Institut d'Estadística de Catalunya.

Santacana, C. 1995. El pensament nacionalista d'ERC (1975–1992). In *El nacionalisme com a ideologia*, ed. J. Termes and J. Casassas, 143–157. Barcelona: Proa.

Scharpf, F. 1997. *Games Real Actors Play*. Boulder: Westview.

Schmidt, V. 1990. *Democratizing France: The Political and Administrative History of Decentralization*. Cambridge: Cambridge University Press.

Schmuecker, K. and J. Adams, eds. 2005. *Devolution in Practice 2006: Public Policy Differences within the United Kingdom*. Newcastle: IPPR.

Schöpflin, G. 1992. The Rise and Fall of Yugoslavia. In *The Politics of Ethnic Conflict Regulation*, ed. B. O'Leary and J. McGarry, 172–203. London: Routledge.
———. 2000. *Nations, Identity, Power: The New Politics of Europe*. London: Hurst.
Scott, J., and M. Hughes. 1980. *The Anatomy of Scottish Capital*. London: Croon Helm.
Scottish Constitutional Convention. 1995. *Scotland's Parliament, Scotland's Right*. Edinburgh: Scottish Constitutional Convention.
Seawright, D. 1999. *An Important Matter of Principle: The Decline of the Scottish Conservative and Unionist Party*. Aldershot: Ashgate.
———. 2002. The Scottish Conservative and Unionist Party: 'The Lesser Spotted Tory'? In *Tomorrow's Scotland*, ed. G. Hassan, 66–82. London: Lawrence and Wishart.
Sepúlvedra, I. 1996. La eclosión nacionalista: Regionalismos, nacionalidades y autonomías. In *Historia de la transición 1974–1985*, ed. J. Tusell and A. Soto, 409–443. Madrid: Alanza.
Serrano, S. 1997. La victòria per sorpresa de Pujol. In *Memòria de Catalunya*, ed. L. Bassets, J. B. Culla, and B. de Riquer, 201–213. Madrid: El País/Taurus.
Seyd, P. 1987. *The Rise and Fall of the Labour Left*. Basingstoke: Macmillan.
Shafer, D. M. 1994. *Winners and Losers: How Sectors Shape the Developmental Prospects of States*. Ithaca: Cornell University Press.
Share, D. 1999. From Policy-Seeking to Office-Seeking: The Metamorphosis of the Spanish Socialist Workers Party. In *Policy, Office, or Votes? How Political Parties in Western Europe Make Hard Decisions*, ed. W. Müller and K. Strøm, 89–111. Cambridge: Cambridge University Press.
Sharpe, L. J. 1993. *The Rise of Meso-Level Government in Europe*. Beverly Hills: Sage.
Shulman, S. 2002. Challenging the Civic/Ethnic and West/East Dichotomies in the Study of Nationalism. *Comparative Political Studies* 35 (5 June):554–585.
Simeon, Rachel. 2003. The Long-term Care Decision: Social Rights and Democratic Diversity. In *The State and the Nations: The Third Year of Devolution in the United Kingdom*, ed. R. Hazell, 215–232. Exeter: Imprint Academic.
Simeon, Richard. 2006. Federalism and Social Justice: Thinking through the Jungle. In *Territory, Democracy and Justice: Regionalism and Federalism in Western Democracies*, ed. S. L. Greer, 18–43. Basingstoke: Palgrave Macmillan.
Simeon, Richard., and D.-P. Conway. 2001. Federalism and the Management of Conflict in Multinational Societies. In *Multinational Democracies*, ed. A.-G. Gagnon and J. Tully, 338–365. Cambridge: Cambridge University Press.
Sked, A., and C. Cook. 1993. *Post-War Britain: A Political History*. 4th ed. London: Penguin.
Skocpol, T., and M. Somers. 1994. The Uses of Comparative History in Macrosocial Inquiry. In *Social Revolutions in the Modern World*, ed. T. Skocpol, 72–98. Cambridge: Cambridge University Press.
Smith, A. 1995. *L'Europe Politique au Miroir du Local: Les fonds structurels et les zones rurales en France, en Espagne, et au Royaume-Uni*. Paris: L'Harmattan.
———. 1998. The Sub-regional Level: Key Battleground for the Structural Funds? In *Regions in Europe*, ed. P. Le Galès and C. Lequesne, 50–66. London: Routledge.

Smith, A. D. 1991. *National Identity*. Reno and Las Vegas: University of Nevada Press.

Smith, G. 1995. Mapping the Federal Condition: Ideology, Political Practice, and Social Justice. In *Federalism: The Multiethnic Challenge*, ed. G. Smith, 1–28. London: Longman.

Smith, M. 1994. *Paper Lions: The Scottish Press and National Identity*. Edinburgh: Polygon.

Smyrl, M. A. 1997. Does EC Regional Policy Empower the Regions? *Governance* 10 (3):287–309.

Snyder, J. 2000. *From Voting to Violence: Democratization and Nationalist Conflict*. New York: W. W. Norton.

Sobrequés, J., and S. Riera. 1982. *L'Estatut d'autonomía de Catalunya 1979*. Barcelona: Edicions 62.

Solé Tura, J. 1967. *Catalanisme, i Revolució Burgesa*. Barcelona: Edicions 62.

———. 1986. *Nacionalidades y Nacionalismos en España: Autonomías, Federalismo, Autodeterminación*. Madrid: Alanza Editorial.

———. 1999. *Una Història Optimista: Memòries*. Barcelona: Edicions 62.

Solé Tura, J., and E. Aja. 1977. *Constituciones y períodos constituyentes en España (1808–1936)*. Madrid: Siglo Veintiuno.

Soto, A. 1996. Conflictividad social y transición sindical. In *Historia de la transicion 1975–1986*, ed. J. Tusell and A. Soto, 363–408. Madrid: Alianza Editorial.

Stepan, A. 1999. Federalism and Democracy: Beyond the U.S. Model. *Journal of Democracy* 10(4):19–34.

———. 2001. *Arguing Comparative Politics*. Oxford: Oxford University Press.

Stokes, W. 1998. Regional Finance and the Definition of a Financial Region. In *Issues of Regional Identity: In Honor of John Marshall*, ed. E. Royle, 118–153. Manchester: Manchester University Press.

Sturm, R. D. 2006. The Adventure of Divergence: An Inquiry into the Preconditions for Institutional Diversity and Political Innovation after Political Decentralization. In *Territory, Democracy and Justice: Regionalism and Federalism in Western Democracies*, ed. S. L. Greer, 139–156. Basingstoke: Palgrave Macmillan.

Subirats, J. 2006. The Triumph and Troubles of the Spanish Model. In *Territory, Democracy and Justice: Regionalism and Federalism in Western Democracies*, ed. S. L. Greer. Basingstoke: Palgrave Macmillan.

Tarradellas, J. 1999[1989]. *Ja sóc aquí*. Barcelona: Planeta.

Tarrow, S. 2004. Center-Periphery Alignment and Political Contention in Late-Modern Europe. In *Restructuring Territoriality: Europe and the United States Compared*, eds. C. Ansell and G.DiPalma, 45–65. Cambridge: Cambridge University Press.

Tarrow, S., P. Katzenstein, and L. Graziano, eds. 1978. *Territorial Politics in Industrial Nations*. New York: Praeger.

Taylor, B. 1999. *The Scottish Parliament*. Edinburgh: Polygon at Edinburgh.

Termes, J. 2000. *Historia del catalanisme fins al 1923*. Barcelona: Pòrtic.

Thatcher, M. 1993. *The Downing Street Years*. New York: HarperCollins.

Thomson, J. K. J. 1992. *A Distinctive Industrialization: Cotton in Barcelona, 1728–1832*. Cambridge: Cambridge University Press.

Tiryakian, E. A., and R. Rogowski, eds. 1985. *New Nationalisms of the Developed West: Toward Explanation*. Boston: Allen and Unwin.

Tomaney, J. 2006. Histories of English Regionalism. In *The English Question*, ed. R. Hazell, 158–173. Manchester: Manchester University Press.

Tusell, J. 1999. *La transición española a la democracía*. Madrid: Historia 16.

van Creveld, M. 1999. *The Rise and Decline of the State*. Cambridge: Cambridge University Press.

van Houten, P. 1999. The Relevance of Political Determinants of Regional Assertiveness: Flanders as Illustration. Presented at the American Political Science Association Annual Meeting, Atlanta, Georgia, September.

———. 2003. Globalization and Demands for Regional Autonomy in Europe. In *Governance in a Global Economy: Political Authority in Transition*, eds. M. Kahler and D. Lake, 111–135. Princeton: Princeton University Press.

Varshney, A. 2001. Ethnic Conflict and Civil Society: India and Beyond. *World Politics* 53 (April):362–398.

Vergés, J. C. 1998. Com podem alliberar Catalunya de l'Estat neocentralista? In *Catalunya i Espanya: Una relació ecomòmica i fiscal a revisar*, ed. Òmnium Cultural, 231–276. Barcelona: Proa.

Vernet i Llobet, J. 1998. L'Autonomía i les competències de la Generalitat. In *El Sistema Polític de Catalunya*, ed. M. Caminal Badia and J. Matas Dalmases, 231–248. Madrid: Tecnos.

Vicens i Vives, J., and M. Llorens. 1958. *Industrials i polítics del segle XIX*. Barcelona: Editorial Vicens-Vives.

Vilalta i Ferrer, M. 1998. El Finançament de la hisenda autonòmica i local a Catalunya. In *El sistema polític de Catalunya*, ed. M. Caminal Badia and J. Matas Dalmases, 367–404. Madrid: Tecnos.

von Beyme, K. 2000. Federalism in Russia. In *Federalism and Political Performance*, ed. U. Wachendorfer-Schmidt, 23–39. London: Routledge.

Wagstaff, P., ed. 1999. *Regionalism in the European Union*. Exeter and Portland: Intellect.

Watts, R. L. 1998. Federalism, Federal Political Systems, and Federations. *Annual Review of Political Science* 1:117–137.

———. 2000. Federalism and Diversity in Canada. In *Autonomy and Ethnicity: Neogitating Competing Claims in Multi-Ethnic States*, ed. Y. Ghai, 29–52. Cambridge: Cambridge University Press.

Whatley, C. 1994. *Bought and Sold for English Gold? Explaining the Union of 1707*. East Linton: Tuckwell.

White, B. 1994. Training Medical Policemen: Forensic Medicine and Public Health in Nineteenth-century Scotland. In *Legal Medicine in History*, ed. M. Clark and C. Crawford, 145–165. Cambridge: Cambridge University Press.

White, R. M., and I. D. Willock. 1993. *The Scottish Legal System*. Edinburgh: Butterworths.

Williams, R. M., Jr. 2003. *The Wars Within: Peoples and States in Conflict*. Ithaca: Cornell University Press.

Wincott, D. 2006. Social Policy and Social Citizenship: Britain's Welfare States. *Publius* 36(1):169–189.

Wood, F. 1989. The Scottish TUC: Scotland's Assembly of Labour. In *Forward! Labour Politics in Scotland, 1888–1988*, ed. I. Donnachie, C. Harvie, and Wood, 130–155. Edinburgh: Polygon.

Woods, K., and D. Carter, eds. 2003. *Scotland's Health and Health Services*. London: The Nuffield Trust/TSO.

Wright, K. 1997. *The People Say Yes: The Making of Scotland's Parliament*. Glendaruel, Argyll: Argyll.

Wright, V. 1997. Relations Intergouvernementales et Gouvernement Régional en Europe: Réflexions d'un Sceptique. In *Les Paradoxes des régions en Europe*, ed. P. Le Galés and C. Lequesne, 47–56. Paris: La Découverte.

# Index